The People In Between

THE PEOPLE IN BETWEEN

THE PARADOX OF JEWISH INTERSTITIALITY

ROBERT J. MARX

C2C Publishing

NEW YORK

Cover to Cover Publishing
P.O. Box 128
Katonah, NY 10536

First Edition

Library of Congress Cataloging-in-Publication Data

Marx, Robert J., 1927-
The People in Between /Robert J. Marx
p. cm.
Includes biographical references and index.
ISBN-13: 978-0-9711626-3-1 (Hardcover)
LCCN: 2013920911

Printed in the United States of America

Book Design by Mark Hess, FullVoiceMedia.com

CONTENTS

Chapter 1

Between the Parts

First there is the word. And then words. The word "between" acknowledges the complexity of language. Word seldom stands alone, seldom exists independent of words, sentences, ideas. Words form a community. The emergence of "between" acknowledges complexity, differentiation. There are distinctions, differences. We speak of the difference between things — the most elemental of things — light and darkness, justice and injustice, happiness and misery. The between is that which mediates, which stands as close to the middle as it dare come. The word "between" is contingency and connectedness, at once powerful and exceedingly vulnerable. This is the story of the People In Between. It starts with a word.

The word is a tool. The word is a weapon, a shield. The word precedes action even as it often follows action. As threat, the word is a call to violence. As an apology it disarms. The word yearns to be heard. But it need not be formed into sound in order to be understood. It can be implied by the unuttered motion that precedes it, the clenching of the fist, the shrug of the shoulder, the smile, the frown. Yet the word needs to be heard; it demands to be freed from its silent prison.

The hearing of the word is interpretation. The word is heard differently in different moments, in different moods. It is never static. Its meaning is always contingent, contingent on its source, contingent in time. Flattery, welcome one moment, turns into saccharine fawning. A joke, a jest, may provoke laughter; yet it may also hurt and infuriate. The ethnic joke, hilarious when offered by an insider, a friend, becomes tasteless and offensive when narrated by an outsider.

History and circumstance translate the word. The insult jestingly thrown out to a good friend signifies camaraderie; thrown at an enemy, becomes a gauntlet. The word calls out for appropriateness. Is it the right moment, the right spokesman? Is it revealed at a time when it can be heard and appreciated?

"Jew." That simple three-letter word is heard differently in different places, in different times. Is it a loving word? Is it a spiteful word — a blessing or a reproach? Is it a word that pleads to become an adjective? The

Jewish people — the Jewish religion — community — pride — mother. Jew! Does the simple three-letter word point to heaven — or to Auschwitz?

Jewish interstitiality is Jewish history. More specifically it is the story of a people separated from its national homeland, yet maintaining its cohesiveness. In this sense it is a post-national history and a pre-national history and a supra-national history. But interstitiality cannot be studied simply through the lens of history or religion, though history and religion certainly provide its constitutive material. The interstitial role needs to be understood in both its external and internal manifestations. This involves the recognition that Jews not only suffered from antisemitism; they were transformed by it, and they often abetted the very forces that sought to turn them into victims. The effort to understand antisemitism was never a simple one, was invariably a frustrating one, was inevitably a disheartening one. Though many solutions were offered, answers remained elusive.

How shall we spell the word that describes the topic of this study? The historian Hannah Arendt, who devoted much of her life to the study of antisemitism, insisted on that spelling of the word rather than the usually hyphenated anti-Semitism. Arendt argued that the word "Semite" was first used pejoratively by the German Jew hater, Wilhelm Marr, around 1870. From that time on antisemitism became understood as unique reproach attached solely to Jews and not to any other Semitic group.[1] It is tempting to believe that feelings of repulsion against the Nazi death camps have made antisemitism totally antiquated. But antisemitism has remarkable staying power, and it has proven a useful tool for both governments and individuals who find themselves under attack.

Studies of antisemitism need to understand the interstitial role. An analysis of this role invites an encounter with the ways Jews faced antisemitism, and demands an examination of how they first suffered from it, then internalized it, and, finally, and in strange ways, took possession of it. Victimization lay in the fact that many Jews, too many of them, came to accept the negative aspects of their "between" position as a reality — and they did so even when they had the knowledge and the tools with which to dispute their powerlessness.

Interstitiality, then, shapes and defines Jewish suffering even as it suggests mechanisms for Jewish survival. But the interstitial role defies efforts to confine it to any one sphere of human endeavor. To insist that interstitiality can only be understood in terms that transcend history or religion is to admit that the role may well involve such mundane aspects of life as mannerisms of speech and humor, family cohesion, and even the physical characteristics of the human body. It invites a comparison of personal relationships discernible within the Jewish community as well as outside of it. In other words, interstitiality will be seen to involve not only the outward study of antisemitism, but also the internalized consequences of that historic malady. It also offers the hope that neither the Jewish community nor humanity at large are condemned to remain in that vicious cycle of hatred whose consequences have proven so historically pernicious.

The unique role of interstitiality in Judaism has become the characteristic, and sometimes defining, quality of a people, dispersed from its original homeland, yet determined or compelled to maintain its own separate and distinctive religious and social traditions. As Jews began to establish settlements throughout the Western world, notably following the Roman conquest of Judea, but beginning even earlier, the distinctive pattern of the interstitial role began to emerge. Or rather, one should say, indistinct and sometimes contradictory patterns began to emerge. Like the image on a modern computer's screen saver, interstitiality is a concept that may seem perfectly clear one moment and quite blurred the next.

The consistent thread running through the story of the Jewish people in its diaspora existence is the permanence of its "between-ness." The Jewish community has historically stood between the parts of a society. The parts themselves may be variable, may change shape as they become powerful or weak. At first it is the dyadic nature of these parts that remains invariable — even when dimly perceived there is always a duality. Every society eventually finds itself confronted by an element opposed to its power structure. Whether the opposition is internal or comes from the outside, monolithic structures are eventually challenged and modified. No civilization has ever been so powerful that it did not evoke its opponents. Throughout history great nations and powerful movements emerge, grow strong, and then diminish. Their power seldom goes unchallenged. Into the resulting conflict, the appearance of a third party always represents the element of surprise. The triad, the significant third party, may function in a variety of ways. It may, for example, support one of the two leading powers or it may even prosper from the confrontation. In this sense the adage "two is company; three's a crowd" may be profound in a large social context. It would be a mistake to assume that the third party finds its calling only in situations of conflict; it may also benefit from a diminution of social tension and from a time of peace and tranquility. Significant divisions — between rich and poor, powerful and powerless, Christian and Muslim,

Protestant and Catholic — suggest the terrain in which the interstitial power is shaped and defined.

In a mundane sense, all immigrant groups struggling to survive in an alien culture exhibit interstitial characteristics. To claim that Jews are interstitial is not to deny that other groups, too, can manifest characteristics of a people living "between the parts." What is crucial to understand is that post-Exilic Jewish history, in its totality, is an interstitial history and that the positive as well as negative aspects of its saga do not find significant parallels in the history of any other civilization. The reasons for this relate not only to Jewish homelessness, but also, as we shall see, to Jewish usefulness.

The word "interstitial" must not be regarded as pejorative — though it may become so under certain circumstances. The interstitial analysis represents an effort to understand an aspect of Jewish history that is too often overlooked or rationalized. And it also raises questions that cannot be ignored. Is it fair to insist that all Jews occupy interstitial roles? Individuals act in unique ways. To say that the Jewish community is interstitial is to affirm a singularity that individual Jews may well seek to deny. Is not the Jewish community more complex than the interstitial analysis acknowledges? There is some justification for the question. For Jews do not invariably respond as a single group, nor do they conveniently fit into a single social class. In addition, the relationship between the Jewish community and the "general populace" fluctuates under a wide variety of historical circumstances. An era replete with overt acts of antisemitism may be followed by a decade of inter-religious amity and cooperation. Yet the hydra-headed nature of antisemitism invariably retains in its malevolent power to erect ever new social walls designed to define and limit "the people in between." At times the partitioning walls are all too visible as they physically confine the Jewish community and circumscribe its options. At other times the ghetto walls of Jewish existence like a chimera seem to fall away entirely. Jewish life enters into what is all too tempting to call a "golden age," only to later plunge into a new dark age of despair.

Like a bacillus resistant to penicillin, antisemitism injects itself into unanticipated issues at unpredictable times. Tensions as varied as those stemming from black-Jewish relationships, the appointment of a Jewish justice to the Supreme Court, the emergence of a Jew as a candidate for high political office, Jewish vulnerability in periods of economic instability, and, most controversially of late, Jewish defense of the State of Israel — all harbor the virus. It is precisely the resiliency as well as the durability of antisemitism that demand a study of the interstitial role.

To speak of traditional social roles is not to deny that an individual or groups of individuals may operate outside the interstitial pattern. (It need hardly be pointed out that the often heard plaint "I am not like other Jews" qualifies as neither a legitimate exemption nor an effective prophylactic). What is important to note and to study is the persistence of the interstitial pattern. What are its characteristics? What accounts for its durability? And why, over the centuries, have so many Jewish communities willingly, and sometimes unwillingly, submitted to it by accepting its most demeaning strictures?

It would be a mistake to regard the interstitial role in only its negative dimensions. A historic commitment to study, a reverence for the holiness and mystery of the universe, an openness to reason and fresh ideas, and above all, a deep commitment to justice — these are merely some of assets of the people who stand between the parts. These positive dimensions of the interstitial role cannot be ignored, and it is these dimensions of the role that need to be appreciated and nurtured. To stand between the parts can be an opportunity and not merely a burden. Positive interstitiality emerges as the repudiation of the negative role. Ideally, it seeks to develop a social agenda that replaces the drive to accumulate with a desire to share, one that promotes altruistic values rather than unbridled self-interest. The people who are positively interstitial learn that they can question values that are selfish or dysfunctional. And they can be skeptical — skeptical even of their own financial and political motives. A community that is interstitial in this sense will respond to the cries of those who are hungry and powerless. It will not be afraid to form alliances. A community that is positively interstitial seeks its own historic heroes. It turns to the moral message of its prophets. It listens to the word.

It was Hegel, the father of German Idealism who understood how the clash of ideas can produce profound consequences. Hegel, whose ideas so excited thinkers at the beginning of the nineteenth century and repelled them by the end of the twentieth, popularized the idea that history moves in patterns that are inevitable even while appearing to be accidental. Beginning with the publication of his Phenomenology of Mind in 1807, Hegel was devoted to the idea that individual thought sensations were destined to develop into a grand consciousness of the entire world. Despite the abuse Hegel has suffered in recent generations — his critics have accused him of being the progenitor of both Nazism and Communism —

his understanding of the dyadic nature of conflict has had a profound effect upon Western thought and remains relevant. Hegel was filled with no small measure of nationalistic hubris when he posited German civilization as the apex of the dialectic process. Yet he staunchly maintained that his goal was not to predict the future, but merely to analyze historical truths. And in his determination to find these truths, he opened the door to a modern appreciation of the interstitial analysis. Thesis, antithesis, synthesis — these were the elements of the Hegelian dialectic. "Antithesis" — the word seemed an apt description of the Jewish people — the middle part of the eternal hypothesis, the part that was eternally replaceable.

Following in the tradition of Spinoza, Hegel discerned the roots of all religious claims to absolute truth in the very earliest biblical narratives. "The great principle of the Jews" he wrote, is to be found in their claim to possess a truth that was exclusively its alone. "This Jewish religion must necessarily possess the element of exclusiveness, which consists essentially in the belief that only the One People which adopts it recognizes the One God and is acknowledged by him."[2] It is this claim to the possession of a truth available to no one else, a claim quickly imitated by both Christianity and Islam, which early created a legacy of religious conflict and persecution. It need hardly be added that, in the race to assert possession of exclusive truth, Judaism was quickly outshone by its own offspring.

It would be an oversimplification to think of the dialectic process merely in terms of the great Western religions just as it would be a mistake to trivialize the importance of the interstitial party. The third party often plays a decisive role in personal relationships as well as in historic ones. Yet it is the historic paradigm of Jewish history that persistently demands our attention. There are times when conflict between the dyads becomes so intense that the interstitial party is obliged to intervene on behalf of one side or the other. In Spain during the fourteenth and fifteenth centuries, hostilities between Muslims and Christians provided numerous opportunities for third-party involvement and even intervention. The Jewish communities of Spain were famously wooed by both Muslims and Christians. That the courtship did not always go smoothly became apparent long before the famous expulsions of 1492.

It is never easy to distinguish between the passions prompted by personal conviction and those inflamed by tyrants and demagogues. And in the area of religion where the imagination and emotions are most susceptible to stimulation based upon fear and superstition, divisions that separate one religious faith from another manifest themselves in a thousand different guises. The clash of ideas, as of cultures, creates a perilous resting place for the party that occupies the middle position. And when the interstitial party claims an exclusive purchase upon an authenticity already preempted, then an incendiary situation is not hard to predict. The universal religious dream of peace and tranquility more often than not wakes up to a reality of hatred and bloodshed.

At times the middle power may be approached, begged to offer its support. More often however, the interstitial party is destined to be overwhelmed by historic and complicated tensions that eventually threaten its very existence. Tensions which, on the surface, appear amenable to rational solution can easily become infected with a virus incubated in ancient hatreds and resentments. The allegiance of the third party may move to one side or the other, may even funnel members into both sides, yet its distinctive interstitial character will not be diminished. Its survival seldom depends upon the victory or defeat of its allies. A distressing paradox of Jewish history lies in the counterintuitive fact that Jewish cohesiveness owes more to enemies than to friends. It is the dark periods of Jewish history more than the golden ones that have challenged the community to persist and to thrive. The recognition of this historic fact, if it is to be understood in new and constructive ways, may offer a path, not to despair, but to genuine confidence and even optimism.

How the Jewish community perceives antisemitism and sometimes even accommodates it, is a phenomenon yet to be fully understood. In its simplest manifestation, it may be asserted that negative interstitiality arose as a result of Jewish victimhood. Compelling Jews to wear a yellow badge or move into a ghetto are merely the cruder manifestations of this process. Nazi Germany revealed how the negative depiction of interstitiality could be carried to its disastrous and fatal conclusion.

But one need not evoke the Holocaust to be convinced of the persistence of negative interstitiality. Overt or even subtle patterns of housing segregation, religious discrimination, and social prejudice find remarkable staying power, even in countries as hospitable to freedom and cultural differences as the United States. "What are the Jews doing in Palm Beach?" asks the anti-Semite. "Don't they belong in Miami Beach?" Legislation may make discrimination illegal, but discrimination has the tenacious ability to humiliate even the most well-intentioned legislation.

The negative interstitial role has a reflexive quality. It throws back upon its victims the prejudices of the oppressor. It is this reflexive quality that is as destructive as any overt manifestations of antisemitism. The victim is not only colored, but is also discolored, by the hatred of the oppressor. Victims of oppression often incorporate into their own behavior the very negative characteristics that their oppressors attribute to them. The historian Simon Dubnow recognized this reality over a century ago when he analyzed how the intermediary roles forced upon Jews living in Russia and Poland had come to play a decisive factor, not only in determining their fate, but also in molding their personality and character. Jean-Paul Sartre carried this analysis of the "boomerang" pattern of anti-Jewish sentiment one step further, as he dissected the prejudices of his own countrymen. He became convinced that anti-Semites were often doing little more than projecting their own fears and self-loathing upon the victims of their historic prejudices.

To place arbitrary boundaries upon the freedom of a people inevitably limits them psychologically and emotionally as well. Discriminate in a way that affects a people's housing or job options and you cripple their psyche. African-American history provides painful examples of the connection between early discrimination and later social and economic frustration. And the failure of the white community to fully comprehend how dehumanizing slavery can really be remains a barrier to complete racial reconciliation. In the process of discrimination, each new insult augments the sense of defensiveness and bitterness and often precipitates an imperceptible turn inward. Caution matures into fear. Jewish history provides ample evidence of the perniciousness of this process. Jews learn to act one way when among their own co-religionists; entirely differently among non-Jews. Again, it is humor that both reveals and conceals its own sordid reality. The story about a "Jewish princess," a joke about a Jewish scoundrel, a joke with a Yiddish punch line — all so enjoyable when told among friends; so offensive when repeated by a stranger. The street language of black rappers, often misunderstood by their white listeners, is but a manifestation of this same syndrome.

The internalization of the negatively interstitial role has consequences that become programmatic as well as psychological. Community priorities become centered on issues of Jewish defense. The synagogue, in full retreat, allows the Anti-Defamation League or the American Jewish Committee to become the defender of the Jewish psyche and even the interpreter of Jewish theology. Concerns are based upon mathematics rather than ethics. "Why are we losing our young people" becomes a more pressing question than: What are we offering our young people? What insights that are inspiring? What values that can evoke excitement and dedication? It is not our children but we who are the problem. Temerity trumps imagination, and the few endeavors designed to help the poor or confront the pursuit of justice or evoke genuine commitment are offered with a rush of publicity that does little more than declare how unusual they really are.

The interstitial role that is negative has its seductive qualities. Aside from inviting participation in alliances that may be economically advantageous but of questionable moral value, the very fight against antisemitism can lead to a distortion of the Jewish agenda. Antisemitism creates a thriving subculture within the Jewish community. It stimulates a proliferation of organizations that offer employment and even financial rewards to the people involved in the noble fight. The antisemitism industry thrives; it comforts its sponsors with promises of defense while disturbing them with specters of destruction. This is not to belittle the struggle against hatred; that struggle is important and its goal is admirable. But too frequently its target is wrong — limited to the battle against individual enemies or nations of enemies. There is a broader context for the understanding of antisemitism, one that forces us to look at Jews in their historic role as an interstitial people.

The institutions involved in the antisemitism industry sap the resources and the emotions of a Jewish community that would be well advised to concentrate on its hopes rather than its fears. For example, anxiety about the beatification of a pope who may or may not have been silent in the face of the Holocaust is certainly a matter of concern for the Jewish community. But how much energy should be devoted to protests about the hero-choices of another religion? The well respected organizations devoted to the fight against antisemitism are quite vocal about external enemies but quite silent about internal ones, specifically those few but powerful Jews whose financial irresponsibility lends itself to their own enrichment while doing little to help fashion a just society. Fear, however, is a powerful taskmaster, and the collective memory of oppression and oppressors causes understandable but regrettable distortions in the Jewish agenda.

Is there not a defect in this line of reasoning? If antisemitism is a constant presence in Jewish history, are not efforts to confront it ultimately meaningless? More importantly, if it is a constant why should Jews remain so concerned with what others think of them? And finally, there is the ultimate question engendered by the creation of the Jewish State. If antisemitism is such a persistent virus, is not *aliyah*, a return to the Jewish national homeland in Israel, the only effective Jewish response?

The call for a "positive" program as a response to the interstitial analysis invites scrutiny on many levels. It can easily be ridiculed as an act of surrender to an enemy that can never be placated. Is it not ultimately a craven act of capitulation to admit that hatred of the Jews is partially the result of Jewish behavior in addition to the ignorance and prejudice of those who afflict them? Is not any call for a transformation of the Jewish agenda ultimately a tacit admission that calls into question the very social and moral values that Jews have always held sacred?

There are challenges to be confronted. The first task is to understand how antisemitism thrives in the interstices, and then to create a response that both treats the disease and transcends its ability to cause pain. A beginning is to recognize that the interstices in which antisemitism flourishes are not merely those which can be identified by studying national or ethnic groups. The gaps between the strong and the weak, the rich and the poor, the powerless and the powerful — all offer arenas which invite thought and action. The positive interstitial role is not a call for volunteers to serve in food pantries, though surely it does not disparage such individual efforts. Rather it calls for the creation of a society that acts to make food pantries unnecessary. With Maimonides, it envisions a program that has faith in the people whose lives it seeks to benefit. And with Maimonides it has faith that the best way to help is to enable people to help themselves.

In Judaism the word is never static. Even for the most traditional of Jews the "holy word" may be unalterable, but never static. It welcomes expansion; it invites Midrash. There is dynamism in Judaism that encourages reflection and transformative action. Talmudic law, rabbinic commentaries and the "way of the people" have always stood in dialectic relationship to the revelation at Mount Sinai. In this sense "hearing" has always been everything. The watchword of Judaism, the *Shema*, may have focused Israel upon its God, but the emphasis upon hearing has always been an invitation to interpretation.

The Jewish ability to listen, to really listen, has been constricted by powerful historic and social forces that have had a crippling impact. Under pressure from the outside, Jewish life and Jewish consciousness has often turned inward. The places where Jews lived have often become synonymous with the Jewish community itself. These places called ghetto, Pale of Settlement, and *Judengasse,* reveal stories of degradation in their very names. There is also a tension between the open society and one that advocates self-segregation, and it is important to understand the appeal of each in order to fully appreciate the impact of the interstitial role.

That even segregation had its positive aspects would be hard to deny. Isolation provided insulation, and Jewish history offers many insights into the ways in which the cohesiveness of Jewish life was sustained by a combination of antisemitism and internal organization. Values such as personal piety, ritual purity, and religious solidarity can be fortified in a society where the temptations of an open society can be resisted. It is these values that gave strength and vigor to a community that remained separated from, but not untouched, by the world around it. Intermarriage and religious heresy were traditionally regarded as particularly threatening. Throughout the Middle Ages and well into modern times, community loyalty remained a matter of utmost importance. Only among the most "exceptional" of Jews were deviations tolerated or possible. As recently as the seventeenth century, Spinoza could be excommunicated for promoting ideas considered heretical by his Amsterdam synagogue. As historically significant as Spinoza's excommunication was, it was only the most noteworthy example of how the interstitial people often reviled their most noteworthy rebels only to later claim them as their own.

Chapter 2

Separate but Sacred

For Jews each word in a sacred text welcomes its own Midrash, its own commentary. The word has power. Its power is to be discerned not only in its clarity — but also in its ambiguity. This is why the narrative of the Bible, important as it is, remains servant to the words of the Bible. Religious fundamentalists often fail to appreciate this possibility. For them the narrative is everything. They miss the ambiguity and the magic of the word.

How may we hear the words? A subject cannot exist without an object, a speaker without those who hear what is spoken. Between the two stands a third participant — meaning. Meaning is always conditional, always ambiguous, and inevitably controversial. It hovers between subject and object. It is both their master and their servant. There are unforeseen consequences. Words intended to comfort may provoke rather than console. Thoughtlessly addressed to bereaved parents, the words "I know how you feel," may well prove hurtful. The same sentence with five small additional words may become cathartic: "I have been there too." The word finds comfort in being shared. Or rather it brings comfort in being shared. But it is shared on the assumption of a common universe of discourse — an assumption that is not always discernable.

During World War II, so the tale goes, American and British naval officers met aboard an American destroyer. Buffeted by North Atlantic storms, they all agreed that they had only a few days to reach a decision that might well impact the future of the entire war. Although both sides thought they were in agreement, the British officers urgently wanted to "table the motion," while the Americans with equal vigor argued against the motion to table. The disagreement was a semantic one; each side heard the same words differently. For the Americans, "to table a motion" was to set it aside; for the British it was to put it on the table for immediate consideration. The meaning of the word is conditional; it needs to be heard, to be understood. The word can be a jealous master as well as a generous one.

For Judaism and the Jewish people the encounter with the word is never static. Ever since Abraham heard a voice telling him to leave his home, ever since Moses stood at Mount Sinai, the word has had a unique role to play in Jewish history. Religious Jews dedicated themselves to exploring the undulating ripples created by those ancient biblical encounters. The word still has the power to comfort and inspire. The essential Jewish prayer, the *Shema*, is a challenge to pause, to listen, to understand the word, to obey it.

The word struggles to be heard in every generation. In its religious manifestation it becomes a vital power, elevating the simple from the profound, the holy from the profane. And in its prophetic manifestation it willingly lends itself to a particular brand of protest, one that consciously stands opposed to the vulgar appetites of the age, one that sees through the pretenses of those consumed with the hunger for power and the hunger for wealth. This protest penetrates the thoughts of Amos and Elijah, Isaiah and Jeremiah. The durability of the prophetic message testifies to the fact that the word is capable of being made relevant, is capable of being made "modern."

For a people whose survival is always a question, the moral voice of the prophet is often a difficult one to hear. It is so harsh, so uncompromising. In recent centuries, two competing forces within Jewish life threaten to drown the prophetic word. These intruding forces are the fear of antisemitism and the temptation of assimilation. Fear and temptation — the Scylla and Charybdis of Jewish history! To navigate between the two has been the burden and blessing of contemporary Jewish life. The contrast between these two impulses is not as stark as it may first appear. For both antisemitism and assimilation are by-products of the interstitial role, the between role, that characterizes so much of modern Jewish life.

The Hebrew word "bayn" ("between") achieves new significance. As the primal act of creation God creates a distinction "bayn" light and darkness. The small preposition looms large in Jewish history. And its importance becomes magnified as the consequences of the traumatic dispersion of Jews from their ancient homeland begin to be understood. The between is a connection. It requires the presence of "the other," of two others. The 'between" struggles to stand alone, but it can never do so. The word is one of dependency — that is, unless it finds a way to surmount its role as a preposition and become a noun, or perhaps even a verb. "How long halt ye between two opinions?" asks the prophet Elijah. (I Kings 18.21) The prophet's challenge implies a choice. But Jewish history —

beginning symbolically with the destruction of the Temple in Jerusalem —
witnesses the transformation of the "between" from an option into a
necessity.

The date of the destruction of the Jerusalem Temple in 70 CE is
memorialized as a day of profound sadness. It was the fall of the Temple
and not the fall of the state that became etched in Jewish consciousness.
How interesting it is that the national tragedy would be preserved in
memory through nostalgia for religious rather than secular symbols! The
Jewish Memorial Day, *Tisha b'Av*, the ninth day of the month of Av,
commemorates the destruction of the Temple, not the destruction of
Jerusalem. Even though the masses of Jews yearned for a return to the Holy
Land, the religious reaction to the destruction was surprisingly apolitical.
The rabbis of the era were not naïve. They understood that Jewish survival
depended upon a religious rather than a political agenda. And so the Jewish
texts dealing with the destruction seemed almost reluctant to criticize their
own defense forces or to acknowledge the power of their Roman adversary.
Instead blame was turned inward; it was assigned to the failed morality of
the Jews themselves.

Midrashic stories illustrating this tendency sometimes took the form of
morality lectures, and sometimes they merged on the bizarre. A wealthy
man wanted to invite his friend Kamtza to a lavish dinner party. But by
mistake the servant responsible for the invitations went to the wrong house
and invited a man with a similar name, Bar Kamtza. Kamtza was a friend
of the wealthy man; Bar Kamtza an enemy. So bitter was the enmity of the
host that he rudely drove Bar Kamtza from his house. Infuriated by his
rejection, Bar Kamtza, so the texts inform us, initiated a train of events that
culminated in the destruction of Jerusalem. Because of poor manners and a
denial of hospitality Jerusalem was destroyed.[3]

More familiar than any of the preserved stories about the fall of
Jerusalem is the legend of Rabbi Yochanan ben Zakkai. His followers
carried him out of the besieged city in the middle of the night so that he
could meet with the Roman general Vespasian, and plead for a place to
start a new center of learning. The hero of this rabbinic story seems more
interested in establishing a seat of learning at Jabne than fighting for his
beleaguered city. It was left for the secular historian Josephus to provide the
details of Jerusalem's destruction. In retrospect both Yochanan and
Josephus could have been charged with disloyalty. Josephus, the military
leader responsible for the defense of the Galilee, had abandoned his post
and cast his lot with the Romans. And Yochanan had abandoned his

besieged city in order to initiate his own peace talks with the enemy. In the Jewish imagination Yochanan was honored; Josephus was reviled.

But both Yochanan and Josephus presaged an important development. The Jewish religion would survive even if the nation perished. The transformation was amazing; and yet the speed with which it occurred probably guaranteed the survival of Judaism. The pilgrimages to Jerusalem, once a prominent feature of the three major festivals now became dim memories. Animal sacrifices, acts that formerly could be offered only in the Jerusalem Temple, were abruptly terminated, relegated to a few memorial lines in the liturgy. Instead, Rosh Hashanah and Yom Kippur with their emphasis upon personal piety emerged as the quintessential Jewish holidays. "The nation has perished, but Judaism has survived." Rabbinic literature heralds the survival even as it rationalizes the tragedy which dramatically reshaped the ancient faith.

The crushing of the nation was a blow that impacted Jewish destiny on three levels: social, political, and religious. The survivors of a disintegrating Judea found themselves transformed into an isolated people, a people struggling to blend into a new life while simultaneously acting to preserve their own distinctive character and faith. They became "the people in between." In its most painful manifestation, the word "between" becomes a synonym of vulnerability. Jews clothed as beggars, forced to wear the yellow armband of powerlessness! The between is a sign of helplessness. Can it also become a sign of renewed vitality and moral authority?

Conceived in national tragedy and nurtured by centuries of suspicion, the interstitial role is the destiny of a people estranged from power. The interstitial model is primitive, as primitive as Cain and Abel, Jacob and Esau. Two forces confront one another, stoic, intractable. They are alone; there are no witnesses to their conflict, no allies, no one to help them. Duality precedes any possibility of a triad. Yet the third party inevitably emerges. When that happens society is created.

Two mountain peaks soar over a fertile valley. The walls of the mountain, conceptual as they are, symbolize the power to limit, the power to contain. Huddled under them is the valley, confined by towering peaks, fearful of the mountains' power, yet grateful for its protection, vaguely conscious that in time, even the most formidable of walls may erode and disappear. The valley may become a plain. But who can tell what avalanches will decimate it, what floods overwhelm it, what mud slides devastate it? The placid green valley snuggled between the peaks remains a pleasant vision and a fragile hope.

Social walls may be more malleable than physical ones; still the metaphor of the valley remains appropriate. The third party, the triadic third party, finds its opportunities circumscribed by Alpine prejudices. Alliances, and sometimes even wars, resolve the old conflicts, yet historic animosities retain poisonous vitality. The interstitial role is inevitably defined by others even as it often deludes itself into thinking that it enjoys complete freedom. Its third-party function may be that of the mediator, attempting to resolve the conflict in nonviolent ways. Social conflicts do not invariably necessitate an intermediary, although they often welcome mediation. They may melt into more passive forms of competition, more dangerously, into the creation of a scapegoat. But the very hint of a third party inevitably creates a new reality. Whether welcomed or rejected, the mere presence of a third party establishes and defines the interstitial role.

"Interstitiality," the essence of existence "between the parts," characterizes the role of a people that is situated between two or more segments of society, segments that are differentiated from it by any number of variable or permanent factors. These factors include race, religion, and politics, as well as economic or social status. To be interstitial is to stand between the boundaries. It is to be literally *in medias res* — in the middle of things. The interstitial condition is not static. The malleability of its existence is one of its primary characteristics.

An individual may be said to be interstitial. But his or her role, notably that of the inspiring leader, is different from that of the interstitial group. The leader becomes significant, not only by dint of personality or military prowess, but as a result of a genuine uniqueness. Such leadership, to invoke Max Weber's classification, is inevitably charismatic rather than bureaucratic or hereditary.

To illustrate the difference between an interstitial leader and an interstitial people, examine the life of the one human being who perhaps did more than anyone else to define the meaning of Judaism. Moses epitomized the interstitial role at a critical turning point in Jewish history. Living in Egypt, he rose to a leadership position despite the fact that he was a quintessential outsider. An initial alienation from his own family was followed by a traumatic break with the royal Egyptian family that had adopted him. In his controversial study, *Moses and Monotheism*, Sigmund Freud even went so far as to argue that the great leader of the Israelites was in reality not a Jew at all.

The pariah status that initially left Moses rejected by both Jews and Egyptians might have been a fatal blow to a lesser human being. But in reality it was his uniquely interstitial position coupled with his charismatic personality that ultimately allowed him to become the leader of his fragmented people. To picture Moses at Mount Sinai is to illustrate the concept of the religiously interstitial leader in its most mystical and also its most essential form. With God thundering commandments from above and the people anxiously waiting below, Moses becomes both the receiver and transmitter of a revolutionary and dramatic revelation.

The depiction of Moses as a model of interstitial leadership is in no way tantamount to claiming this role as an exclusively Jewish one. How many other great personalities moved from the periphery into the center of their people's destiny as they ascended to power! There are countless examples of spiritual leaders whose unique powers enabled them to transcend the social divisions of their era, and bring complex and contentious forces together.

But the acknowledgment of individuals who may be described as interstitial is only minimally useful in the effort to understand the "interstitial group." Leaders who are uniquely interstitial fulfill their destinies and then leave the stage to others who invariably settle into a style that is bureaucratic rather than charismatic. Yet, as Jewish history reveals, distinctions between followers and leaders are neither simple nor inevitable. When applied to an entire people, the concept of interstitiality achieves a complexity and resiliency that is anything but commonplace. And the roots of this complexity are philosophical as well as social.

The theological roots of interstitiality are to be discerned in a simple idea that has infused not only Judaism, but much of Western civilization as well — the idea of separation. First revealed in the account of the biblical cosmology, the full manifestations of the interstitial role were suckled by many of the philosophical systems that came to define Western civilization. Its modern excesses, encouraged by a wide variety of ideologies, find an unhealthy outlet in national chauvinism and class conflict.

The act of creation which launches the Bible is one of separation — of "between-ness." The Bible begins with a duality which immediately admits the possibility of an intermediary. The waters of heaven and the waters below are separated by a firmament, which defines and limits their authority. The division of heaven and earth may be the poetic invention of a primitive cosmology, yet it is also the symbol of a unique way of viewing the world. The very frequency of these divisions is what distinguishes biblically based religions from other belief systems. "Separation" itself emerges as a religious goal. It points the path toward sacred purity; it is an essential element in defining humanity's unique relationship to God. To be holy is to be *kadosh* — to be separate.

At its most elemental level, the biblical use of the separation idea reveals its social usefulness. Distinctions between the stranger and the home-born, between the priestly Levites and masses of Israelites, and most notably, between Israel and everyone else — all provide ample evidence of primitive divisions within ancient social structure. The stranger may be welcomed, but strange communities are to be avoided. The Hivites, the Perizites, the Jebusites, and above all, the Amalekites are to be shunned, not only because they are enemies but also because they are a threat to the purity of the covenant between God and God's chosen people.

Born of a search for religious integrity, yet seldom consciously acknowledged, the idea of separation, to be found in Judaism as well as Christianity and Islam, has had a profound effect upon every aspect of Western civilization. To be chosen is to be separate. To take part in the ritual of communion, to submit to the will of Allah, to join in a Passover Seder — all contain aspects of separation as well as affiliation. The idea, too often taken for granted, is all too seldom accorded the significance it deserves.

The rules of separation touched every aspect of biblical life. Wool and linen were not to be mixed; a mother bird and her offspring were not to be eaten at the same meal, nor were milk and meat. But of all the Jewish rituals it was the act of circumcision that most dramatically revealed the separation idea. Removing the foreskin of an eight day old male child became a distinctive act of Jewish commitment, and throughout the ages it remained the primary symbol of Jewish separation as well as Jewish affiliation. Even enemies understood this fact. As early as the first century of the Common Era, there are indications that Roman officials would sometimes examine the genitals of those suspected of trying to escape payment of the *fiscus Judaicus*, a special tax imposed upon all Jews living in Rome. "I recall being present in my youth," the historian Suetonius remembers, "when the person of a man ninety years old was examined before the procurator and a very crowded court, to see whether he was circumcised."[4] And as recently as the twentieth century, circumcision could become a life-threatening act. Nazi soldiers frequently required male detainees suspected of being Jewish to undergo a humiliating examination of their genitals. For these Nazis circumcision was regarded as *prima facie* evidence of Jewishness. But for their unfortunate victims, the ceremony that was intended to be a life-blessing often became a sentence of death.

18

The Sabbath is the most important day of the Jewish religious calendar and, as is to be expected, its very emphasis on worship and study are features that mark it as a separation symbol. As distinguished from the secular part of the week, the Sabbath is a day of rest; it is a time to do things that are not done on the weekday; it is a time to be godly. The lighting or extinguishing of a candle marks not only the beginning and ending of Sabbath, but also dramatizes the sharp distinction between the Sabbath and the rest of the week. Sabbath and Havdalah candles penetrate the darkness, isolate the Sabbath, and establish barriers dividing the holy from the profane.

The importance of Jewish dietary laws can only be appreciated in the context of the separation idea. Jewish tradition came to regard what you put into your body as a mirror of what you do with your body. Thus, the laws of kashrut, including the rules of ritual slaughter and dietary purity, acknowledge the holy space between God and man. What shall be eaten, when it may be eaten, who should fast and who refrain from fasting — these were all part of a well-tuned system of dietary regulation. And within these regulations, no rules were more significant than those regarding the dietary use of blood. Blood is the crucial symbol, the sign of life, the one thing that distinguishes an eternal and undying god from temporal and mortal human beings.

The prohibition against blood is ordained in the very first chapter of Genesis. The menu is vegetarian. Adam listens to the description of the things that may be eaten; notably absent from the list is meat. It is only generations later as Noah's great flood comes to its end that the voice of God announces a quite significant change in the human diet: "from now on, Noah, you may eat meat." There is, of course, one reservation: no blood shall be consumed by any human being. The reason is crucial: the *nefesh*, life itself — is in the blood. (Gen. 9.4) No biblical warning is repeated more insistently than the one forbidding the eating of blood. "Only be steadfast in not eating the blood; for blood is the life; and thou shalt not eat the life with the flesh." (Deut. 12.23. See also, for example, Lev. 3.17; 7.26-27 and Deut. 12.16)

Prohibitions regarding blood lie at the heart of the most basic separation of them all — the separation of man from God. For that which is most holy finds its representation in blood, the *nefesh*, the soul, the divine. For Judaism, humans may have been created in the image of God, they may imitate what they think is godly, but they cannot be God. It is at this point that Judaism and Christianity diverge most sharply, and it is their attitude toward ritual wine that reveals the depth of their division. Both Christianity and Judaism use wine for religious purposes — Christianity for the rite of communion, Jews for the Sabbath and Passover. But the significance which the two faiths impute to the drinking of wine reveals their profound differences. In the Christian communion, the wafer (the Passover *matzo*) together with wine became symbols of the savior's body and blood. Judaism, on the other hand, historically insisted that the two symbols be treated literally and not figuratively. Thus, matzoh and wine were regarded not as reminders of a crucified savior or of a mysterious incarnation, but simply as foods reminiscent of the Jewish experience as slaves in Egypt. As these memories of slavery became ritualized in the Passover Seder they were augmented by reminders that Jews should be concerned for the poor, the sick, the homeless, the "other." Thus Jews could acknowledge matzoh and wine as reminders of the divine impact upon human beings; they could not accept them as the symbols of a human being become divine.

What irony, then, is to be seen in the incredible accusation that Jews use blood in the baking of Passover matzoh! The infamous "blood libel" is more than preposterous when it is remembered that even the symbolic drinking of blood, as in the ceremony of communion, is something Jews would never contemplate. What is fascinating in a macabre way is to follow the path of the Jewish prohibition against the consumption of blood as it first becomes converted by its daughter religion and then corrupted by its enemies. The blood libel, particularly with its insinuation that the blood of a child would be required in the baking of matzoh is one of those amazing perversions that only the most insidious of propagandists could appreciate. Surely it is an awesome and awful tribute to the power of propaganda, that Judaism's dietary laws could be transmogrified and desecrated in such a grotesque way.

But perhaps this ugly transformation should not surprise us. Throughout history ethnic and religious concepts and descriptions have proven to be surprisingly malleable. Blessings become curses and curses blessings. Was it not Balaam, hired by Balak to curse Israel, who ended up offering the most sublime of blessings? The once pejorative word "black" becomes transformed by the civil rights movement into an expression of racial pride: black is beautiful! And of course, the most benign of ideas bear the potential for being turned into something quite ugly. Pacification becomes oppression; re-education is a prison sentence. Yet the blood libel remains a unique perversion — a perversion, it can hardly be denied, that has achieved incredible staying power.

These thoughts must not divert attention from the more profound manifestations of the separation idea. Good and evil contest one another for the human soul. The important point is that the earliest biblical attempts to define ethical behavior established the framework for an interstitial analysis. Here there is a remarkable similarity between Judaism and Christianity. More is involved than an initial Judeo-Christian appreciation of seminal personalities. Invariably the leader stands apart, rises above the masses of followers. Moses and Jesus each climb the mountain. Their followers remain behind yearning simply for food, for manna or fish. The leader is in the clouds; the followers are hungry. The geography of mountain and valley is present again but it is merely suggestive of the moral dichotomies which religion invariably addresses. Jeremiah rightly understands the chasm between the vision and reality when he laments: "'Peace, peace,' they cry, but there is no peace." (Jer. 6.14; 8.11) The rebellious grumbling in the desert is as predictable as the pure inspiration at the top of the mountain. Whatever forms the polarities take, whether social or religious or economic, they inevitably invite something or someone to fill the space between their parts. Out of this invitation, the interstitial model is created.

It is not surprising that the same patterns that mould religious life figure prominently in the philosophic systems that dominate Western civilization. It was Western philosophy's preference for dualistic theories that gave substance to the interstitial concept. As the greatest of the classical philosophers became attracted by different aspects of the dualistic hypothesis, few of them remained attached for long to the ancient forms of monism. For Plato the basic dualism was that of body and soul; for Aristotle, mind and matter. Inevitably, it was Aristotelian thought, as given theological interpretation by Thomas Aquinas, that dominated Western civilization throughout the Middle Ages. Even Descartes, seeking to break away from the classical Aristotelian tradition, could not avoid the temptation to think in terms of dualities. For him the concepts of extension (matter) and thought needed to be understood in a way that could accommodate modern science and still offer a rational justification of traditional Christian belief. It remained for Spinoza to confront the dilemmas of the dualists and to fashion a unified theory in which God and nature became one. Yet, despite the advances of modern science, Spinoza's thought remains outside the mainstream of Western philosophical thought.

Within the classic dualities interstitiality became more than an ideological postulate. It assumed a social reality. The people whom we may label as interstitial are traditionally divorced from any national entity that they might claim as their own. They inevitably seek a place of comfort between opposites. Without being conscious of the effort, the interstitial community tacitly acknowledges that the dualities of the philosopher have become reified in the difficult social conditions that now limit and define it, conditions that have grown slowly throughout the centuries to form what may be called a "national character."

Three elements enter into the creation of a national character and they consequently serve also to shape the interstitial role — a shared history, a shared culture, and a shared faith. These elements are never so distant from one another that any one of them can be dismissed as irrelevant. Groups that do not participate fully in any one of these elements can be thought of as foreigners and be subject to overt or covert discrimination. This was the situation of Jews throughout much of their diaspora history. What characterized societies where a dominant group sought to suppress a troublesome minority was even more discernible in a society where comparatively equal groups struggled for dominance. This was the scene in Spain in the years prior to 1492.

Long before Hegel's dialectic conceptualized the process, the interstitial community sought to escape the clash of thesis and antithesis which formed the basic condition of their existence. And optimism was never wanting. For Jews, every new synthesis could be greeted as if the end of the process were at hand, as if a messianic age had arrived. But the elimination of every Haman brought new concerns and renewed anxieties. Even the establishment of a Jewish state in Israel has produced no real solution to the Jewish problem. That all dreams inevitably prove to be no more than chimeras is the great disappointment of Jewish history.

If political life was the arena in which the interstitial role became most apparent, it was in the world of art that the earliest symptoms of Western dualism can be clearly perceived. The art of Western civilization may be said to profoundly influence, and even to precede, the articulation of Western thought. Sharp differentiations, first observable in Egyptian and Greek depictions of the human body, are characteristic of much of this art. Using Grant Wood's familiar painting *American Gothic* as a reflection of American thought, F.S.C. Northrop has argued that the art as well as the philosophy of any given civilization provides clues to a nation's generalized pattern of behavior. In *American Gothic*, the staid couple standing before a simple structure reminiscent of a church makes us look at what Northrop critically described as our blank souls "with all their rigid ethical virtues, but devoid of a hearty human spontaneous expression of feeling, compassion and the emotions."[5]

Northrop insisted that particular philosophical theories had real and historic consequences. The theory of an atomic bomb, for instance, could be developed by German scientists steeped in the philosophies of the German Idealists such as Kant and Hegel. In the hands of these scientists, however, the bomb existed only as an idea. It took the practical know-how of American scientists, steeped in the pragmatic empiricism of Locke and Hume to turn the idea into a reality.

In much of Western art, the figures are "differentiated" — the central object of attention stands sharply separated from the background. In Rembrandt's portraits or da Vinci's *Mona Lisa*, not to mention *American Gothic*, the subject of the painting dominates and seems to obliterate a background that we hardly notice. The contrary is true of the typical Asian painting whose characteristic feature can be described as "undifferentiated." Asian art is replete with expressions of passivity and contemplativeness — a gentle stream is more familiar than a roaring Niagara. Not here do we find Amos's impassioned call to "let justice roar down as waters, righteousness as a mighty stream." The figure in the Asian painting is typically indistinct; it is a perfect representation of the serenity the picture seems to idealize. These distinctions are relevant to any analysis of interstitiality, for it is the very prominence of the differentiations that give substance to the role.

The sharp delineations, so characteristic of Western art, may be a more accurate depiction of Western religion than may be suspected. The history of these religions is a history of confrontation and conflict. In the process of defining their differences, Western religions sought clarity and shunned ambiguity, venerated the martyr and burned the heretic at the stake. The consuming vision was of an ultimate unity — a unity, paradoxically, that could be realized only at the altar of duality. And the ultimate unity was God. But whose God was to be venerated, whose customs to be observed, whose heresy to be eradicated?

Western philosophers, beginning with Plato and Aristotle, extending through the German Idealism of Kant and Hegel and even Karl Marx — all sought their own meaning of "ultimate unity." Alchemists of the soul, they struggled to find the one true answer. Yet they invariably had to be satisfied with some form of dualism. Even the monads of Leibniz came to be seen as the last gasp of a traditional philosophy that was ready to be buried though no one seemed to notice that it had expired. Only with the empiricism of Locke and Hume was the door of contemporary thought opened to new and exciting possibilities. It was through science, through observation, that important truths might be discovered. The search for unity moved from the realm of religion to the realm of science, and along with it the great hint that neither monism nor dualism, but a new form of pluralism was the path to take if ultimate unity was still to be regarded as a worthy goal. The welcome impact of empirical thinking upon the Jewish community of the United States invites further exploration.

Of course, the struggle between the one and the many persists. "Thou shalt! Thou shalt not!" These imperatives are the moral companions of a duality inherent in most societies. But beginning with Greek thought, and later adopted by Judaism and Christianity, the idea of heaven became the most impressive symbol of the dualism which had permeated religious thought. Again it was Plato who gave the clearest interpretation to this form of duality and crowned heaven as the ultimate reality. It began with an effort to solve the problem that had troubled the earliest of Greek philosophers, the problem of motion as expressed in the question, "How do things change?" Plato's solution was to posit a perfect world, a world "out there" — a world of ideas — paralleled by the imperfect world all of us experience. The dualism which Plato had fashioned proved congenial to Judaism's own insistence on the separation of God and man and gradually found a welcome home in the foothills of Judea. By the first century Plato's ideas had come to permeate Judaism and, through it, Christianity and Islam. Heaven was born, a new metaphysical heaven, and with it a new vision of immortality.

Heaven and earth, heaven and hell — these are the metaphysical dualities that accompany the marriage of the Greek idea of beauty with the Jewish idea of God. We are accustomed to being told to reach toward the heavens; the things that are high become laden with value. The mountain itself becomes the logical place for decisions to be made. The Ten Commandments are given on the mountain. The great sermon of Jesus is delivered on the mountain. And more contemporaneously, Martin Luther King was able to proclaim that he had "gone to the mountain." One "stands tall," possesses "high moral principles," or reaches the "highest ladder of success." The heavens and the earth, the mountain and the valley, the rich

24

and the poor, the powerful and the oppressed — out of the dualities the interstitial idea is born.

Chapter 3

Biblical Shadows

Can an interstitial people — so precariously balanced between the parts — find a moral voice that is uniquely its own? The people in the middle do not have to remain in a state of ethical hibernation. Like Israel at Mount Sinai they may be challenged to respond to new moral and social situations they may not yet completely understand, but nevertheless involve them in intricate ways. Alliances may be formed, not only with those dedicated to solving global issues such as the health of the universe and international warfare, but especially on a local level with those who are concerned with the welfare of those who are poor or ill or abused. In all of these grand schemes the painful task of opposing those in our own midst who exploit others needs to be undertaken with the same seriousness mustered to deal with the harm that results from generalized patterns of selfishness and social indifference.

There are important differences that separate the Jewish interstitial experience from that of others. Jewish interstitiality has been infused with three characteristic patterns: an unusually intense self-awareness, a rich cultural tradition, and nostalgia for a socially cohesive past. These qualities (unspectacular when reviewed in isolation, but quite significant when present collectively), were not allowed to flourish unchallenged. They were overwhelmed, suffocated by a viral and unrelenting form of persecution, one that sought to punish as well as to use its Jewish victims.

When the indomitable Benjamin Franklin was serving his country in England he experienced a challenge to his integrity that proved to be embarrassing to him and his family. For a few months public criticism of Franklin was unrelenting, and was even widely reprinted in American newspapers. To comfort his concerned daughter, Franklin is reported to have written a letter back home in which he said something like this: "When I see young boys casting stones at trees, I am but little distressed, for their stones tell me there must be apples in those trees." The ability to find the good in the midst of adversity, as Franklin's letter attests, is an admirable personal trait. When it enables social groups to survive and flourish, even in the face of persecution, it is all the more remarkable. What is painfully negative may frequently harbor the potential to be reborn as something fresh and quite positive.

The roots of Judaism's ability to transform negatives into positives are quite ancient. They can be discerned in the radical, self-evaluation which followed the destruction of the national state in the first century. Out of a tragedy that was perceived as cataclysmic, there developed a profound devotion to study, a deepened reliance upon family networks, and an ongoing commitment to the search for community and individual morality. Because persecution acts as a poison gradually paralyzing its victim as it proceeds on its fateful path, the consequences of the new role became apparent only gradually.

Antisemitic stereotypes have hobbled the ability of Jews to become totally whole, and have created fractures within the Jewish psyche that have persisted through the ages. The fragmentation can be seen on many levels. The destruction of the Jerusalem Temple signaled a Jewish turn inward. The turn inward was not a voluntary one, but the very real isolating pressure from the outside did evoke a response from the inside. The Jewish communities of Europe became insular; their grand ethics reduced to parochial issues largely concerned with the two P's, purity and preservation. The contradictory nature of the stereotypes invariably defied any rational effort to confront them. Pejorative adjectives became devastating. "The rich Jew, the clannish Jew, the Hollywood Jew, the Wall Street Jew" — each stereotype possessed its own destructive psychological power; and each assaulted the image of Jew as simple human being. Self-consciousness and self-doubt became the genetic inheritance of a people that must not be allowed to define themselves.

The interstitial role may not be limited to any one people. But it is the necessary role of the Jewish people. In its simplest form negative interstitiality occurs when Jews are oppressed and assume the posture of helpless victims. Antisemitism creates the interstitial role as it acts to oppress Jews on the basis of their distinct social and religious status. Positive interstitiality, on the other hand, occurs when Jews move beyond their sense of powerlessness and exercise a talent, born in a biblical tradition and nurtured by a history of persecution, the talent that enabled them to feel the pain of others. Whether the negative role can be transformed into a positive one remains a question and a challenge.

Antisemitism, with all of its historic narratives and social complexities, remains a disease that resists any simple analysis. Its persistence throughout history, however, has been well documented. Whether its roots extend back to the trial and execution of Jesus or to the subsequent competition between two closely related religious communities is a matter that continues to be debated. Although, as we shall see, expressions of anti-Jewish sentiment are to be found in very ancient records, it was the sustained attack on Jews and Judaism following the birth of Christianity that left its near fatal wound. That the martyred savior was Jewish and that his followers gradually separated from their fellow Jews has been well documented. But the bitterness that separated the two religions is hard to rationalize, particularly in view of the early traditions that both shared. Both ardently expected the arrival of a messiah. The compatibility of their earliest prayers and holiday schedules was not matched by any consensus as to the substance of their expectations. What had begun as a Jewish hope for a military-political deliverer quickly was supplanted by the Christian expectation of a personal savior, one who could be worshipped as the Son of God.

Early biblical references to a messiah picture him as an ordinary mortal who is selected to be king. He became *mashiach* — an anointed one. It was under the rule of King David that the monarchy achieved its greatest glory. David came to be regarded as the king *par excellence* — the king who might come again to save his people. By the first century of the Common Era, the legends about King David had assumed a new religious significance. A descendent of David will deliver us — a *mashiach ben David.* Inspired by this quasi religious idea of a messiah, Jews rebelled against their Roman rulers As Jews fought for their freedom they yearned for their deliverer, a human deliverer, one fashioned in the mould of the mighty David. The new Christian leadership, settled now in Rome, transformed the idea of the messiah. The military model was replaced by a spiritual model. King David, no longer viewed as the military-political prototype of a national future, retained his importance only as the progenitor of the promised savior. Paradoxically, the lineage of Jesus, the child of a virgin, is traced through his father, back to the idealized king. The actual father is a mere presence; the mother is venerated.

Early Christians and their Jewish contemporaries could often be found in the same family. Over time, however, any semblance of family unity was to prove illusory. The reasons for the break between Judaism and Christianity are profound and they have been well rehearsed. But their relevance to the development of Jewish interstitiality must not be overlooked. Early in its history, Christianity accepted those aspects of Judaism which offered widespread appeal — its monotheism, its biblical

28

narratives, its concept of heaven and of personal salvation. Simultaneously, it rejected those aspects of Judaism which could be problematic for converts — particularly circumcision and the dietary laws. After the destruction of the Jerusalem Temple in 70 CE, and more significantly, after the failure of the Jewish rebellion led by Bar Kochba in 135 CE, major segments of the Jewish community began to emigrate from Judea and settle in various parts of the Roman world. These Jews carried with them their religious practices, practices that could be adopted, adapted or abandoned by the adherents of the new Christian faith.

Regrettable, yet inevitable, perhaps, was the growing rivalry and then bitterness that more and more divided the two faiths.[6] Circumcision was an obvious practice that could have discouraged those who might otherwise have chosen the parent of the two monotheisms. Significantly, and evoking the spirit of the prophet Jeremiah, the apostle Paul called for a circumcision of the heart instead of the flesh. The dietary laws, too, were soon deemed to be cumbersome as well as unnecessary.[7]

As competition between Christians and Jews accelerated, so did the bitterness. The Hebrew Bible was demoted to the "Old" Testament; Sunday replaced the Sabbath as the preferred day of worship; the date of Easter, historically so connected with Passover, was reformulated so that it no longer coincided with the Jewish holiday. And tainting these ritual and calendar alterations was the zealous propagation of a virulent form of religious hatred, a hatred that would plunge Jews into a position where their negative interstitial role, once a mere possibility, had now become a painful reality.

Invidious comparisons were concocted to further divide the two faiths from one another. The Jewish Bible was invariably depicted as the Bible of stern justice; the New Testament was the Bible of love. The Jewish Bible's "eye for an eye" was vindictive; the New Testament's "turn the other cheek" was merciful. Above all, the stain of the trial and execution of Jesus was to be reckoned as an eternal and collective curse upon the people who had rejected the messianic claims of the new faith. The charge of deicide was to tincture Jewish-Christian relations through the ages.

The consequences of this growing hatred defined and permeated antisemitism throughout the ages. As early as the fourth century in Spain, Jews and Christians were prohibited from marrying one another. For the first time, but surely not for the last, Jews were forced to wear a yellow badge so as to be easily identifiable. Opportunities for earning a livelihood were severely restricted as community after community experimented with new ways to force their Jews to live in confined areas of a city or country. Whether they became prisoners of the ghetto or world travelers, the economic rules set by outsiders continually defined their possibilities and limited their potential. Invited into one area so that they could stimulate the economy, Jews would inevitably be forced into exile when they were no longer deemed useful.

In spite of these limitations, or perhaps because of them, some Jews managed to translate adversity into opportunity. As a result of family contacts in scattered parts of the world, many Jews became travelers and traders. Because they were denied membership in trade guilds and were restricted in their employment, Jews often found that by lending they could gain entry into a world that was reluctant to acknowledge their presence. But until the nineteenth century, success in handling money had an inverse relationship to success in social life. Furthermore, as Jews experienced segregation, they discovered that in the eyes of the European world around them they had lost more than their freedom; they had lost their human individuality. Jews had become a "thing," an object of contempt. In the eyes of the whole world and in their own eyes too, Jews became a "thing" that was unique and different. Sometimes exotic, often mysterious, more often dangerous, they had become separated from the "normal" parts of society. They had become interstitial.

Illustrations of the interstitial role can be quite simple and anecdotal. Lillian Wald, the pioneering social worker was the founder of New York's famous Henry Street Settlement. Writing in 1915, Wald recalled a conversation one of the teachers overheard at the Settlement House. "An Irish boy observed to one of our residents that on Easter Day, he intended to kill his little Jewish classmate. Having had long experience of the vigorous language and kind heart of the young Celt, she paid little attention to the threat, but was more startled when the soft-eyed Francesco chimed in that he was also going to destroy him 'because he killed my Gawd.' 'But,' said the teacher, 'Christ was a Jew.' 'Yes, I know,' answered the young defender of the faith, 'he was then, but He's an American now.'"[8]

Does Lillian Wald's narrative have any relevance for us today? There are those who would insist that anti-Jewish sentiments are a relic of a distant past, that the international flow of populations has found substitute victims, recent immigrants or vulnerable Muslims. Particularly in America where religious freedom is so cherished, the threat of any kind of an antisemitic outbreak seems ever more remote. Anecdotal accounts of religious prejudice are easily dismissed, particularly by Jews who live in urban areas where prejudice is regarded as déclassé. And there is that 2006 Gallup Poll suggesting that Americans feel more favorably disposed to Jews than to any other single religious group. There is even a movement of "Pro-Semites" who "seriously favor things Jewish."[9]

All of this can be quite seductive. The crude forms of antisemitism may appear less and less frequently, but this assumption, true as it may be does not conceal an anxiety that surely persists. And so the question remains relevant: is antisemitism still something that must concern us? Throughout their history Jews have never lacked friends. It is the persistence of their enemies that is so threatening. The hibernation of prejudice is hardly proof of its demise. Overt tensions related to Israel are not necessarily antisemitic but they often deteriorate and transmogrify. The continued vitality of so many Jewish defense agencies testifies to the endurance of a hatred that refuses to die. And any examination of the internet reveals that the virus of antisemitism is very much alive.

James Baldwin observed key differences between the experiences of American Jews and African Americans. Jews came to a land dedicated to religious freedom and diversity. They faced minimal obstacles as they sought to enter the mainstream of American life. In sharp contrast, Africans came to America as unwilling slaves. Their immediate introduction underscored the humiliation and degradation that marked so much of their later experience. Despite these very real differences, Jews could easily understand the pain and certainly the anxiety experienced by those whose history marks them as "different." Their compassion reveals an anxiety. There is a shooting at a college campus. Six students are killed. "Who did it?" — a universal question. "I hope he wasn't Jewish" — a Jewish prayer.

Despite the wishful thinking of the optimists, concerns about antisemitism remain a discernible feature of the American Jewish agenda. These concerns become particularly acute when there are discussions about sweatshops, about the control of Hollywood, about the power of the liberal Eastern media. On a more sophisticated level, they infiltrate discussions of Jewish involvement in corporate mergers, or the ownership of athletic teams, or financial speculation in the markets. And, most urgently in recent times, these concerns hover over any discussions of Israel and the "powerful Jewish lobby."

It can seem gentle, even good-humored and manageable, in one era, this anti-Jewish sentiment, and yet it can suddenly become ferocious in another. How do seemingly sane and sensible people suddenly become infected with its most radical manifestation? How can the Germany of Goethe and Beethoven so easily become the Germany of Hitler and Goebbels? It is the durability of antisemitism, despite all rational reasons for it to disappear, that continues to perplex and to trouble. Efforts to deal with this agonizing phenomenon have colored Jewish history for two thousand years.

The historic survival of the biblical people becomes all the more remarkable when viewed within the context of Jewish powerlessness. The discontinuity between the power that was always ascribed to them and their actual powerlessness has been an enduring feature of Jewish history. Jews were never to become feudal lords. They were never allowed to become members of a trade guild. They were not wealthy, nor, compared to so many of their contemporaries, could they be described as poverty stricken. And they certainly could never be considered powerful. They survived between the parts. That they survived in the face of expulsions and crusades and pogroms is in itself — if there is such a thing — a miracle.

The survival of a Jewish people finds its explanation as much in its early theology as in its early history. The biblical narrative, as Spinoza was to point out, is full of repetitions and contradictions; its miracle stories read best as allegories. Yet there is an undeniable beauty in the morality of the prophets, the rhetoric of the Psalms, the wisdom of the Proverbs, and the insights of Ecclesiastes or Lamentations. And despite the skepticism of Spinoza and generations of Bible critics, there remains a beauty in the text itself that confounds any purely rational analysis.

Genesis is largely occupied with the history of a troubled family. The word "dysfunctional" is hardly a term the biblical narrator would recognize, but how else can one describe the story of a young man who murders his own brother, a father who offers his own son as a sacrifice, or a group of young people who sell their youngest brother into slavery, and then torment their father by convincing him that the beloved child is dead.

The freedom narrative of Exodus cannot be understood without first confronting the interstitial narrative that unfolds at the end of Genesis. It matters little whether the book of Exodus is a fictional account, as some historians have recently suggested, or an actual historical event. The narration assumes meta-historical proportions that transcend any factual analysis. Here is a story of family hatred, of a father Jacob whose love of his youngest son. Joseph inflames the hatred of his brothers so much that they sell him to a band of passing merchants who bring him into Egypt as a slave. Joseph seems destined to bring his family into Egypt just as surely as

Moses is destined to bring it out. The Egypt of Joseph's time may not have been the land of milk and honey but it was a haven where food could still be purchased by those who were facing starvation. And, back home with his flocks and his quarrelsome sons, Jacob was surely facing starvation. Joseph, the rejected brother, became the savior of his family, the savior of Egypt, a hero and also a source of ultimate disaster.

Appointed by the pharaoh as his chief advisor, Joseph finds himself in charge of the distribution of grain in a time of famine. His is the most essential, the most crucial task of all — the job of feeding a hungry and restless populace. The pharaoh is no fool. Who better to face the hungry, and increasingly angry, masses than a handsome foreigner? Joseph is wise too, and a skillful diplomat. With his family now placed in key positions, he possesses the agrarian knowledge and bureaucratic skills that are desperately needed and also uniquely capable of resisting the intrigues of the royal household. But is this condition sustainable? Joseph was, and remains for all time, a symbol of the stranger. He stands between pharaoh and the people, between the rich and the poor. He is the powerful leader who lacks power. And with the passage of years his extended family is destined to experience the consequences of his fatal alienation.

"And there arose a new king over Egypt who knew not Joseph." Biblical commentators devote much attention to this early verse in the book of Exodus. Was this the same pharaoh who had elevated Joseph and had second thoughts about him? Or was it a successor who had forgotten how much Joseph had once meant to Egypt? The dangerous results of Joseph's role as an interstitial personality have been obscured by generations of Bible readers, content to close the book on him as they read the last verses of Genesis. But in so many ways, Exodus begins exactly where Genesis ends. An isolated Jew occupies a position of power in the royal court. There is a poetic symmetry in the parallel lives of Joseph and Moses, an eidetic imagery. Joseph moves from family to alienation to power; Moses moves from power to alienation to family. The career of Joseph led to the ultimate enslavement of his people, that of Moses led to the liberation of his people. In the two lives nestles the difference between interstitiality in its positive and negative guises.

The contrast between Joseph and Moses must not be allowed to obscure the fact that the intentions of both men were virtuous. The results of their virtue, however, produced quite different consequences. It is useful to examine other Jewish prototypes that stand in opposition to the negative interstitial role. The typical biblical prophet offers just such a prototype.

Alienated from society at large, the prophet sought a moral justification for his isolation. To turn to the prophet is neither to demean nor to dismiss other moral voices that have moved and challenged Jews throughout the ages. Nor is it to dismiss halachic and rabbinic efforts to find moral solutions to important social and religious problems. Indeed, the insights contained in the Babylonian and the Palestinian Talmud as well as thousands of later commentaries, constitute formidable contributions to human morality. The many books and articles devoted to an analysis of these modern moral problems give ample testimony to the relevance of modern Judaism.[10]

It is the stubborn independence of the prophet that commands attention. In their characteristic defiance of authority, the prophets offer a useful insight into both the problems and the promises inherent in any modern effort to create a just society. To be sure, the concerns of the prophets were ritual and theological as well as social, but the clarity and the poetry of their ethical commitment lays an undeniable claim upon our moral conscience. What is the reason for "the current neglect of the Prophets in favor of rabbinic texts?" asks Eugene Borowitz. The rabbinic texts have surely shaped our Jewish destiny, but they "will not teach us how to speak truth to power. We whose social ethics is so centrally involved with government can have few better guides to our duty than these fearless champions of Adonai's demands on rulers and the ruled."[11]

The prophet was the "lonely man of faith" — that phrase of Joseph Soloveitchik will be encountered later, but for now it can introduce a model of leadership that can often be emulated but seldom duplicated. The prophet's words give substance to an interstitial role that is positive. But an immediate warning must be issued. The prophets were products of their time, not ours. It would be a mistake to assume that they spoke with a single voice or that social justice was their sole preoccupation. They castigated and comforted; they criticized and consoled. And they did this as individuals, not part of any power bloc or professional group.

In view of his unbending commitment to justice, it is hard to understand why Spinoza disliked the prophets so intensely. Spinoza dismissed the prophets as "religious amateurs," gifted orators who all too glibly attributed their message to an imaginary divine source. It was how the prophets rationalized the source of the message, not the message itself, which evoked Spinoza's ire. Did the voice belong to God or to mortal man? Spinoza's question still has its power to concern us, but for all the passion of his criticism, Spinoza's view of religion was not so distant from that of the prophet. The primary task of religion, insisted the Dutch philosopher, was to seek justice, and on this score surely he would have found pleasant companionship in the presence of Isaiah and Jeremiah.

The prophets issued stern demands for social reform even as many of them sourly predicted a time of disaster, "the day of the Lord," as Amos famously called it. Eschatology and deontology — the end of things and the "ought" of things — married together in the prophet's unique rhetoric. Angry predictions of doom were joined to moral imperatives: take care of the widow and orphan; feed the hungry and the poor; put an end to corruption and the misuse of power. The prophets were offering more than formulas for change; they were challenging the abuses that debase God's creation. Their vision was often "messianic," and it was in this context that they often understood "the end of days." Whether the "end" would be glorious or catastrophic remained a matter of urgent speculation.

The words "chosen people" reveal a biblical idea whose sweet nectar conceals a bitter hemlock. From the moment Abraham is aroused from his comfortable life in Haran, commanded to leave his home and go to an undesignated land, the special character of Israel begins to take form. Israel is to be exalted over all other peoples. There are privileges and responsibilities, and also unforeseen perils. The book of Deuteronomy spells out the relationship most succinctly: "For you are a people consecrated to the Lord your God. Of all the peoples on earth the Lord your God chose you to be His treasured people." (Deut. 7.6) This special relationship between Israel and God permeates the entire Bible, stimulating devotion among those who are within the covenantal pact, bitterness and resentment among those outside of it.

It was the Age of Enlightenment that inspired Jewish thinkers to reassess the idea of the chosen people. With their stress upon the kinship of all human beings, Enlightenment thinkers forced religious people to question old assumptions. Here, too, it was Spinoza together with Voltaire and Rousseau who challenged the idea of religion as heritage rather than responsibility. Beginning with the middle of the seventeenth century, liberal Jewish thinkers began to cite biblical passages in order to emphasize Israel's responsibilities rather than its exclusiveness. The new Enlightenment thinking began to emphasize service to humanity as a religious goal. What became important now was a mandate that had universal appeal. And what is required? "Only to do justly, and to love mercy, and to walk humbly with thy God." (Micah 6.9)

It is hardly surprising that the early champions of the most liberal interpretations of Judaism were eager to affirm their companionship with "universal man." Reform-minded rabbis began to preach that the chosen people were chosen to bless rather than be blessed, to give more than to receive. These liberal rabbis had a glorious vision of a world they wanted to help create. And if their pronouncements could be generous, they could also be grandiose: "Let us step forth, and with uplifted standards of victory win the waiting world." The words are those of Kaufmann Kohler, Isaac Wise's successor as president of the Hebrew Union College. "Let us proclaim and practice, and by practicing successfully, teach the true religion of humanity and thus contribute our share towards making man what he is made for — God-like."[12]

This was radically different from the much older messianic ideal. By the nineteenth century, the dream of a personal messiah who would bring about a national restoration had been replaced by the vision of a messianic age, a time of universal peace and religious harmony. At least this was the understanding of most liberal Jew. Orthodox Jews remained indifferent to such ideas, firm in the conviction that these universalistic fantasies were little more than a chimera; worse, that they inevitably opened a door that led out of Judaism rather than into it. What neither liberal nor traditional Jews were willing to face was the diaspora reality of the interstitial role. What neither group could understand was that even in a time of enlightenment, the third party status of the Jewish community was to remain unchanged. The third party, the people in between, the other — no matter what it was called — the interstitial status was to remain simultaneously a burden and a blessing.

"Everything is not a Jewish issue," proclaimed Edward Bernard Glick. Writing in 2007, this Temple University professor denounced what he labeled as "Darfurism" and suggested that Jewish reactions to the brutal treatment of refuges in the Sudanese area of Darfur had become typical of the meaningless Jewish way of responding to many social problems. "Besides the rhetoric, do the Jewish Darfurians have any practical suggestions for stopping the slaughter in the Sudan?" For Glick, Jewish issues needed to be more sharply defined and more limited in focus. Israel is a Jewish issue; intermarriage is a Jewish issue. But ecology? "The environment is a problem, but it is not a Jewish problem. It does not belong on the Jewish agenda."[13]

What can be said about such a critique, one that evokes widespread approval in large segments of the Jewish community? The most obvious response is that a commitment to Jewish issues need not exclude other social concerns. There is ample room for both. "If I am not for myself," asked Hillel two thousand years ago, "who will be for me?" That Hillel immediately answered his question with another question reveals his dual focus, one which remains relevant: "And if I am for myself alone, what am I?"

But there is a more urgent response to those who advocate Jewish insularity: social justice is the ultimate guarantee of Jewish security. Jewish life flourishes when justice is ascendant. It might be argued that economics more than morality has historically affected Jewish well-being. Indeed, history seems to support the judgment that Jewish life appeared most vigorous in societies that were economically prosperous. But prosperity has often been proven to be a fleeting thing. When economic expansion was followed by economic collapse or by corruption or by social oppression the gold could quickly became dross. As important as economic expansion was for Jewish prospects, it was always the perpetuation of justice that offered Jews their most reliable hope. Justice emerges once again as a Jewish issue — not a minor one, an essential one. Here the historic vision of the prophets meets the complexities of modern civilization. The same evils that Isaiah and Amos railed against, poverty and inequality, remain as toxic social ingredients that portend a future of fear and insecurity. For modern Jews, justice is not a slogan, not a wishful dream; it is the guarantor of the future.

Like "love" and "peace," the word "justice" evokes universal admiration. What is so easy to praise in the abstract reveals itself to be quite controversial in its execution. There are dangers along the way; the journey requires both intelligence and courage. Start with the earliest of the prophets, Nathan, who confronted King David over his sexual exploitation of Bathsheba. Nathan's condemnation combines two basic elements of the prophetic mission — moral indignation and moral courage. More reprehensible than his seduction of Bathsheba is David's treatment of Bathsheba's husband, Uriah, the Hittite. Uriah is sent away from his home and into a battle where he is marked for death, a death ordered by a monarch whose power seems limitless. Nathan's insight into the abuse of power is profound. That the ill-fated Uriah remains a faithful soldier to the very end of his life makes David's deception all the more reprehensible. "Thou art the man!" Nathan hurls the accusation at his king — the first, but surely not the last, of the prophetic condemnations of arrogant power.

In the name of religion the prophets attacked religion. And even as they castigated misbegotten political alliances or military ventures, they understood the connection between politics and poverty, between international negotiations and domestic oppression. The military disaster that overtook King Ahab, for example, was directly related to the abuse of power which led him to expropriate Naboth's vineyard.

Nathan, Elijah and Elisha — these are the significant "non-literary" prophets whose alienation from secular life mark them as seminal figures in the development of a new moral standard. Politeness was hardly the hallmark of these early pioneers. "In the place where dogs lick the blood of Naboth, even there shall dogs lick your blood" — Elijah hurls the curse at King Ahab after the king and his wife Jezebel provoked the lynching of Naboth. (I Kings 18.20-40) The prophet is remote from any group of elites. With few exceptions the prophet lives alone. He invariably flees to some kind of a desert as does Elijah after his confrontation with Ahab. His social alienation reveals the very real dangers that often adhere to the positive interstitial role.

It was Amos whose poetic call for "justice to well up as water, righteousness as a mighty stream" set the tone for the literary prophets who followed him. His ringing pronouncements, which at first appear to contain few specifics, are actually filled with moral challenges as relevant today as when the prophet from Tekoa defiantly strode into the sanctuary a Beth-el. Warning against wanton greed and the exploitation of the poor, Amos condemns those who are conspicuously wealthy, "who lie on beds of ivory." He castigates those who multiply their real estate holdings at the expense of the poor, who "sell the needy for a pair of shoes." (Amos 2.6; 3.15; 4.1; 5.24; 6.3) The timelessness of this message becomes apparent with every new revelation of fiscal recklessness on the part of those who are expected to be the epitome of responsibility. The victims, now as always, are the poor and the powerless.

Nowhere is the interstitial role of the prophet more firmly illustrated than in the encounter between Amos and the priest Amaziah. Not only is Amos an alien in Israel, having traveled northward from Judea; he also refuses to allow himself to be stereotyped. He is a prophet, yet not a prophet. He is not a member of the professional group of prophets who tour the country and offer predictions about the future. "I was not a prophet, nor the son of a prophet," he insists, "but a simple pruner of sycamore trees."(Amos 7.14-15) His words come from God, Amos asserts. His ear is tuned to the people who suffer rather than those who worship at the altar of wealth and power. "I hate; I despise your festivals," Amos thunders (Amos 5.2) and his attack reveals again that he stands not only between the political elites and the populace, but also between the religious establishment and the wealthy people who have come to worship. In a similar vein, Isaiah compares the upper classes to Sodom and Gomorrah. Their sacrifices will be offered in vain. (Isaiah 1.11-14) Twice interstitial — religiously as well as socially — the prophet emerges as the idealized voice of morality, a voice that is as timeless as it is contemporary.

No clearer example of this unique mediate role can be found than Isaiah's stirring Yom Kippur challenge. On the holiest day of the religious year, he comes before his fellow Jews and bitterly castigates them: "Is this the fast that I have chosen?" Is it a day to wear sackcloth and ashes, to bow your head and pretend to be pious? Isaiah is aware of the incendiary nature of his words and he is prepared with an answer. "Is not this the fast that I have chosen? To loose the fetters of wickedness, to undo the bands of the yoke, and to let the oppressed go free? Is it not to deal thy bread to the hungry, and that thou bring the poor that are cast out into thy house?" (Isaiah 58) Isaiah's sermon is unsparing in its criticism of the mores of his society. But it is also relevant to our contemporary social scene. So too is his demand that worshippers "hide not from thine own flesh." His ancient words remain pertinent to our own Western civilization where wealthy consumers are becoming increasingly estranged from the workers who produce the products that enrich them.

Although some of the prophet's metaphors may sound archaic, their moral indignation is as timely now as it was in ancient Israel. Avarice is still a disease that touches those who close their ears to the cries of the poor. "They add house to house" — the words of Amos. They conflate power and wealth — not all, but a significant number of those who are exceedingly rich — and they rationalize the persistence of vast economic disparities as just rewards for their talents. They add corporation to corporation and have little regard for the consequences of their speculations. They fly on private jets between homes in Palm Springs and New York, and then off to visit an estate in Provence — the avocation of the superrich. Huge profits are realized through speculating on the funds of others. At a tragic cost to our entire world economy, the mortgages of poor homeowners are still sliced and diced, and then sold again. The poor are still "sold for a pair of shoes" — their incomes kept well below a living wage. When working men and women seek to protect their rights, or to form a union, they are exposed to the harsh realities of a society that has little sympathy for their efforts to organize.

Of course there is nothing inherently immoral about wealth itself. But there is something terribly disturbing about a society that lavishes huge tax advantages on the very rich while simultaneously reducing much needed health and welfare benefits so desperately needed by the poor. The problem is social as well as moral. Huge economic distortions in a nation suffused with democratic ideals invariably lead to painful social disruptions. And the most recent statistics do reveal alarming income imbalances. Five percent of national income in the United States goes to families in the upper one hundredth of a percent of the country's population. This means that an elite few earn incomes of $5.9 million or more each year while millions of children go to bed each night lacking any assurance that in the morning there will still be a place they can call home.[14]

The language of the prophet could be florid, but the word pictures they drew were incisive. Isaiah compares his listeners to a carefully tended vineyard that produces only rotten fruit. Hosea likens Israel to a harlot. The people, he insists, have abandoned their most basic principles and have violated the ethical rules that they ought to have held most sacred. For Jeremiah, on the other hand, the purchase of a plot of land in the midst of the city becomes a harbinger of an urban renewal that is ethical as well as political.

The prophetic tradition has not been without its detractors. For some it is too dismissive of prayer and ritual. A few modern commentators have been heard to complain that the prophets were too critical of their own people. Their criticisms are akin to those directed against Jews who question the proliferation of Israeli settlements in the occupied territories.[15] "Self-hating Jews" is the term easily thrust upon those Jews who dare question the wisdom of the Jewish establishment. And it is an accusation often assigned to the prophetic personality. Despite these criticisms, the message of the prophet remains an essential component of any effort to define positive interstitiality.

In writing about the prophets, as he did often, Abraham Joshua Heschel used to argue that the prophetic role was a response to God's pathos. By "God's pathos" Heschel insisted that God was not a passive force. Pathos was an acknowledgement of "God as involved in history, as intimately affected by events in history, as living care."[16] It would be hard to point to a twentieth-century Jewish leader who represented the prophetic call to justice more valiantly than did Heschel. To predicate prophetic action on God's pathos, however, is to place a burden upon both divinity and prophecy. It is to attach an unnecessary anthropomorphic quality on God. For despite Heschel's protest that God's pathos is not to be conceived of as an essential attribute of God but rather a "functional reality," there is a temptation to do what Maimonides warned against, namely to attribute human qualities to divine being. Much tidier and more direct is the earlier endeavor of Spinoza to identify the totality of religion with the totality of social justice. Spinoza's view of religion may have lacked the modern urgency of Heschel's but their mutual devotion to the idea of justice cannot be underestimated.

In recent years, there has been a tendency to replace the clear voice of the prophet with a less strident and more ambiguous call to social action. The idea of *tikkun olam* — the repair of the world — has become a familiar part of the Jewish social action vocabulary. The phrase which first appeared in Talmudic literature and later played a prominent part in Jewish mysticism is appealing in that it seems to be luring its listeners into some great cosmic venture. But there is a vast difference between the clarion call of the prophet and the more subdued premise of *tikkun olam*. There is also a troubling element of condescension in the idea of *tikkun olam*. For all its good intentions, the phrase *tikkun olam* is a pessimistic one — the world is broken, not at all whole. Again it is contemporary philosopher Eugene Borowitz who suggests that there are so many worthy causes thrust upon us that our ethical activism gives way to ethical humility. "Is that what we are hinting at in translating *tikkun olam* as merely 'mending the world,' that is, at best leaving it a thing of patches, when not too long ago we hoped for more grandiose human accomplishment?"[17] It was not a patchwork quilt that the prophets envisioned. Theirs was a more glorious goal. "In the end of days," they repeatedly intoned, humanity will reach the very summit of God's world, "the mountain of the Lord's house." Their dream was of a godly world, a peaceful world, and above all, a just world.

The prophetic word need not always be strident and critical. There are times when the prophetic voice becomes soft and gentle. A great tragedy occurs. A city is shattered by a tornado. A country is devastated by a flood, a terrorist attack. The interstitial voice may be the voice of compassion. It may be the calming voice of a mature Jeremiah urging patience rather than vengeance, consolation rather than condemnation. The prophets were not monochromatic. Predicting the downfall of Jerusalem, an angry Jeremiah could declare: "I have set my face against the city."(Jer. 8.10) But after the fall of the city, he could join the exiles as they leave for Babylonia. He finds words that offer healing and hope: "For I will pardon them whom I leave as a remnant."(Jer. 50.20) In a similar spirit a later Isaiah offers the consoling words that a suffering people need to hear: "Comfort ye, comfort ye, My people, saith your God. Bid Jerusalem take heart."(Isaiah 40.1)

The interstitial voice of the prophet, so often abrasive and occasionally florid, is nevertheless a perfect model for a world in which injustice and greed still masquerade as virtue and achievement. To be sure the words of the biblical prophet will not be identical to those so urgently needed in a technological society such as the one we inhabit. Humility is always a worthy companion for anyone who would try to wear the mantle of the prophets. The ability to listen is to recognize the possibility of mistakes. It is to remain open to new insights. The positive interstitial role requires that we open our hands and minds and hearts to the "other." It demands a willingness to grow and to learn.

What it does not require is acquiescence in the face of injustice. Rather, the positive interstitial role invites a regular process of self-examination — one in which motives as well as deeds are weighed in the moral balance. Specifically, for modern Jews, it represents an opportunity to re-examine cherished and possibly outmoded priorities. Good advice may still be found in the words of Isaiah: "Wash yourselves; make yourselves clean; learn to do good; seek justice, relieve the oppressed; defend the fatherless; plead for the widow." (Isaiah 1.16-20)

Chapter 4

Confronting the Problem

"**Things fall apart**; the centre cannot hold." William Butler Yeats' famous line may be a summation of Jewish diaspora history. When things do fall apart, as they do during periods of social or economic stress, the position of the people in between becomes perilous. Interstitiality may, but does not necessarily, entail antisemitism, but antisemitism invariably entails interstitiality. The role itself is a neutral one; its essential feature is simply its position — a position eternally in the middle.

At least four different forms of antisemitism become immediately identifiable. The first, and most readily understood of these, is religious antisemitism. "The Jews killed Christ!" or "The Jews betrayed Mohammed." Variations of charges such as these are infinite, ranging from affirmations that the "Old Testament" stresses law and not love, to the still troublesome accusation that even modern Jews bear a collective responsibility for the death of Jesus. Most perplexing and outrageous of all is the durability of the charge that Jews engage in the practice of "ritual murder." It can be argued, not without reason, that it is these religion-based hostilities that initiated ancient animosity toward Jews, and that they continue to nurture modern anti-Jewish attitudes.

A second form of antisemitism is political and social in content. Hostility toward Jews existed in the ancient world long before the great religious rupture between Judaism and Christianity. A brief examination of these early tensions will expose an aspect of the interstitial role that is of crucial importance — antagonism toward Jews based upon their "separateness." This sense of separateness was arguably as much social as it was religious.

As early as the first century, Josephus felt the need to defend his co-religionists against the bitter attacks of Apion on this issue, but criticisms of Jewish separateness can be found many centuries earlier. Apion, who was born in Alexandria and lived from about 35 BCE to 48 CE, was filled with enough animosity that he did not need to replay the discredited tales of others. Yet the lure of imitation was hard for this acerbic Alexandrian to resist and he ended up by willingly repeating the most incredible tales of others, including those aired by the ancient Egyptian Manetho, who lived

43

in the third century BCE. Reconstructing Manetho's account, Apion offered with certainty the knowledge that the Jews were driven out of Egypt because they were lepers. Even Moses himself was a leper.

Apion gives early encouragement to the ritual murder charge, solemnly repeating the rumor that every year the Jews take a foreigner into the forest, fatten him up, and then kill him for religious purposes. But the most credible point of his bitter polemic, and the one that Josephus felt compelled to answer, was his insistence that the Jews of Alexandria had no right to citizenship, that they were basically foreigners, and that their loyalty was always to be regarded with a suspicious eye. It is worth noting that the Alexandrian Jewish philosopher Philo had traveled to Rome in the year 38 to plead for the restoration of Jewish rights in his native city. It need not surprise us to learn that Apion had traveled to the same court to denounce the very Jews that Philo, Alexandria's most illustrious Jewish leader, had come to defend. That Josephus felt the need to write an entire book in response to Apion provides evidence of the tremendous pain that this Alexandrian logician had been able to inflict on the Jewish community. *Contra Apionem*, written thirty years after the death of Apion, reveals the persistence of the accusation that Jewish ideas and Jewish practices justified excluding Jews from the larger Roman community.

Was the idea of separateness an essential aspect of the Jewish belief system, or was it something imposed upon Jews as a result of their position as outsiders? As important as the answer to this question is, it is clear that the ubiquity of "separateness," both as idea and reality, is crucial to an understanding of the interstitial role.

Early manifestations of interstitiality may be found in the way the pagan world gradually came to view the Jews, particularly those Jews who lived outside of the Holy Land. Not surprisingly, there is a lack of agreement as to the causes of early anti-Jewish hostility. Peter Schafer and Louis Feldman, respected scholars, come to sharply different conclusions about the ancient origins of antisemitism. Schafer discerns a variety of views among scholars studying anti-Jewish attitudes in the ancient world. He identifies two of the more prominent theories, labeling them "substantialist" and "functionalist." Substantialists, he suggests, argue that ancient anti-Jewish sentiments stemmed from the religious practices of the Jews, that is, the "substance" of their belief system, particularly those that led them to separate themselves from other people. Functionalists, on the other hand, while still recognizing the importance of a separate and distinct Jewish role, maintain that ancient antisemitism had little to do with the essential beliefs of Judaism, but rather stemmed from particular political events (functions) which produced hostility between Jews and their neighbors.

Among substantialists, Louis Feldman certainly plays a leading role. He insisted that most pagans "viewed the Jews as a group, making almost no differentiation among subgroups." Even in the oldest texts "there is always a facile generalization about the Jews . . . based on the perception . . . that Moses introduced to his Jewish followers a way of life that was hostile to foreigners . . . so that they might not have social contact with non-Jews."[18] Feldman's substantialism emphasizes that it was Jewish religious practices that provoked resentment among pagan peoples.

Peter Schafer accuses Feldman of being overly apologetic, even as he stakes his claim on the middle ground while acknowledging the merits of both functionalists and substantialists. Elements of both schools are true, Schafer suggests, but a crucial aspect of early antipathy toward the Jews has generally been overlooked — and that element is revealed in the title of Schafer's book, *Judeophobia*. It is hatred coupled with fear that formed the basic components of ancient hostility toward the Jews.

Acknowledging the combustible mixture of national homelessness and intense religious rivalry does not diminish the unique importance of either Jewish beliefs or of politics in the formation of the interstitial role. On the contrary, both elements are essential. Schafer offers an example of how both factors combined to create a violent, but little-known confrontation that occurred far from the main stage of Jewish history. In the year 410 BCE, the Jewish community of Elephantine, a military colony on the southernmost border of Egypt was traumatized by an outburst of anti-Jewish feeling. Religious tensions had been brewing for many years. The priests of the ram-god Khnum wanted to prevent the Jews of Elephantine from worshipping God, and from offering sacrifices in their temple. While these tensions were building there was rising antagonism between the Persian rulers of Elephantine, and the Egyptians who resented the power of their foreign oppressors. The Jews of Elephantine were interstitial. The Egyptians saw them as allies of the hated Persians. The strange worship in the temple was a pretext. When the Egyptians finally rebelled against their Persian oppressors, it was the Jewish temple of Elephantine that bore the brunt of Egyptian animosity. That animosity was not satisfied until the temple had been burnt down to its foundation. "It is the triangle between the Egyptians, the Persians, and the Jews, in all its religious and political dimensions and implications, within which the hatred of the Jews has to be defined. From the very beginning of this complicated relationship between native Egyptian, Persian oppressors, and Jewish mercenaries, the Jews always appear on the side of the Persians."[19]

Again, it is important to recognize that there are significant differences between pagan anti-Jewish feelings and the type of antisemitism that gradually came to inform the interstitial role in medieval and modern times. Two crucial events marked the transformation which occurred relatively simultaneously: the loss of a national Jewish homeland and the rise of a new religion, a religion that came to regard its progenitor not as parent but as adversary. These two phenomena cannot be separated from one another. It is the combination of the two that invests interstitiality with its unique significance. It is also this combination that distinguishes Jewish history from that of other minority groups.

Every Jewish religious school student memorizes the year 70 CE, as the quintessential tragic moment in Jewish history. But the destruction of the Jerusalem Temple in that year was both preceded and followed by waves of Jewish emigration from the historic homeland. The diaspora was a process, not a one-time event. That it was accompanied by growing competition between powerful religious forces resulted in a cataclysmic transformation for the Jews of the entire world. The miracle of Jewish survival, if one can ascribe the word miracle to historic phenomena, was that the destruction resulted in a moral re-examination of the entire faith. Neither the temptation to assimilate, nor the tendency to blame the political powers of the age — though both tendencies both could be noted — stemmed the moral recriminations which strangely provided catharsis as well as hope.

Rooted in history, sociopolitical antisemitism also transcends history. It is not dependent upon any single event. It invariably fashions the event to reinforce an assumed reality. It insists that Jews are too wealthy and powerful, or conversely, too poor and dirty. Crass and exploitive at one moment; they are Communists and radicals the next. It was these apparently contradictory aspects of antisemitism that achieved a strange rationality with the passage of the centuries. By the middle of the nineteenth century, the most sophisticated country of Europe witnessed the birth of a new form of antisemitism. It was in France rather than in Germany that the contradictions of modern antisemitism began to assume political dimensions. Nurtured by the fears of clergy and military leaders, and sustained by a propaganda program that remained undaunted even by its own irrationality, hostility toward Jews became, for the first time, a

46

matter of national security. And it was in France that Jews became conscious of their vulnerability to attacks from the left as well as the right. From the right the charge could be made that the Jews were allied with the anti-military, anti-Catholic forces threatening to join liberals and intellectuals in an assault on the ancient traditions of France. Was it not Jewish refugees from Eastern Europe who were bringing vice and social unrest into Paris as well as other leading cities? From the left the accusations were equally ominous. Jews were the harbingers of a new type of religion, a religion whose god was money. Even some of the previously friendly socialist movements began to picture Jews as parasites feasting upon the French body politic.

That these contradictory tendencies should have erupted with such passion during the Dreyfus trial need hardly surprise us. The trial represented an effort to defend the old order, an order that at times seemed senile rather than merely "old." The French Revolution had merely been the first of the attacks on the Catholic Church, much of whose authority could be seen to have already slipped away. And the power of the Rothschild family had already become more the stuff of legend than of reality. The days when they could provide governments with the funds need to purchase a Suez Canal or to finance the construction of utilities and railroads were fast coming to an end. The Rothschilds remained notably silent during the Dreyfus trial, a reminder of the delicate path they had chosen to take in order not to alienate any of their potential enemies. Yet the vision of their wealth could still be associated with images of world domination. For the anti-Semite, every Jew was a Rothschild. Most Jews could only wish that they were.

The third, and, in terms of its modern consequences, the most devastating form of anti-Jewish sentiment stemmed from the development of genetic theories during the last decades of the nineteenth century. Taking their clue from the "scientific" ruminations of Joseph Arthur Gobineau and his successors, racial bigots could begin to picture Jews in a new and much more ominous light. Jews could now be regarded as racially inferior. No longer merely a political or religious threat, the new theories opened the door to a much more ominous view of antisemitism. Jews came to be seen as the incarnation of a disease; a disease that had to be eliminated. Racial antisemitism, of course, achieved its full devastating power in Hitler's Germany, where the fanatical hatred of one man met ancient stereotypes and succeeded in convincing an entire people that the very Jews who had lived and worked in their midst for centuries had suddenly become a virulent cancer. Overnight, it seemed, Jews had become doubly vulnerable. Not only were they disloyal to country, but they were also physically dangerous, a dire threat to the character and existence of an entire society.

The fourth form of antisemitism, which, for want of a better term, may be labeled as psycho-social, permeated and also gave cohesion to each of the first three forms. The phrase "psycho-social" is used to convey the complex psychological factors, real or imagined, as they encounter all kinds of social reality. This type of antisemitism, which, as we shall see, Jean-Paul Sartre tried to analyze, was based upon the generalized socialization of personal experience. "I simply don't like Jews. They are too pushy. They are noisy." Or, "I like individual Jews. Get them together, though, and I can't stand them." Reactions such as these, putatively based on unpleasant personal experiences, easily transformed themselves into stereotypes — stereotypes useful in reinforcing the very antisemitic attitudes from which they sprang. It must be added that Jews themselves have not always been averse to invoking some of these very stereotypes in describing their co-religionists.

This type of anti-Jewish sentiment, so characteristically stereotypical, was invariably deductive rather than inductive. Individual experiences, it assumes, spring from some universal truth. "Sam is a cheater; what do you expect, he is Jewish," or "No dear, Hannah is not to be invited to your birthday party; she is a Jew." The more frequent formula was painfully generalized: "You can never trust a Jew." Cradled in religious and social assumptions, this form of prejudice nourished its own cherished assumptions. The result is that the individual Jew became, not a person, but an abstraction.

The varying forms of antisemitism may invite distinctions and welcome historical analysis. But, as we have seen, there is one element that is always present — the consistent and persistent fact of Jewish separation. The moral implications of this separation remain to be studied. The interstitial role is not a simple one. Janus-like it has two faces. And the two faces reveal important and distinct aspects of the role. The first bears the name "negative interstitiality." The word "negative" acknowledges the painful and dysfunctional nature of antisemitism. It feeds on its victims and ultimately determines that they are less than complete human beings. To study negative interstitiality is to comprehend its causes and to understand its impact upon its perpetrators as well as its victims.

48

A traditional way for Jews to escape antisemitism was to turn inward. A life confined by the geographic and social limitations of a ghetto or *Judengasse* could provide security and comfort. When the hostile environment around them proved too oppressive, Jews could find solace within themselves, within the relatively safe world of religious piety and study. But regardless of whether their faces turned inward toward the comfort of their own community or outward toward society in general, there were significant personalities who would emerge from time to time as leaders and spokesmen. Who were these leaders and what were the qualities that brought them to prominence?

The interplay between leader and people invariably emerged as a drama acted out on the larger stage of Jewish interstitial life. The power available to any one individual was traditionally fashioned and limited by a wide variety of external forces, forces that were often taken for granted even if they could seldom be fully articulated.

Solomon Zeitlin, who never achieved the scholarly recognition many feel that he merited, taught history at a small college of Jewish studies in Philadelphia. Dropsie College was founded in 1913, with a faculty of three professors. A small, prestigious institution, Dropsie eventually became the Center for Advanced Judaic Studies at the University of Pennsylvania. During the 1940s as Hitler was decimating European Jewry, Zeitlin began to explore the changing patterns of Jewish leadership. His particular focus was upon the dichotomy between secular and religious leaders. His analysis of leadership patterns convinced him that the tensions between these two types of leaders revealed much about the thinking as well as the everyday life of ordinary Jews. Leaders, in other words, both reflected and affected the lives of those who came under their influence. The historic tensions which Zeitlin studied can still be discerned. These tensions are particularly evident in the persistent competition between rabbis and federations and welfare funds, as well as in the often tenuous relationships between rabbis and the lay leaders of their congregations.

Parallel to any study of competing patterns leadership, and perhaps more decisive in terms of the Jewish masses, would be an examination of the economic factors that dominated Jewish life. Was Karl Marx expressing his deepest anti-Semitic thoughts when he suggested that Jews had survived, not in spite of history, but because of history, and that Judaism and capitalism were synonymous? Certainly his early works revealed more than a hostile tone toward the religion of his parents, yet his analysis cannot be dismissed out of hand, and his disciples testify to the power of his shattering analysis.

Abram Leon was one of those Marxists who tried to understand the entire history of Judaism in terms of its economic history. Leon, who joined the Belgian resistance during World War II, was captured and murdered by the Nazis before he could finish his probing analysis. His study, *The Jewish Question*, represented a general attempt to understand the economic fate of the Jews as they existed in various stages of world economic development. Leon's dramatic condemnation of capitalism, a critical part of his Communist Marxist orientation, led him to be dogmatic at times, but the broad range of his economic analysis invites further scrutiny.

Isaac Deutscher was a different kind of radical yet his critique of religious Judaism brought him close to Leon's economic determinism. Deutscher, who died in Rome in 1967, was an authority on Trotsky and Stalin, and remained a life-long Marxist, even though he became sharply critical of Stalin and of the Soviet Union. In a rather lengthy essay published shortly after his death, Deutscher's widow Tamara described the exact moment in which this son of Polish Orthodox Jews realized how religiously alienated he had become. A young friend, who was an atheist and a communist, dared Isaac to skip Yom Kippur services and to join him in a visit to the cemetery. Standing at the grave of a revered rabbi on the holiest day of the Jewish year, the young man pulled out a sandwich made of ham and butter and dared Isaac to eat it. After but a moment's hesitation, the fourteen-year-old Isaac Deutscher began to eat the sandwich. For years after, whenever he recounted the story he admitted to his anguish and embarrassment. It was not that he had deceived God; but that he had deceived his own beloved parents.[20]

Deutscher's alienation from Judaism is noteworthy here, not only because it reflects the indifference of many modern Jews, but precisely because his religious alienation combined with his search for a meaningful Jewish community exposes a critical aspect of the interstitial analysis. What makes me a Jew? Deutscher asked. "Religion? I am an atheist. Jewish nationalism? I am an internationalist. In neither sense am I therefore, a Jew. I am, however, a Jew by force of my unconditional solidarity with the persecuted and exterminated. I am a Jew because I feel the Jewish tragedy as my own tragedy; because I feel the pulse of Jewish history; because I should like to do all I can to assure the real, not spurious, security and self-respect of the Jews."[21]

The primary challenge was to secure the safety of the Jewish community. But it was not an easy challenge to meet. The leaders Jews selected for themselves, or had selected for them, were not a simple lot. There was strength and helplessness, altruism and selfishness, inspiration and opportunism. By examining the actions of some significant Jewish leaders it becomes possible to discern an important aspect of the interstitial role. It was not merely the Jewish community that existed "between the parts." Its leaders were also interstitial, but in a dual sense. If the Jewish community found itself influenced and shaped by external forces, its leaders, as the face of that community, inevitably depended upon support from within and approval from the outside. That support was not always forthcoming, nor was it consistent. No wonder that Jewish leadership often proved to be such a perilous undertaking.

What, then, are the factors that fashioned the interstitial role? Posing this question invites a host of others. How did individual leaders respond to their interstitial roles? What external influences modified or stimulated the actions of specific Jewish leaders? How did these factors affect the non-Jewish community as well as the Jewish community, and how were they perceived similarly or differently by each? An approach seeking the answers to these questions needs to avoid the temptation to minimize the importance of personal deeds or religious aspirations. On the contrary, an understanding of how external forces influenced Jewish history serves to augment an appreciation of individual accomplishments even as it makes the search for positive interstitial roles more meaningful and more urgent.

Since the interstitial analysis is so steeped in the history of antisemitism, it is important to recognize that anti-Jewish feeling is seldom related to the actions of any one individual. Rather, this form of prejudice is generally the product of various social conditions that Jews may influence but never control. The Vietnam War, for example, was one of the most unpopular of all American wars. As President Nixon's secretary of state, Henry Kissinger was responsible for U.S. foreign policy. Yet Kissinger's Jewishness hardly emerged as an issue during this entire controversial period. On the contrary there have been times when an outburst of antisemitism could apparently be stimulated by the actions of a single individual. Angry protests doomed Joseph Suess Oppenheimer in Germany, and the trial of Alfred Dreyfus in France was accompanied by mass anti-Jewish demonstrations. But even these outbreaks, and countless others like them, were the products, rather than the sources, of existing antisemitism.

Regardless of whether Jewish leadership has often alternated between secular and religious personalities, as Zeitlin has suggested, a distinct factor in these alterations was invariably the absence of Jewish political autonomy. This loss, beginning centuries before the destruction of the Temple in Jerusalem, was accompanied by a pattern of steady Jewish emigration from ancient Judea and by the inevitable subordination of Jewish leaders to the dominion of others. Jews did not need a Herzl to remind them of the pain precipitated by their dispersion from the historic homeland. "Next year in Jerusalem!" became the culminating prayer of the Passover ritual. The words were not merely a fervent hope; they also represented a constant acknowledgment of the heavy social and emotional toll that their exile had imposed upon them.

It was not solely the destruction of the Temple in Jerusalem that caused the critical upheaval in Jewish life. The deterioration of the economy that had become painfully apparent by the dawn of the new millennium had made life in Palestine increasingly difficult. The destruction of the Temple in 70 CE certainly was a psychological and religious trauma. But subsequent Jewish history, and particularly the history of Jewish suffering, magnified the significance of the Temple to the point where its destruction became such a vivid symbol of powerlessness that simply mentioning the date "70" required no other commentary. It is certainly true, that upon the destruction of Jerusalem, the Roman commander Titus brought thousands of Jews as captives back to Rome. What is equally noteworthy, however, is that these captives were quickly ransomed by the thousands of Jews already living and prospering in Rome. As merchants and artisans, Jews brought skills to Rome badly needed by a society convinced that the whole world was its empire.

And so, even before the destruction of the Jerusalem Temple, patterns of interstitiality were emerging from the rapidly changing conditions of Jewish life. In some detail, Josephus describes an incident that occurred in Rome, probably around the year 33 CE, during the reign of Tiberius. A renegade Jew recruited three equally disreputable Jewish companions who were able to persuade a wealthy and dignified lady by the name of Fulvia to make a significant contribution to the Temple in Jerusalem. Fulvia had recently converted to Judaism, an act which of itself casts light upon the comparative freedom of religion Jews were able to enjoy in Rome. Unfortunately, Fulvia's well-intentioned generosity was aborted when the four scoundrels spent her money on themselves. Their corrupt behavior was soon exposed and punishment was immediate and severe. Josephus tells us that Tiberius "ordered all the Jews to be banished out of Rome....Thus were these Jews banished out of the city by the wickedness of four men."[22] The contrast between Fulvia's right to convert to Judaism, and the subsequent mass expulsion of Jews, raises questions about the real quality of Jewish life in Rome, and also perhaps about the reliability of Josephus in this instance. Were the four Jewish scoundrels a symptom of a deeper corruption within the Jewish community, or was the blanket punishment imposed upon Jews as a group an early example of the stereotyping that was to become so characteristic of later antisemitism?

The gradual dispersion of Jews from Palestine was accompanied by long, and sometimes bitter, power struggles within the Jewish community itself. These struggles between secular and religious leaders often provide hints about the degree of freedom any given community was allowed to enjoy. Although the pattern was not totally consistent, secular Jewish leadership tended to flourish during those times when civil and religious rights were being expanded. Conversely, persecution usually resulted in a Jewish turn inward with its accompanying idealization of piety and scholarship. During these periods of oppression religious, rather than secular, leaders tended to prevail.

Not the least of the blows caused by the loss of autonomy was the blow delivered to Jewish universalism. Isaiah's vision of an "end of days" became an object of derision in the face of the pressing need for Jewish survival. The creative energies of the Jewish community became preoccupied with the need to defend the community from its real or perceived enemies. Leaders, even the most competent among them, were expected to do one thing and to do it well — defend their people. Even writers and intellectuals were expected to defend the community, and, at the very least, do it no harm. Thus, the acceptability of these leaders by the non-Jewish community became as important as their credibility within the Jewish community. In many eras this meant that Jews abdicated complete control over the selection of their own leaders and had to suffer quasi leaders who were appointed by, or acceptable to, non-Jewish authorities. The credibility of these leaders took a variety of forms, some of them more legitimate than others — their wealth (the Rothschilds), their scholarship (Rashi or Maimonides), or their political acumen (Hasdai ibn Shaprut or Samuel ha-Nagid). Their survival invariably depended upon the tenuous relationship between society at large, and an amorphous Jewish society — between non-Jewish expectations and a Jewish search for equilibrium.

Standing between Jew and Roman or between Jew and Christian or between Jew and Muslim, the mediating role of the leader may seem inconsequential beside other characteristics. Family connections and personal charisma are always qualities attached to genuine leaders. But the interstitial role creates its own illusions. One illusion was that the interstitial leader was acting as free and independent agent. Coupled with this illusion was the even more ingenuous conviction that diaspora Jews had actually succeeded in becoming an indigenous part of the larger non-Jewish society in which they dwelt. Both assumptions were to prove tragically disappointing. In reality, the interstitial character of their leaders often masked the limitations of Jewish power.

To study historic Jewish leaders solely in the light of the interstitial roles they occupied would slight the unique and creative energies that propelled them to prominence. Yet to ignore the overwhelming reality and debilitating power of the intermediary role is to fail at another level. It is to remain indifferent to an aspect of Jewish history that has previously been neglected. It is also to allow the consequences of many actions taken in the name of the Jewish community to remain unexamined. And so a closer look into the lives of a few significant historical personalities may not only provide a fresh view of some important events of the past but may also offer insights that might well prove useful in the future.

In ancient Judea following the destruction of the Jerusalem Temple in 70 CE, the distinction between religious and secular authority became a matter of increased importance precisely because the suppression of Jewish nationalism resulted in an increased emphasis on scholarship and religious life rather than political activity. But it should immediately be observed that the divorce of these two aspects of Jewish life was never as complete as it might appear. What is indisputable is that Palestine itself was suffering through a period of political and social decline. Unpredictability marked the political status of the Jewish community. A decade of persecution might well be followed by a few years of comparative tranquility — all dependent upon the disposition of the administration in Rome. Under these circumstances, dedication to scholarship, rather than military prowess, became the acknowledged path to Jewish leadership. But the fact that these leaders were distinguished primarily by their religious rather than their secular qualities did not prevent them from acting in the political arena as well.

With the approval of the Roman government the control of Jewish life was placed in the hands of religious leaders and especially the *nasi* or

Patriarch. The word *nasi*, however, connotes two distinct leadership roles. For the Romans the leader of the Jews was simply the "patriarch," but the word *nasi* itself also carries the quite secular connotation, "prince." Judah ha-Nasi fit both roles perfectly. A patriarch by birth and by bearing, he soon acquired both the trappings and the power of royalty. By the year 165 CE, Judah had come to be recognized as the undisputed leader of the Palestinian Jews. He was a brilliant scholar as well as a capable administrator. Not the least of his talents was his remarkable ability to get along well with the administration in Rome.

The work of Judah ha-Nasi has to be understood in light of the suffering experienced by Jews under the oppressive tyranny of the emperor Hadrian. In the beginning of his reign Hadrian appeared to be a friend of the Judean Jewish community, The amicable relationship, however, soon turned sour as Hadrian revealed his determination to turn Jerusalem into a Roman city and to rebuild the Temple as a shrine to Jupiter. He also enacted laws severely limiting the Jewish rite of circumcision as well as academic freedom. The rebellion that broke out in 132 was led by Simon Bar Kochba, whose claims to leadership were little hurt by the conviction of many of his followers that he was actually the long awaited messiah. These claims were not impaired; in fact they were famously encouraged by the support of the brilliant and charismatic scholar, Rabbi Akiba ben Joseph.

Surprising to no one, save the rebels themselves, the revolt was brutally if not quickly suppressed. In addition to the deaths that occurred during the three years of the rebellion, thousands of Jews were sent to Rome as captives or exiled to Egypt. Jerusalem itself, according to the legends, was plowed over by a team of oxen, and Jews were allowed to visit the city only on the 9th of Av, the traditional day of Jewish mourning over the destruction of both the First and Second Temples. Writing some seventy years after the events themselves, the Roman historian Cassius Dio provided a chilling account of the suffering that resulted from Bar Kochba's defeat. "Five hundred and eighty thousand men were slain in the various raids and battles, and the number of those that perished by famine, disease and fire was past finding out."[23] Even granting that numbers used by ancient historians are always suspect, the losses were undoubtedly staggering.

Less symbolic, and therefore less well commemorated than the destruction of the Temple in 70, the failure of the Bar Kochba revolution was nevertheless a decisive event in Jewish history. With Bar Kochba's downfall, the last visages of autonomy were crushed, and Jews had to begin the search for new patterns of leadership. Legends about the destruction of the Jerusalem Temple became ever more popular and mystical. The reasons for this development, however, were hardly mystical. After Bar Kochba, Jewish survival depended upon its religious leaders, not its military or political ones. From now on hopes of a national restoration could only be taken seriously if they were couched in religious terms.

If the failure of the Bar Kochba rebellion marked the end of Jewish national aspirations, it had little deleterious effect on Jewish religious endeavors in other parts of the country that now began to be known by its ancient name of Palestine. Following the death of Hadrian oppression seems to have diminished. It was in this new and more open context that Judah ha-Nasi emerged as the seminal Jewish personality of his era. His genius lay in the way he was able to maintain his powerful influence within his own community while simultaneously gaining the respect and trust of the Roman leadership. Rabbinic literature even contains a legend alluding to a personal friendship between Judah and the enlightened Roman emperor Marcus Aurelius. Whether Judah enjoyed this relationship with Marcus Aurelius or more likely a later emperor of the Severan dynasty, the closeness of the Jewish leader to Roman officials proved to be of great importance both for Judah personally and for the welfare of Palestinian Jews.[24]

Under the guidance of Judah ha-Nasi the compendium of Jewish law known as the *Mishnah*, was debated and codified. This tremendous creation which was to become the basis of the Talmud, owes much to Judah's scholarship and leadership. The contents of the *Mishnah* cast a light upon the concerns that were occupying the Jewish academic world as well as the Jewish community at large. The six major tractates or sections bear names that reveal both the scope of Jewish legislative power and its limitations:

1. *Zeraim* — seeds
2. *Moed* — festivals
3. *Nashim* — women
4. *Nezikin* — damages
5. *Kedoshin* — holy things
6. *T'harot* — purification

Agriculture and worship and personal purity — these are the areas encompassed by the Talmud. The *Mishnah* reveals a Jewish world wavering between an idealized past and an uncertain future. Past rituals, many of them involving a Temple that is no more, are painstakingly described; economic and social regulations are offered in great detail. But the omissions are as significant as the inclusions. What is missing is anything that has to do with self-government or political power. Thus, the creation of the *Mishnah* marks an important transition in Jewish life. It is a work of memory and also of expectation.

The books of the *Mishnah* and later the Talmud reveal a process in which the desire for self-government is gradually replaced by a new reality — the reality which came to define the interstitial people. Political autonomy and rules of national governance are replaced by codes of personal conduct and inner-group relationships. Absent from these codes, then, are precisely those characteristics of an independent nation that Thomas Jefferson included in the final paragraph of the Declaration of Independence: "That they have full Power to levy War, to conclude Peace, contract Alliances, establish Commerce, and to do all other Acts and Things which Independent States may of right do."

Judah ha-Nasi's authority was limited to those functions tolerated by Rome. In this respect, his activities reveal an early form of the interstitial role — that of the individual positioned between his own people and a dominating foreign power. His rise to power was not the result of class struggle or family intrigue. No cataclysmic clash with existing powers is to be found here. Judah was respected because his scholarship made him acceptable to Jews, and his diplomatic skills made him acceptable to the Romans. Jewish leadership after the destruction of the Jerusalem Temple is seldom one of opposition — often one of accommodation or even of "mediation."

Judah's power was impressive. He held the authority to appoint judges and teachers to positions all over the country. He could determine who sat on the Sanhedrin. His ability to place scholars in rabbinic positions was seldom subject to question so long as these appointments did not involve someone who might be seen as a threat to the Roman government. Not to be overlooked were Judah's economic connections. Commercial alliances were formed that rewarded Judah for his loyalty and also proved beneficial to the administration in Rome. Evidence suggests that Antoninus entrusted Judah and his staff with several of his estates and joined him in a cattle-breeding venture.[25]

Judah, however, was ambivalent about helping the poor. In his pioneering *History of the Jews*, Graetz offers two stories from rabbinic literature illustrative of Judah's wealth and also his arrogance. During a time of famine Judah agreed to open up the vast warehouses that he controlled. But he stipulated that food be given only to those who were committed to scholarship. Angry at this decision, Jonathan ben Amram came to see Judah disguised as an am-ha-aretz — a non-scholar who typified the majority of the people. "Feed me," he demanded, "as you would feed a hungry dog or a raven." A similar story is told about the daughters of Aher who were reduced to begging for food. Aher was a brilliant scholar and also a reviled apostate. Aher's hungry daughters were denied food at Judah's orders. "Rabbi, forget our father's deeds," they implored, "and remember instead his scholarship." In both of these cases, whether because of his own sensitivities or public pressure, Judah was forced to relent, and provide help to those who sought it.[26]

To highlight the interstitial aspects of Judah's leadership does not diminish an appreciation of his scholarship. On the contrary, the fact that he and his colleagues could produce such an enduring compendium of Jewish law is a tribute to their ability to create great legislation under conditions that must have been far from ideal. Toward the end of his life, Judah ha-Nasi and his academy moved north toward the Galilee. The move was more than geographical. An old order was coming to an end and a most uncertain one was looming over the horizon. Galilee and not Jerusalem was now the center of Palestinian Jewish life. Many of the accounts of Judah's life indicate that the move to Galilee was motivated by Judah's declining health. Simon Dubnow, however, suggests that the academy was impelled to move, or perhaps even "compelled," in order to be closer to the seat of Roman authority, now relocated in Sepphoris in the Galilee. When the government issued its orders, even the prince of the Jews had to obey.[27]

In Babylonia, unlike conquered Palestine, leadership of the Jewish community fluctuated between secular and religious personalities. The gaon was a religious leader; the exilarch, a secular one. Conflicts between the two could be long and bitter. But victory in the struggle was not always evidence of moral or intellectual superiority. External political movements, the strength of the caliphate, and the perceived need to place limitations upon an "alien" people were invariably factors that shaped Jewish life in Babylonia. The heads of the two great academies at Sura and Pumbeditha became the acknowledged leaders of the Babylonian Jews at a time when Jews had turned inward and were struggling to remember their past and as they sought to fashion a legal framework that would guide them into the future.

During the period following the compilation of the Talmud and for many centuries thereafter, secular and religious leaders, the exilarch and the gaon, vied for supremacy. Again it was Zeitlin who analyzed the difference between patterns in Palestine and Babylonia; he also described how leaders tried to use Judah ha-Nasi as well as history to justify their later aspirations. "Thus, as we have shown, in Palestine after the destruction of the Temple the entire authority of the Jewish community was vested in the hands of a single person, the Nasi, Patriarch, thereby avoiding conflict between the secular and religious authority. In Babylonia, however, these two powers were separate, i.e., the exilarchs and the scholars (the heads of the academies), thus creating friction as to their supremacy. In the later period of Amoraim, the scholars succeeded in wresting authority from the exilarchs by maintaining that they were the actual successors to Rabbi (Judah the Patriarch), who held civil authority by virtue of his descent from David and religious authority by the unbroken chain of tradition which descended from Moses."[28]

The emergence of Islam in the seventh century created dramatic changes as Jewish leaders became increasingly subject to the will of Muslim authorities. Jews enjoyed comparative freedom despite their second-class status. It must be remembered that under Islam, the traditional distinctions between church and state, religious and secular were no longer applicable. The theocratic state tolerated its "alien" element, but only up to a point. Continued Jewish existence became a gift rather than a right.

The dispersion from the ancient homeland carried with it a considerable price. Whether in Rome or Damascus, Jews became conditioned to cast a cautious glance over their shoulder in order to discern the limitations of their own power as well as to identify and mollify the people who were capable of either protecting them or attacking them. As members of an identifiable minority, they learned how important it was to tender their respect to kings and caliphs, to landgraves and princes. They formed alliances with royalty, seldom with the masses.

Just as in Babylonia, where Jewish leadership fluctuated between religious and secular, so too in the countries of Europe, patterns of leadership proved to be variable. In Muslim Spain secular leaders predominated, while in France, Jews could be seen turning to more religious personalities. There were good reasons for these variations, of course, and they had everything do with the social and historical conditions which Jews encountered in their chosen homes.

Jewish colonies were to be found in Spain as early as the third century CE. These early settlers became merchants and artisans. They traded in silks and gold, metals and olive oil. In all of this, their family connections were of paramount importance. There were contacts in Syria and Egypt, Palestine and Babylonia — and a common language provided the communication link so vital to successful commerce.[29] These skills proved to be a vital asset to the Moorish leaders of Spain who found themselves continually faced with the necessity of expanding, or, at the very least, preserving their threatened domains.

Under these conditions, Jewish secular authorities, with their commercial and intellectual skills, were able to serve both their Muslim rulers and their own people. Two of these leaders, Hasdai ibn Shaprut (915-970) and Samuel ha-Nagid (933-1056) attained impressive personal power, accompanied, as it invariably was, with equally impressive power over their fellow Jews. Hasdai ibn Shaprut excelled as a doctor, a linguist, and ultimately as the foreign policy advisor to a Caliph who proved to be warmly disposed toward the Jews in his kingdom. Abd-ar-Rahman III ruled for fifty years and was regarded as the most powerful caliph of the Umayyad dynasty in Spain. He needed prestige, and in a daring break with the rest of the Muslim world he gave himself the title "caliph." He needed his harem, and by the end of his life he was criticized for maintaining both a male and female harem. He needed wealth, and for this he needed Hasdai ibn Shaprut.

The combination of skills which Hasdai brought to Spain was impressive indeed. He knew Hebrew and Arabic as well as Latin. He was a skilled doctor who actually began his rise to power as Abd-ar-Rahman's personal physician. The caliph was quick to recognize Hasdai's other talents and within a few years Hasdai was given responsibility for collecting taxes at Spain's ports. It was an office that enabled him to amass tremendous wealth for both his master and himself.

From a Jewish point of view Caliph Abd-ar-Rahman III was an enlightened ruler, one whose benevolence helped create what has so often be called a "golden age" for the Jews of Spain. What is less well documented is the Caliph's involvement in the trading of slaves. During his reign, men, women, and children were seized in Slavonic cities and sold to wealthy patrons in southern Europe and North Africa. The trade was a lucrative source of income for German settlers who, during the tenth century, migrated into Bohemia and made the flourishing city of Prague the center of their commercial activity. Jewish slave traders were among the immigrants. In this unpleasant role they were abetted by members of the German clergy who prospered from the trade. Captured slaves were transported in Greek or Venetian vessels. The Spanish ports were crucial to the smooth functioning of the trade, and Caliph Abd-ar-Rahman III directed its operation from his palace in Cordoba. Famously suspicious of his highest-ranking officers, he nevertheless entrusted Hasdai ibn Shaprut with the management of his ports.[30] That Hasdai was an "outsider" was highly congenial to the increasingly suspicious caliph.

The liabilities inherent in the interstitial role are often ignored in the face of the temporary benefits the role is able to produce. Hasdai possessed the dubious virtue of being more generous to his foes than to his friends. Capable of protecting his people while at the same time serving his masters, Hasdai was looked upon as the "guarantor of his people's survival." Yet his arrogance simultaneously provoked jealousy out in the community and anxiety in the Jewish one. Jealously was one of Hasdai's least admirable qualities.

It was in his treatment of the Jewish poet Menachem ben Saruk that jealousy and power met to disastrous effect. Not unlike his Caliph employer, Hasdai was chronically suspicious of those who worked for him. Something Menachem wrote evoked his anger, and his stern condemnation of the poet was swift and awesome. Hasdai's servants seized Menachem in his home, severely beat him, and then sent him to prison. As if that were not punishment enough, Menachem's house was razed to the ground by Hasdai's agents.[31] Menachem's poem of complaint which he addressed to Hasdai remains a moving plea against the misuses of authority. "They beat me before your eyes," wrote Menachem, "divesting me of my robe on the holy day of rest and plucking my hair on the holy Sabbath…And on the festival day you ordered my home to be destroyed, not by gentiles, but by their own [Jewish] hands."[32] The Jews of Spain, indifferent to Hasdai's shortcomings, were awed by his ability to protect them. They regarded it as a sign of divine providence.

A singularly unique pattern of Spanish Jewish leadership was that which characterized the life of Samuel ha-Nagid, also known as Samuel ibn Nagdela. Samuel's unusual talent was that he was a military man. In the years following the death of Abd-ar-Rahman III, in 961, Moorish rule in Spain became fragmented. The center in Cordoba had declined in power, even as smaller territories such as Granada rose to prominence. It was in this small kingdom that Samuel ibn Nagdela managed to gain unique prestige. Always the outsider, Samuel was able to use his dazzling knowledge of military matters and of people to great personal advantage. He too was a poet and linguist, as well as a brilliant political tactician. Samuel b. Joseph ha-levi, to use his full name, began his political career as an insignificant merchant. Through his skill and knowledge of languages, he came to the attention of the vizier and ultimately of King Habus. For over thirty years he conducted the foreign as well as domestic affairs of Granada. He proved to be so uniquely talented that King Habus honored him with a title that no Jew before him could even dream of possessing. The king bestowed upon him the title "vizier." In appreciation, Samuel composed a saccharine poem of praise to the King in seven different languages.

Samuel turned out to be a more than competent military tactician. In his capacity as vizier, he assumed command of the army and on more than one occasion successfully led his forces in battle. Habus and his son and successor King Badis could be tyrannical and profligate. Badis proved to be so uninterested in ruling his kingdom that for a time Samuel ha-Nagid became the *de facto* king.[33] As a result of his position, he was able to enjoy an extravagant lifestyle. King Habus and his son needed the support of the Jews in their wars, and Samuel was able to provide that support despite the fact that the Jewish community of Granada had initially been hostile to him.

Samuel's personality cannot easily be defined. According to the available sources, he could be kind and generous one moment and quite merciless the next. Legend has it that during the days of his service to King Habus, a jealous merchant insulted Samuel. The king ordered Samuel to cut out the tongue of his detractor. Instead, Samuel decided to pardon the offending merchant and give him a gift. The amazed king asked Samuel why his order had not been carried out. Samuel responded: "I did carry out your order. I cut out the offending tongue and gave him a kindly one." Samuel's skill with words was matched by his love of literature. He was a patron of the arts. In addition to his own poetry, he aided the career of the great Jewish poet Solomon ibn Gabirol.

Samuel prided himself on the quality of his contacts, the beauty of his home, and the ostentatious display of his humility. Despite his reputation as a merciful executive, Samuel's actions evoked enmity within the Jewish as well as the community. He was openly disdainful, for example, of those who wore their Judaism too ostentatiously. He ridiculed those who "imagine that by fringes and beard and tall turban a man is qualified to head a yeshiva." In his own palatial home Samuel was anything but modest.

Contemporaries describe a huge home with a "water fountain which fell from above in the shape of a dove onto a floor of marble and alabaster. And they placed lights within the dome ... a wax candle at the head ... There was also a fire burning before him on winter days with shapes of birds around it."[34] For many years, speculation persisted that it was Samuel ha-Nagid and his son who were responsible for building the famous Alhambra in Granada.

The Jews of Spain relied on Samuel to protect them. They also feared him. Samuel liked to picture himself as the guardian of his people. Yet his actions ultimately exposed his people to great danger. "From Samuel's poetry," Yitzhak Baer reports, "it would appear that he was entirely absorbed in this world of wars, uprisings, murders, intrigue and treachery. In domestic affairs, Samuel did, as his enemies charged, utilize every available means to get rid of opponents, and to elevate his friends."[35]

The fears of Granada's thoughtful Jews proved to be well founded. The tyrannical system of which Samuel ha-Nagid was a part, crumbled soon after his death. In 1066 the people of Granada rebelled against their oppressive rulers. Samuel's son was assassinated by the rioters. Fifteen hundred Jewish families were murdered at the same time.[36]

The influence of poetry in the life of Spanish Jewry cannot be ignored. For it was poetry, both in terms of its structure and its content, that had become the favored form of artistic expression. Many of the Moorish rulers loved poetry; many of them wrote it themselves and they also welcomed poems written in their honor. Both Hasdai and Samuel ha-Nagid enjoyed writing poetry. They generously rewarded poets they liked, and they punished those that disappointed or angered them. Yet even during this golden age of Jewish life in Spain, a discernable note of anxiety could be perceived in these artistic endeavors. From Hasdai's patronizing and sometimes tyrannical treatment of his "house poets" to Samuel's fawning praise of his king, the power of poetry was not to be underestimated. But the poets never seemed to be entirely comfortable with their place in either Spanish or Jewish society. The most distinguished of them, Judah Halevi, famously wrote: "My heart is in the east, but I am in the far, far west." And Solomon ibn Gabirol, the poet-philosopher whose works were read by Christians perhaps even more than by Jews, often thought of abandoning Spain entirely. He would write, "My soul thirsts to see the sons of my people."

For Spain's Jewish intellectuals at least, Spain was home, but never, it seems, a completely comfortable one. Apparent in their lives and in much of their work was a yearning for something else, something far away, something that offered them that kind of security that even a "golden age" could not quite provide. The discovery that there was a kingdom of Jews tucked away somewhere in southern Russia made this yearning seem both exotic and tangible. Hasdai ibn Shaprut wanted to know more about this faraway kingdom of converts that evoked such curious excitement. He sent emissaries and letters of inquiry.

So great was the general fascination with the faraway kingdom, in fact, that Judah Halevi took its name as the title for his most comprehensive philosophical work. *The Book of Kuzari* is a magnificent polemical illustration of the interstitial role as conceived by one of Spanish Jewry's major thinkers. The king of the Khazars wants to choose a new religion. Standing between Islam and Christianity is Judaism. Unlike these two more dominant faiths, argues Halevi, Judaism is a religion of action, not of creed. It is noteworthy that Judah Halevi's idealized kingdom is located far away from his own home. The choice of a distant kingdom is not incidental. At the very end of the dialogue between the Kuzari and his rabbi-tutor, there is a hint of what is behind its author's thinking. The king speaks to the rabbi: "I thought you loved freedom, but now I see that you are finding new religious duties which you will be obliged to fulfill in Palestine."[37] Judah Halevi finished his major work in 1140. That September he left his home in Spain. Legend has it that as he caught sight of the gates of Jerusalem, he was run down and slain by a lone horseman.

Hasdai ibn Shaprut and Samuel ha-Nagid were both products of a feudal society that valued their knowledge and economic skills. And both were tremendously competent executives. While these men were able to accumulate much power, their positions were always vulnerable. It is clear that they were seen as protectors of their people, and in this sense their prestige within the Jewish community was enormous. But it was equally clear that there were significant differences between their transitory power and that possessed by the true rulers of the country. They were always regarded as Jews and therefore always different — even when tremendous responsibility was placed in their hand. These Jewish elites always seemed to be casting a suspicious look backwards even as their considerable talents urged them to seek new outlets for their grandiose aspirations.

Chapter 5

Rashi and Maimonides

The two acknowledged giants of medieval Jewish life were Rashi (1040–1105) in France and Maimonides (1135 or 1138–1204) in Egypt. Both left an indelible mark on Jewish life, though their styles differed quite significantly. Yet both were products of societies that became increasingly indifferent to the painful conditions which were beginning to confine and limit the communities of which they were a part.

Rabbi Shlomo Yitzchaki, known to Jews throughout the world simply by his synonym, Rashi, wrote commentaries on the Bible and Talmud which made these works accessible to Jews all over the world. For his time, Rashi was a new kind of leader, one who achieved greatness not as a result of wealth or family, but through recognition of his intellectual superiority. Prior to his time, leaders of the French Jewish community were appointed by the king. This fact is important to realize in order to appreciate the tremendous changes wrought by Rashi's religious example. Before his time, in the various areas of France, a wealthy or influential Jew would often be honored with the title *rex judaeorum,* or "king of the Jews." These officials, appointed by the Carolingian kings, were also known by the Hebrew name *nasi,* "chief dignitary" or "prince." *Nasi,* of course, was the name associated with the head of the Palestinian Jewish community, a community, as we have seen, whose leadership following the Bar Kochba defeat, became primarily religious. It was not religious functions, however, but quite secular ones that occupied the Jewish "kings." Each of them had a dual role — to protect the community and to guarantee the payment of tithes to the government. These leaders often became quite wealthy and also quite powerful. Beginning with Charlemagne, these appointed leaders of the Jewish community were given large land holdings as a reward for their efforts.

Even Rashi's own grandson Jacob Tam, himself an impressive scholar, benefitted from the privileged position he enjoyed as an agent of King Louis VII. "I am heavily occupied," wrote Rabbenu Tam — "the work of others is put upon me, as well as labor in behalf of the king." And again, responding to a request for information that arrived during the time the king was visiting in Rheims, Rashi's scholarly grandson penned a hasty note apologizing for his all too brief reply. He worries that he has so much to do "until this ruler of mine departs."[38]

If Jacob Tam was able to benefit from his dual role as a scholar and an agent of the king, he owes much to his distinguished grandfather. For Rashi was not only responsible for the dramatic change in the way Jews looked upon their leaders, but he also can be credited with helping generations of Jews gain insight into the meaning of their most sacred texts. Almost single-handedly, he elevated the role of the rabbi while simultaneously fighting for the right of each community to set its own rules. He also endorsed the radical proclamations made by Rabbenu Gershom forbidding polygamous marriages and protecting the right of wives in any divorce actions. In doing this Rashi brought dramatic changes to the domestic lives of French Jews. The time gap of several generations separating Rabbenu Gershom and Rashi is less significant than it may at first appear, for the sanctity of marriage remained a Jewish issue as well as a Christian one throughout the tenth century, controversies surrounding marriage rites and practices provide evidence of how closely connected Jewish issues were with those of society in general.

Historians of the eleventh century describe dramatic changes that were then occurring in France and western Germany. Travel became significantly easier. Scholars could be found journeying to far off places in order to find new books or editions of books they had heard about. Forgeries were plentiful. Documents were "more copious than exact," and so the search for authenticity took on a special urgency. In addition, agricultural developments involving new ideas about rotating crops as well as the introduction of new and improved farm implements stimulated a new interest in the cultivation of the soil and the development of vineyards.[39]

In all these areas, Rashi was a man of his times. He proved to be not only a brilliant scholar but a young man skilled in many trades. He was familiar with the banking trade, with soldering and engraving, with weaving and embroidering, and with currency exchange rates. He also studied agriculture, and his ownership of vineyards was ultimately to provide him with a comfortable living.

The search for authentic religious texts was one which engaged Christian scholars as well as Jewish ones. Early in his academic life, Rashi traveled to Mainz and Worms in search of an authoritative copy of the Talmud. It was in these cities that were then still considered part of Lorraine that he found the texts he needed, and he also familiarized himself with the work of the famous rabbi Gershom ben Judah. Rabbenu Gershom was known as the "light of the exile," and was responsible for the famous edict that put an end to polygamy. Rashi was fond of declaring: "We are all students of Rabbenu Gershom." When he had found the texts he needed, Rashi returned to his home in Troyes and established an academy that soon began to attract students from all over Europe. The teachings of Rabbenu Gershom came with him.

In France during this period language often proved to be a problem especially for the common people who found official communications baffling. Latin was the language of the scholars, and documents needed for everyday transactions of all kinds were available only in Latin. The masses had little idea of what these documents contained. Rashi, too, faced a language problem. He needed to write in a language that the majority of Jews could understand. And so, in his commentaries, he often introduced French words, called *la'azim*, where no suitable Hebrew or Aramaic equivalent was available. As a result of these innovations and his own ability to simplify and clarify, Rashi's commentaries on both the Bible and the Talmud enabled Jews to understand their holy texts.

Marriage and domestic life, as we have noted, were central preoccupations of clergy and lay people throughout the tenth century. Changes within Jewish life reflected similar transformations occurring within French society in general. As simple a question as who may officiate at a marriage could become a central focus of concern for both Jews and non-Jews. It certainly was a concern for Rashi. His struggle to guarantee rabbinic control over marriage finds its parallel in an incident involving the Archbishop of Lyons and King Philip of France. Historian Georges Duby suggests that the conflict between bishop and king was more than a struggle between two strong personalities; it had its profound impact upon the whole institution of marriage. And Rashi was certainly influenced by the dramatic events centering on a royal marriage and an attempt to dissolve it.

King Philip had married Berthe de Frise in the year 1074. Twenty years later, the King repudiated Berthe and confined her to one of the estates that had been provided as a marital dowry. The King was now in love with Bertrade and determined to marry her. The only problem was that at the time, Bertrade was married to someone else, the Count of Anjou. It was not unusual for the nobility to marry more than one wife, or to forcibly seize another man's wife. And so, Bertrade's previous marriage was not a problem for members of the French ruling class or even for many of the French bishops who not only attended King Philip's wedding, but also participated in the marital rites.

But one ecclesiastical figure, Yves the Bishop of Lyons, did object, and he carried his objection so far as to excommunicate King Philip. The king appealed to the bishops, and the Bishop of Chartres appealed to the Pope in Clermont. The ensuing battle redefined French marital attitudes and lead to the "Christianization" of marriage.[40] Ultimately, the Bishop of Lyons was sustained in his objection to the marriage, and from that time forward matters regarding marriage were firmly placed in the hands of the clergy. No longer could a king or nobleman physically seize a desired bride and expect to wed her. The church was successfully asserting its authority over marital matters — and despite occasional challenges to that authority, notably, the challenge which led to the creation of the Church of England — the supremacy of the church in marital matters remained secure for hundreds of years.

During this same period, Rashi was acting to revise the rules of Jewish marriage and to bring them under rabbinic authority. One of the texts Rashi brought back to Troyes was Gershom's copy of the Talmud, authenticated, he claimed, with Gershom's own signature.[41] Rashi brought back more than authentic manuscripts when he returned from Mainz. As a result of his decisions supporting Rabbenu Gershom's decree, monogamy became the firmly established Jewish tradition in France. More significantly, Rashi's actions brought marriage under rabbinic authority. In this, Rashi was acting not only as a pioneer, but also as a product of his times. George Duby insists that the key to an understanding of the many marital disputes that occurred in the eleventh and twelfth centuries lies in recognizing the church's continual struggle to assert its authority over the state in marital matters. The proscription of polygamy within Judaism, therefore, can be understood not only as an effort to define Jewish marriage but as a reflection of a contest between rabbis and the laity for control of Jewish life it was a contest in which rabbinic leadership, like church leadership, had, at least for the moment, emerged triumphant.[42]

When he returned to Troyes after his visits to the Talmudic centers in Germany, Rashi became a successful vintner. In both Christian and Jewish circles it was considered unseemly for religious leaders to be paid for their services. That Jews could own vineyards was considered to be an indication that the France of Rashi's time was hospitable to Jews. In one of Rashi's responses there is a reference to one Jewish landowner who owned four separate vineyards, and these had apparently been part of his family for several generations. Another one of Rashi's responses describes a Jewish woman and her son who held the title of an entire town and the tithe to it. This was a gift given as a reward for "something she had done." These *responsa* picture a successful and prosperous Jewish community in Champagne.

Significant, too, are the accounts of the commercial fairs that began to spring up in certain of France's cities. Troyes, where Rashi lived, was a town of some significance and for a time was the capital of Champagne. Under Rashi's leadership Troyes became a vibrant center of Jewish scholarship. It also gradually developed into one of the towns that hosted popular country fairs. Thousands of people visited these fairs twice each year and so did scores of moneylenders. To acknowledge that most of these moneylenders were Jewish is neither to inflate their numbers (which were quite minimal) nor to detract from the large majority of Jews who were involved in a wide variety of trades and professions. What is relevant here is an understanding of how even a few Jews involved in moneylending can emerge as typical of the larger community. What is also relevant is the rabbinic rationalization of moneylending which seemed to justify Jewish participation in this questionable trade. Rashi himself offered such a rationalization. An important passage in the twenty-second chapter of Exodus summarizes the biblical view of moneylending. "If thou lend money to any of My people, even to the poor with thee, thou shalt not be to him as a creditor; neither shall ye lay upon him interest." Rashi bases his commentary on the single word *ami* — "my people." "An Israelite should receive preference over a non-Israelite, a poor man over one who is better off, a relative over a stranger and the poor of one's own city over the poor of another."[43]

From one point of view, Rashi's vineyards could be seen as precursors of a noble French tradition. In this sense the famous vineyards owned by the Rothschild family can find a pedigree of sorts in Rashi's early agricultural experiments. "All the Jews," wrote Rashi in a hurried note to an acquaintance, "are at this moment engaged in the vineyards."[44] But the connection between Jews and the sale of alcoholic beverages can also be viewed as a precursor of a different kind. Hundreds of years after Rashi's return to France — and far away in Russia and Poland — Jewish prominence in the liquor trade and moneylending were to fuel the pogroms that induced waves of impoverished and terrified Jews to turn their hopes toward a new home, a new world.

The Jews who lived during the time of Rashi were hardly regarded as French, and they certainly were not Christian. They lived between the parts, as a state within a state, their safety dependent upon the revenues they were able to generate for their protectors. It was a precarious existence, but one in which external dangers could all too easily be ignored.

In a sense Rashi symbolized both the apex and the nadir of Jewish history in medieval France. The Crusades that broke out at the end of his life marked the end of one period and the ominous beginning of another. Some of the changes could be blamed on the growing power of the church itself; others were related to frustration over a stagnant French economy. As for the Jews of France, they were continually trapped between the powerful social forces that kept exerting pressure upon them. The power struggles between the church and the government, the kings and the minor nobility, the nobility and the masses, all found one reliable outlet when the pressures became unbearable — the Jews.

Overnight, it seemed, a new and more hostile attitude toward Jews could be seen emerging from the papacy, then centered in Clermont. Religious passions were being aroused, directed against perceived outsiders — against Muslims and Jews. The Crusades were but a symptom of deeper social tensions. The Crusades served the dual purpose of stimulating religious zeal and relieving domestic economic pressures. Antisemitism could be used to foster both objectives. For both church and state, antisemitism had suddenly become "useful." A more disturbing change was that the hatred of Jews was gradually becoming infected with a new element — fear of the Jews. Whereas formerly, antisemitic measures threatened Jewish rights and Jewish property; it now threatened their lives.

The changes did not take place all at once. The Jews of France found themselves on a roller coaster, reviled one moment and courted the next. Rashi's own life ended under the threatening cloud of the Crusades. And in 1182, a mere thirty-five years after Rashi's grandson, Jacob Tam, had served King Louis VII so conscientiously, the entire Jewish community was ordered to leave France, at least the part of France that was controlled by King Philip Augustus. Money was, of course, a factor in the expulsion. Before driving the Jews out of his realm, the king confiscated all the lands that Jews owned and demanded a ransom from the Jewish leaders that he had imprisoned. In the meantime, he annulled all loans that Christians had taken from Jews. And in the process, he took 20 percent of each loan for himself. By 1198, the Jews were back — by invitation of the king. The new regulations regarding their financial activities guaranteed that a large percentage would accrue to the king.

How much of this could Rashi have foreseen? Sitting in his study in Troyes, he could not have heard the muffled sounds of thunder beginning to emanate from Clermont. Under the prodding of Pope Urban, the first Crusaders were gathering their forces and beginning the long journey toward Jerusalem. As they passed through the towns of Germany and France, they brought panic and death to the Jews who lived along the way. A contemporary account captures the feelings of many of these Crusaders. In the fall of the year 1102, a young man named Johannes Dreux converted to Judaism, and became known as Obadiah ha-Ger, or Obadiah the Proselyte. Prior to his conversion he was present at the First Crusade, so his eyewitness report is invaluable. Before starting on their journey, reports Obadiah, the crusaders "said to one another, 'Why should we go to a country far away to fight our enemies while in our own countries, and in our own cities there are our enemies and those who hate our religion? Why should we leave them here with our wives?" Historian Simon Dubnow was to echo this same theme in his *History of the Jews*. Dubnow may have known nothing about Obadiah, but he was certainly familiar with many other similar contemporary accounts. And so eight hundred years after Obadiah first documented them, Dubnow created in his imagination the sentiments a typical Crusader might well have felt: "We are on the way to avenge the Ishmaelites, and here we find Jews, whose ancestors had crucified our Redeemer; so let us first wreck our vengeance on them. Let the name of Israel be eradicated — or let them become like unto us, and recognize Jesus as the Messiah."[45]

Rashi was undoubtedly aware of the impending Crusade. Faced with the task of responding to the fanaticism of the Crusaders without provoking new violence against his people, he turned once again to the texts he knew and loved. In one of his final commentaries he notes that the Bible begins with an account of the creation of the world rather than with the words of the twelfth chapter of Exodus: "This month shall be unto you the beginning of months." The reason the Bible starts with an account of the world's creation, Rashi insists, is to proclaim that it is God, and only God, who owns the land. The choice of the creation story is as contemporary as it is historical. "Should the people of the world say to Israel 'You are robbers because you took by force the lands of the seven nations of Canaan,' Israel may reply to them, 'All the earth belongs to the Holy One Blessed be He; He created it and gave it to whom He pleased.

When He willed He gave it to them, and when He willed He took it from them and gave it to us."[46]

All the earth belongs to God, not to any one people — that was Rashi's message. It was a message the Crusaders would neither hear nor understand, a message the Jews of France, contemplating their own plight, yearned to believe. Rashi lived for nine years after Pope Urban ordered the first Crusade. During his final years, while he was not fleeing for his life, he carefully revised his biblical and Talmudic commentaries — and wondered perhaps why his grapes had suddenly turned so sour.

In another part of the Jewish world, an entirely different interstitial role was being occupied by a scholar who was both a brilliant philosopher and skilled physician. Moses ben Maimon, or Maimonides, (1135 or 1138-1204), as he came to be known, was born in Spain, and eventually came to Egypt by way of Palestine. The city of Cordoba where Maimonides spent his first year had a Jewish population that dated back to Roman times. The Jewish quarter of the city, the *juderia*, was located near the royal palace. This location afforded Jews protection against the constant threat of mob violence. It also created "a bond of mutual dependency between the Jews and the ruling establishment that contributed to popular resentment."[47] And it was resentment combined with a violent form of religious fanaticism that caused the Maimon family to finally abandon Cordoba and seek refuge in other parts of the Muslim world.

It is important to understand and appreciate how much suffering and humiliation was involved in each of these moves. Each was a traumatic event, an event that repeatedly underscored the powerlessness of the Jewish community. After so many disruptions Maimonides was finally able to settle in Egypt, at Fostat, the bustling community that was later to become the heart of Cairo. Located as it was, just south of the area where the Nile forms its Delta, Fostat was admirably situated for all kinds of commerce. While continuing to study and write, Moses also entered into a business partnership with his beloved brother David.

Because he had personally experienced the zealous fanaticism of the Almohads, Maimonides could be sympathetic to those Jews who had converted to Islam out of fear of persecution. After all, it was the Almohad version of Islam, with its fierce rejection of all liberal impulses and strict interpretation of the Sharia that had driven the Maimonides family out of Cordoba. In his *Iggeret Temen*, he suggested how these oppressed Jews could preserve their dignity and their faith. This famous letter, written to the Jews of Yemen, provided a formula for dealing with forced conversions.

Jews who converted under pressure, he declared, should not be regarded as though they had renounced their Judaism. Instead, these Jews should feel an obligation to leave the countries that deny religious freedom as soon as they can. This was to prove more than a dispassionate piece of advice. Maimonides's own safety was to be jeopardized by the very dilemma that he had addressed in his letter to the Jews of Yemen.

Is it possible that Maimonides himself may have been a temporary convert to Islam? Jewish religious authorities have been reluctant to entertain the idea that the author of the famous "Thirteen Articles of Faith" and the *Mishne Torah* could have even contemplated such a step. There is evidence, however, that in Fez, Maimonides may well have converted in order to save himself and his family.[48] Whatever the facts, rumors of a conversion to Islam were to pose a threat for Maimonides that persisted throughout his life.

In view of his own encounter with apostasy it seems strange to note Maimonides's hostility to those Jews who deviated from Jewish tradition. Toward the Karaites he was particularly hostile. That Jewish sect which arose in the middle of the ninth century was distinguished by its rejection of the post-biblical rabbinic tradition and of Talmudic authority. Only the Bible, maintained the Karaites, should be regarded as Judaism's holy text. In Fostat where Maimonides lived, Karaites and traditional Jews lived close to one another; they frequently intermarried. Yet Maimonides regarded the Kairites as *minim*, apostates, and in the spirit of his age, he came down in vigorous opposition to their perceived influence.[49]

In his biography of Maimonides, Solomon Zeitlin points out that following the Spanish Jewish tradition, Maimonides was an advocate of secular leadership. This explanation is only partially adequate. Because he lived in a country where the divisions between the religious and the secular became easily blurred, and although Maimonides achieved power as a result of his medical and political connections, his formidable intellect and religious skills testify to the uniqueness of his life.

It is true that Maimonides successfully opposed Samuel ben Ali, a rabbi living in Baghdad who had argued for the abolition of the secular exilarchate. This was the position that had existed in Babylonia since Talmudic times and was always abhorred by the rabbis as a threat to their religious authority. The argument between the two scholars provides a window into the complexity of Maimonides's thought. Samuel ben Ali felt that his own scholarship qualified him to claim title as the successor to the Talmudic sages who had led the academies at Sura and Pumbeditha.

Therefore, he claimed, an exilarch was superfluous. And he vigorously opposed the appointment of a new one.

Maimonides, who by now had become the physician to the Sultan's Vizier, el Fadil, acted in this case as a strong proponent of secular leadership. He argued that much more than scholarship was required of a community leader. Maimonides emerged triumphant from this dispute, but not before a sensitive aspect of his own theology had been exposed and vulnerable.

Maimonides had consistently maintained that the Bible contained nothing that defied the rules of reason. What role then did resurrection play in a rational theology? Samuel ben Ali seized upon Maimonides's views of resurrection in an effort to discredit his powerful adversary. Maimonides did not really believe in resurrection, Samuel argued. Had not Maimonides written that in the world to come the body would be unnecessary, that the soul could get along quite well without it? Maimonides at first claimed that he had nothing more to say about resurrection than what he had already written. Only later did he become defensive, asserting that, like all things that defied reason, resurrection was an allegory. In truth Maimonides was caught between his own intellectual honesty and his desire to respect the entirety of Jewish tradition. His writings on resurrection were to remain subject to controversy long after the great scholar's death. Maimonides had listed a belief in resurrection as one of his "Thirteen Articles of Faith." Yet it was clear that the doctrine of resurrection did not fit comfortably into his philosophy. Toward the end of his life he returned to the theme. Among the last of his writings was his "Treatise on Resurrection." Here he made the strange argument that the important issue is not whether resurrection will occur, but whether it can occur.

Despite Samuel ben Ali's strong objection to the appointment of a new exilarch, Maimonides prevailed. As a result of his friendship with the Vizier, Maimonides played more than a minor role in the selection of the new exilarch. Samuel ben Ali was furious, and in his anger he wrote an insulting article about one of Maimonides's dearest friends. What response should be made to the insult? Maimonides counseled a compassionate response: "Who would not cry out if he were wounded?" These were the conciliatory words he sent to his Baghdad representative.

Maimonides's numerous writings, including the *Mishneh Torah* and his *Guide for the Perplexed*, won him a devoted following throughout the entire Jewish world. But his rationalistic approach to the Bible and Jewish philosophy also provoked fierce opposition. That Maimonides could call his compilation of Jewish law, *Mishneh Torah*, Second Torah, is an astounding testimony to his self-confidence as well as his prestige among the Jews of Egypt.

It is clear that Maimonides was an elitist. He wrote for two distinct audiences — the masses who needed allegories in order to understand the Bible, and a few intellectuals who could understand his intellectual works. "I do not expect you to understand everything I have written," was his oft-repeated message.

In 1171, the powerful military leader Saladin marched into Cairo and was recognized as caliph. At about the same time Maimonides was appointed *Ra'is al-Yahud*, or Head of the Jews. The position he occupied represented a refinement of the *dhimmi* rules which defined the lives of Jews and Christians in the Muslim world. These rules delimited the separate but protected status for non-Muslim "People of the Book." As a price for their special status, Jews were required to pay a *dhimmi* tax, and in times of governmental stress this tax could be quite arbitrarily increased. In his position as head of the Jewish community, Maimonides was vested with a great deal of power. As *Ra'is*, he was responsible for appointing Jewish judges and religious officials. He would be expected to represent the Jewish community in meetings with government officials. Marriages, divorces and matters of inheritance were also under the jurisdiction of the *Ra'is*. His also was the responsibility of ensuring that Jews dressed appropriately and wore the prescribed yellow badge on their turbans. It was expected that the position of *Ra'is* would be occupied only by a person of unimpeachable integrity, someone who would be "the judge of widows and father of orphans...the hope of the poor and the shield of the oppressed." In every aspect he served as the intermediary between the government and the Jewish community. Records show that Maimonides officially occupied the position for less than two years. Unofficially, he served as the Head of the Jews for the rest of his life.[50]

Many of the Jews who lived in Fostat occupied administrative or professional positions and large numbers of them were merchants and specialists in foreign trade. Maimonides's own brother David was a merchant whose commercial endeavors provided financial security for the entire family. But in the year 1174 disaster struck. The ship on which David was sailing was lost in the Indian Ocean. David himself went down with the ship together with all of his jewelry, his assets as well as the assets that friends had entrusted to him. The loss was a devastating blow for

Maimonides. Years later he tried to describe what had happened. "In Egypt I underwent severe and great misfortunes partly owing to illness and loss of property and partly owing to informers who were scheming to kill me, but the greatest misfortune which finally befell me caused me more grief than anything I have hitherto suffered, that is the death of the just one who was drowned in the Indian Ocean, and with him was lost considerable money belonging to me, himself and others. He left me with his widow and a little daughter. For nearly a year after I received the sad news, I lay ill on my bed, afflicted with fever and despair."[51]

His commercial partnership now tragically ended, Maimonides entered a new phase in his life, a period of intensified intellectual searching. To earn a living, he renewed his dedication to medicine, and in the process he gained lasting fame as a pioneer in the field of medicine as well as in the world of Jewish philosophical thought. Maimonides experienced the dualities of the interstitial role. He was both victimized by its negative aspects and exalted by its positive ones. He was honored beyond his fondest dreams and yet he also lived in constant fear of his life.

What does Maimonides mean when he writes that "informers sought to kill me?" As we have seen, reports that Maimonides had actually converted to Islam were to pursue him all his life. The rumors about his "conversion" became especially threatening when one of his enemies, the Nagid Zuta, indicated his intention to tell the authorities that Maimonides was a lapsed Muslim. Jews were tolerated in Egypt, but not Jews who had converted to Islam and then returned to Judaism.[52] Fortunately, his worst fears were never to materialize.

That Maimonides was protected from the charges of his enemies was partly due to his intellectual prowess and partly due to the prestige that attached to him in his capacity as the physician to the vizier of Sultan Saladin. By now, Maimonides was the attending physician not only to the vizier, but to the family of Saladin himself. Thanks to the unwavering support of Vizier el Fadil, it was determined that Maimonides had never actually converted, but had merely pretended to be a Muslim during the travels that took him to Cairo. This fine distinction was to serve double duty. It protected Maimonides while it guaranteed that the royal court would continue to receive the best medical advice available anywhere in the world.

The friendship between vizier and physician had one other pleasant outcome. In the year 1187, Saladin defeated the Crusaders and recaptured Jerusalem. Within a few years Jews, to the pleasant surprise of many of them, were given permission to return to their holy city. Did Maimonides's position have anything to do with Saladin's generous treatment of his Jewish subjects? It may not have been a decisive factor, but it surely must have weighed in their favor.

If a positive interstitial role could be attributed to any medieval Jewish leader, it certainly would be to Maimonides. From a political and social point of view he acted as a bridge between his people and the government of Egypt. More significantly, his genius expressed itself in his ability to bring ancient and modern Jewish law together in a new and enduring synthesis. Like rabbinic scholars who preceded him, Maimonides recognized that Jewish law needed to be adapted to changing conditions. The words of Jewish faith needed to be interpreted so that a more sophisticated generation could understand them. In his *Mishneh Torah* he summarized Jewish law in a way that had an enduring impact upon the generations that would follow him, and in his *Guide* he would open doors to a new and exciting realm of Jewish thought.

Maimonides was a rationalist. He wanted to reject or reinterpret those narratives and laws that flew in the face of reason. His constant effort was to preserve the tradition but divest it of superstition and magic. Even the most obscure of biblical narratives came under his rational scrutiny. The effort could sometimes prove daunting. "The following," wrote Maimonides, "is a remarkable passage, most absurd in its literal sense; but as an allegory it contains wonderful wisdom, and fully agrees with real facts, as will be found by those who understand all the chapters of this treatise. When the serpent came to Eve he infected her with poison; the Israelites who stood at Mount Sinai removed that poison; idolaters who did not stand at Mount Sinai, have not got rid of it."[53]

In all of his work Maimonides bridged two philosophies, two cultures, two religions. He brought Aristotle and the Muslim philosophers to Judaism and simultaneously, he brought Judaism to the Muslim thinkers of his time. In fact, his influence on three religions is profound. Aquinas quoted him frequently and positively. It was through his *Guide for the Perplexed* that Maimonides introduced Aristotelian philosophy into Judaism. Aristotle's theories he claimed are those "least open to doubt."[54] Nevertheless he criticized Aristotle for not believing in the possibility of *creatio ex nihilo*. Following the biblical account, even as he consistently sought to make it rational, Maimonides insisted that God did have the power to create the world out of nothing. Despite disagreements on this as well as other issues, Maimonides's impressive writings resulted in a synthesis of Judaism with both Aristotelian thought and contemporary philosophy.

An example of this synthesis can be found in the way Maimonides idealized the role of the prophet. But the prophet that Maimonides had in mind was not the prophet most people think of — Isaiah or Jeremiah. He was not a thundering advocate of social justice. The ideal prophet was none other than Moses — and this Moses was as much an Aristotelian creation as a Jewish one. For Maimonides the true prophet is one who is able to achieve his or her full potential as a human being and creation of God. The idea of potentiality is an Aristotelian one. Potency and Act are the two factors necessary for any account of how change occurs. Potency, once its potential aspects have been fully realized, becomes its Act. The acorn, to use the familiar illustration, has the potency to become an oak tree. When this occurs the potency of the acorn becomes the actuality of the oak tree. But the oak tree, in turn, has the potency of becoming an acorn. Maimonides relied upon these Aristotelian ideas of potency and act to describe the ideal prophet.

Moses ended his days, so the Midrash tells us with a kiss from God. "This kind of death, which in truth is deliverance from death, has been ascribed by our Sages to none but to Moses, Aaron, and Miriam. The other prophets and pious men are beneath that degree," but their intellects "remain constantly in the same condition, since the obstacle is removed that at times has intervened between the intellect and the object of its action."[55] This is an example of how Maimonides combined Aristotelian thought with Judaism. When one's intellectual potential is completely activated, then the status of prophet can be achieved. In the final analysis, the prophet turns out to be an intellectual, not unlike Maimonides himself.

What is the relationship of all of this to the interstitial role? The meaning of Maimonides's life can best be understood in terms of the connections that were so much a part of everything he did. His own political and social role in Muslim Egypt underscores the uniqueness of his achievements. Even if his description of the prophet could be seen as self-referential, the brilliant way Maimonides synthesized Jewish, Greek and Muslim thought has had an enduring influence on Jewish and also, via Aquinas, upon Christian thought. At the end of his study of Maimonides's philosophy, David Hartman offers this telling assessment. "Maimonides, the writer of the *Mishneh Torah* and the *Guide*, remains a lonely figure because he believed that a total commitment to the Jewish way of life — Halakah — can be maintained by one who recognizes that there exists a path to God independent of the Jewish tradition. Maimonides was a witness to the fact that intense love for a particular way of life need not entail intellectual and spiritual indifference to that which is beyond one's own tradition."[56]

Maimonides's interstitial role was both legislative and philosophical. Yet there was one other dimension to it that should not be overlooked. His service to the sick and the needy offers a picture of a remarkably altruistic life. As he grew older, Maimonides found himself increasingly besieged with requests for advice. One of these requests came from Samuel ibn Tibbon who also wanted to come and visit the great scholar. In a well-known letter of response, Maimonides described what happened at the end of a long day spent taking care of the Sultan and his family. Upon returning home, he wrote, "I dismount from my animal, wash my hands, go forth to my patients, and entreat them to bear with me while I partake of some slight refreshments, the only meal I take in the twenty-four hours. Then I attend to my patients, and write prescriptions and directions for their several ailments. Patients go in and out until nightfall, and sometimes even, I solemnly assure you, until two hours and more in the night. I converse with and prescribe for them while lying down from sheer fatigue, and when night falls I am so exhausted that I can scarcely speak."[57]

What is remarkable is that at the end of his long and creative life, Maimonides found nothing more fulfilling than serving those who were ill and suffering. Even his scholarly interests gave way before his humanitarian ones. This is not to say that Maimonides was a saint. He could be caustic in his treatment of those he considered his intellectual inferiors and condescending toward those he wished to teach. And even when measured by the standards of his time, his attitudes toward women could hardly be called enlightened. Still, the man possessed a remarkable ability to understand the relationship between his own faith and the society that dominated it. This understanding represented more than an intellectual achievement; the fact that the name of Maimonides continues to be associated with so many contemporary fields of endeavor is an enduring tribute to this unique Jew whose journey took him from persecution and exile to the very center of power. As a physician Maimonides served Jews as well as gentiles, the nobility as well as the poor. In more ways than one, the historic tribute to Maimonides remains relevant: "From Moses to Moses, there were none like unto Moses."

Individual expressions of Jewish leadership varied widely in almost every respect. They involved gentleness and callousness, poetry and military skill, knowledge of agriculture, and knowledge of philosophy. Some of the leaders excelled because of their familiarity with Jewish law and tradition, others because of their political and sometimes even military skills. All had one feature in common: they operated "between the parts" In a real sense they were doubly interstitial. They had to gain the trust of both the secular and religious elements of their own community, and then they had to justify that trust as representatives of their people in the often hostile world at large. Whether it was Rashi or Maimonides, Judah ha-Nasi or Hasdai ibn Shaprut, there was a partner in their lives — a doppelganger — the interstitial role — or, more precisely, interstitiality itself. Each of these leaders was married in a way to the Jewish community, but there was always a third party present at the marriage — a third party whose presence at times was so intrusive as to be offensive, yet at other times so obsequious that it hardly drew notice. Society, the outsider, looked through the window at the wedding, but could never quite join in the festivities.

Chapter 6

The Righteous and Not So Righteous

Maimonides acted as a link between the secular and religious forces of his day. Jewish leaders throughout subsequent centuries emulated Maimonides, and either by power of intellect or strength of character sought to exert a similar impact upon their own unique community. Responding to the lure of freedom and opportunity, Jewish communities arose and prospered in thousands of small towns and rural areas, but primarily in large centers as disparate as Warsaw and Frankfurt, Paris and London, New York and San Francisco, Melbourne and Buenos Aires. Each told its own story, hailed its own heroes, regretted its own villains, and mourned its own martyrs.

How paradoxical it is that religion, the symbol of compassion and peace, the source of "love your neighbor as yourself," has been an excuse for some of the bloodiest battles mankind has ever known. This paradox is so familiar it hardly merits comment. Nor is it surprising that Judaism, too, has experienced conflicts between its various traditions. But there is a difference.

Here are the followers of two of the bitterest antagonists engaged in a relentless conflict — the Baal Shem Tov and Elijah, gaon of Vilna. Their followers hated one another, but the battle was unlike many other religious conflicts. The interstitial parameters of the enmity did not permit these Jewish antagonists to assemble armies to slay their adversaries. No crusade, no battle between Shiites and Sunni, no inquisition, no *auto da fé!* Their weapons were words, bitter words, and sometimes the intervention of an indifferent government that, more often than not, was sympathetic to neither them nor their opponents. The interstitial people can only turn to a hostile government in the midst of their conflict.

The antagonism between the followers of these two spiritual giants was unrelenting. Israel ben Eliezer, was born in 1698 in what is now Ukraine. He used to lead small children to school singing to them, and talking about the future to which they might aspire. The modesty of his life was gradually supplanted by the recognition among his friends and disciples that something profound lay behind his simple songs and stories. They started calling him the Besht, the Baal Shem Tov. Master of the

Good Name, is how the words translate, and so powerful was the goodness of his name that the vast Hasidic movement, anti-intellectual at first, but profoundly emotional, began to spread throughout Eastern Europe.

The popularity of the new Hasidic movement was quick to draw its detractors. Most eloquent of these opponents was Elijah of Vilna, whose associates bestowed upon him the ancient honorific, gaon. A generation younger than his rival, Elijah was nevertheless expected to shut the flood gates of pious zeal that the Baal Shem Tov and his disciples had opened. *Mitnagdim* was the unfortunate name given to the movement the ascetic gaon was called upon to lead. It can be deemed unfortunate because *Mitnagdim*, literally, "those who are opposed," conveys no indication of a positive program, whereas the activities of those they so detested, the Hasidim, signaled by their very name an immediately recognizable and positive outlook.

The two movements could hardly be faulted for their devotion to Judaism; yet they found ample fault with one another. Each group worshipped God with such intense passion and mutual animosity that at times it seemed they each worshiped a different God. Ultimately, their mutual vituperation cast a shadow over all of East European Jewry. Yet it is the political, and not the religious, dimension of their conflict that interests us here. To the extent that they denounced one another to the secular authorities, an offense which they committed with unseemly frequency, they betrayed their own weakness and revealed another negative aspect of their interstitiality.[58]

In a different part of Europe and five hundred years after the death of Maimonides an entirely novel aspect of the interstitial role emerged from the *Judengasse* of Frankfurt. The ascendance of the Rothschild family significantly transformed the face of Jewish leadership even as it both precipitated and acknowledged dramatic and often revolutionary developments in European economic activity. The Rothschild dynasty had the power to simultaneously evoke feelings of admiration and revulsion, envy and contempt. Its critics acted with equal alacrity, either to savage the business or to accept an invitation to dine at one of the Rothschild estates.

The rise of the Rothschilds seemed at times to be both spectacular and inevitable. With breathtaking speed Mayer Amschel Rothschild and his five sons acquired incredible riches and power. The Rothschilds were the ultimate insiders as a consequence of their wealth; simultaneously they were the ultimate outsiders in terms of the suspicions and phobias their successes provoked. *The Protocols of the Learned Elders of Zion*, that infamous Russian forgery picturing a world Jewish conspiracy, found nourishment in the antagonism to the economic dominance of the Rothschilds. And although *The Protocols*, written at the end of the nineteenth century, ultimately served a much more malicious purpose than to decry Jewish commercial activities, they certainly were fueled by a paranoid view of the Rothschild family and their seemingly ubiquitous influence.

The power of the Rothschilds was neither secular nor religious. It was financial. By the time they embarked upon their financial career the stereotype of the Jewish moneylender had become an all too familiar one. The Rothschild family carried the image to an entirely new level. They developed the resources, and they could act decisively while others seemed paralyzed. The well-known story of how Britain acquired a dominant interest in the Suez Canal provides a window into the speed with which the family could respond to most opportunities. When Benjamin Disraeli, the "sort of Jewish" Prime Minister of England, required an immediate loan of four million pounds so that Britain could purchase the Khedive of Egypt's interest in the Suez Canal, he needed only to turn to his friend Lionel Rothschild. The normal channels for borrowing money of this dimension were much too cumbersome. In addition, four million pounds was a huge sum at the time, 8.3 percent of Britain's entire budget. The London branch of the Rothschild family could produce the needed funds — and produce them speedily.

Speed and knowledge — these were the assets that the Rothschilds valued most. Mayer Amschel, the founding father, used his knowledge of antiques and coins to develop a relationship with the aristocrats of his time. His was a mail order business long before it was a banking business. Rothschild biographer Niall Ferguson points out that as late as 1790 Mayer Amschel was merely another one of many Jewish antique dealers. But by 1797, he had become one of the richest Jews of Frankfurt, and was now no longer an antique dealer, but a banker.[59] The Rothschilds were to become "interstitial elites." As a result of their endeavors, the stereotype of the Jew as a grasping moneylender began to be supplemented by the stereotype of the Jew as international banker.

Not enough credit has been given to Gutle, Mayer Amschel's wife. She bore an amazing nineteen children; ten of them survived — five sons and five daughters. It was the five sons who entered into business with their father and began the Rothschild legend. One day Nathan, the third and most independent-minded of the sons, felt that he had been slighted by a visiting English merchant who had refused to sell him some fabric.

Nathan's response to the snub was a defiant one, and years later he reminisced about what he did to retaliate. "I will go to England," he told his father. This was on Tuesday. And on Thursday he was on his way to London. The Rothschild family had become international. And within a few years their influence would be felt all over Western Europe. Salomon went to Vienna, Jacob (James) to France, Kalman (Carl) to Italy, while Amschel, the oldest of the sons, remained at home to work with his father.

The Rothschild endeavors were not uniformly successful, but when they did succeed, the results were spectacular. Most remarkable was the strong bond that developed between the brothers. Their loyalty to one another was sustained by a masculine need to dominate. Rothschild sons were allowed to marry only Jewish spouses; daughters, on the other hand, could marry anyone they wished. Neither daughters-in-law nor sons-in-law were allowed to question any amounts bequeathed to them; nor were they to be given any access to the Rothschild financial records.

If the bond between father and sons was extraordinary, it had its downside as well. The Rothschilds were a close-knit family, and a secretive one. Their tremendous success engendered jealousy among competitors. And this jealousy could be used by competitors to stir up suspicion and resentment among the masses. The Rothschilds must be at the heart of a huge mysterious conspiracy. They are part of a secretive Jewish plot to take over the world. These were ideas that became all too easy to formulate and easier yet to circulate. Suddenly the prototypical Jew had become not interstitial and weak, but interstitial and powerful, fearfully powerful. The power had to be resisted.

Beginning around 1840 a curious and vicious cartoon began to be circulated throughout Germany. The cartoon called *Die Generalpumpe* depicts an obese caricature of a Jew standing knee deep in a pot of gold. The Jew is a money pump, a composite Rothschild. A paper crown on his head lists the Rothschild loans of the last decades, and a badge on his coat indicates that he is the "executor of the court of all the world." The grotesque figure seems to be pulling the strings that control the countries of Europe. Rothschild, the cartoon implies, pumps money into the world, even as simultaneously he sucks it back out.

In the popular imagination the Rothschild name was to become synonymous with a distorted vision of Jewish domination and control. Even among Jews the name evoked fear as well as envy. Indeed, the rise of the Rothschild family signified a new era in the development of Jewish leadership. The most awesome figures on the Jewish scene were suddenly the wealthy bankers, not only the Rothschilds, but also financiers such as Baron Maurice de Hirsch and Gerson Bleichroder. De Hirsch owned homes in London and Paris as well as estates in Hungary, and Bleichroder, who was known as "the Rothschild of Berlin," managed Bismarck's financial affairs.

Much was expected of these Jewish "aristocrats," and their charitable donations evoked both awed appreciation and angry disappointment. The Rothschilds had consistently fought for Jewish rights all over Europe and donated generously to a wide variety of charities. In view of their power the Rothschilds were treated by Jews as if they were royalty. Typical of the awe in which they were regarded was the fawning letter that Gerson Bleichroder's father sent to Anselm Salomon in Vienna. "It is you, most noble Herr Baron, who picked me out of the dust; you most noble one have put me in the position of being able to nurture a large family…. As long as I live, therefore, your picture will live in my heart, and my last breath of life will be devoted to you, my benefactor."[60] Later, to be as "rich as Rockefeller" became an American fantasy. Antecedents to this fantasy may surely be discerned in Jewish attitudes toward the Rothschilds.

But there was a negative side to the Rothschild success story. As early as 1832, the Jewish-born reformer and poet Ludwig wrote that the Rothschilds should be crowned monarchs of Europe because in that capacity they might finally stop floating their oppressive loans. "It is always the same game which the Rothschilds play in order to enrich themselves at the expense of the country they exploit." Boërne's criticism may be easily dismissed — after all, he had rejected his Judaism years earlier when he had become a Lutheran, but his sentiments were shared by many Jews as well, of course, by many non-Jews. It remained for Theodor Herzl to offer a more nuanced insight into the conflicting feelings the family evoked. Herzl desperately wanted the Rothschilds to help with the Zionist cause. He also resented the indifference with which most of the family treated him. But more significantly, Herzl understood that the wealth and power of the Rothschild family posed a serious threat to the safety of the Jewish community. Theirs was wealth that bore the semblance of power but was unconnected to real power. It was wealth that could buy and sell things, but could never be at home with the masses of people. The Rothschilds could purchase ornate estates; they may have been "in residence," but were seldom "residents." Family members reached upward to make contact with nobility and about-to-be-kings, but seldom formed meaningful relationships with the people who lived and worked among them. It is perhaps to expect more of them than of other wealthy families to complain that they believed in charity but did little to promote justice.

Thus Herzl suspected what the anti-Semites knew — the Rothschilds' wealth was a threat and not a blessing. "I merely repeat once again," Herzl wrote in 1895, "the sole way out is to assemble all the secondary Jewish banks and weld them into a formidable money power to fight the Rothschilds." And a year later he was to write: "I am an opponent of the House of Rothschild because I consider it to be a national misfortune for the Jews."[61]

And as the Rothschild power grew, so did the hostility they evoked. "There is — who can deny it — a secret influence behind the throne" — so wrote a Whig member of England's Parliament as early as 1828. The attack of course was an obvious reference to the Rothschilds. "I believe their object to be as impure as the means by which their power has been acquired, and denounce them and their agents as unknown to the British Constitution, and derogatory to the honor of the crown."[62] That Rothschild agents have filtered into governments all over the world was a persistent theme, a theme that refused to die precisely because it was so preposterous. In 1891 in Germany Max Bauer gave voice to these sentiments when he asked: "What physical notion does the world have of Rothschild? He is never seen, just as the tapeworm remains invisible in the human body. The 'house' of Rothschild is a structureless, parasitical something-or-other, that proliferates across the earth from Frankfurt and Paris to London like a twisted telephone wire."

Nowhere was anti-Rothschild feeling expressed more angrily than in France. Amazingly, especially in view of his later defense of Dreyfus, it was Emile Zola who gave voice to contemporary attitudes. At first, Zola seemed an unlikely champion of Jewish causes. In his novel *L'Argent*, the character Gundermann is a vivid caricature of James Rothschild. Gundermann is, says Zola, "the banker king, the master of the bourse and of the world . . . the man who knew {all} secrets, who made the markets rise and fall at his pleasure, as God makes the thunder . . . the king of gold." An entirely more hostile adversary was the passionately antisemitic editor Edouard Drumont who could never suppress his anger at what he perceived as Jewish arrogance. "The God Rothschild," he wrote, is the real "master" of France. Later he added: "the Rothschilds, despite their billions, have the air of second hand clothes dealers. Their wives, despite all the diamonds of Golconda, will always look like merchants at their toilet."[63]

By the end of the nineteenth century an ominous new form of antisemitism was beginning to emerge. Drumont's suggestion that Jews were "hygienically unclean" was but the beginning. In Germany, Max Bauer introduced the word "parasitical" in describing Jews; he began to use the word "Jew" as an object, "something that proliferates across the earth" — these were different and ominous ways of describing Jews. The new antisemitism now began to use the vocabulary of genetics. If Jews could be proven genetically deficient, then who could be concerned about their fate? In matters of the sewer, the rats may be exterminated; no one will mourn their extinction.

Much time has been devoted to the Rothschild family and with reason. Their rise to wealth and power marked an important milestone in Jewish life. Jews had been struggling to achieve their liberation from oppression through political action. The Rothschilds achieved it through economic action. And in doing so they paved the way for other Jewish communities to improve their political as well as their social status. But the triumph of the Rothschilds had its cost. By and large they were far from innocent. And by and large the members of the family were realistic enough to recognize that their successes had also stimulated a new kind of antisemitism. To their credit, they tried to avoid the semblance of partisanship in times of warfare. As Baron James Rothschild observed in a note he sent to Bismarck's Jewish financial advisor in Berlin. Writing to Gerson Bleichroder, he noted that "it is a principle of our Houses not to advance any money for war, and even if it is not in our power to prevent war, then our minds at least can be easy that we have not contributed to it."[64] Yet despite earnest pronouncements such as this, the Rothschilds found it hard to avoid the popular suspicion that their governmental loans financed the major conflicts of the nineteenth century.

The various branches of the Rothschild family tried to combat antisemitism in a variety of ways. Some of them sought satisfaction by challenging an adversary to a duel. Some of them used their political contacts to protest bigoted political leaders, such as those who came to power in Vienna during the final decades of the nineteenth century. The Rothschilds invariably voiced opposition to the anti-Jewish policies of the Russian government. Yet most of the family remained indifferent or hostile to Herzl as he tried to establish a Jewish state. Simultaneously, members of the family donated generously to charities of all kinds. They contributed to hospitals and housing projects, even as they fought against all forms of taxation, taxation that might have resulted in real help to those who suffered from poverty and poor health. The Rothschilds gave generously to the poor. They never thought of forming alliances with the poor.

The Rothschilds and the Rockefellers invite comparison. Both families have endured intense criticism because of their wealth. One difference however is critical. No one has ever complained about an international Baptist conspiracy.

Ever since the destruction of the Jerusalem Temple in 70 CE, secular and religious forces have competed for leadership in Jewish life. The fluctuation of economic conditions, coupled with changing religious attitudes, has had a crucial influence on each leader's career. Diaspora leadership has historically depended upon political factors that Jews could not control and often could not even perceive. The creation of the *Mishnah* and Talmud coincided with the death of Jewish autonomy. The appointment of an exilarch in Babylonia depended upon the will of rulers who may have known little about the inner workings of the Jewish community, but who knew much about maintaining their own power. Hasdai ibn Shaprut and Samuel ha-Nagid in Spain prospered because they were able to maintain the good will of the reigning caliph or king. As singularly outstanding as they were, both Rashi and Maimonides were fashioned and limited by external political forces that permeated and controlled their lives.

To study the various patterns of Jewish leadership is not merely to analyze alternating historic trends. It is important to understand the fluctuating significance of the interstitial role and the ways in which that role responded to external pressures as well as internal expectations. In Europe — and in the Arab world as well — Jews did not lead lives of social and economic isolation. Invariably the design of their leadership was affected by currents and cross currents in the broader community. It would be a mistake to simplify these variable currents. Yet it can be suggested that the secular leadership prevailed more characteristically during times when the bonds of oppression were loosened. Conversely, religious leadership generally emerged during more oppressive years. During "golden ages" as in Spain in the eleventh century, secular leaders were able to flourish, whereas in periods of persecution — in nineteenth-century Russia and Poland, for example — Jews turned inward toward scholarship.

There are exceptions, of course, to any generalized pattern. During the darkest period of Jewish history, the years of the Holocaust, a time when serious scholarship became increasingly difficult, Jewish community leadership virtually slipped away from Jewish control. As Nazis occupied the various regions of Europe, they mandated the creation of Jewish Councils. These councils were secular in nature and they took precedence over older established Jewish community structures. In Warsaw, for example, the traditional *kehilla* which was religious and social in character could be suddenly replaced by the totally secular and totally subservient Jewish Council. The members of the *Judenrat* were first ridiculed, then despised and ultimately feared as they unwittingly became a part of the "final solution." Were these members of the Jewish Councils truly Jewish leaders? "The Community Council is an abomination in the eyes of the Warsaw Community..." Chaim Kaplan wrote these words in his diary on April 23, 1941. "When the Council is so much as mentioned, everyone's blood begins to boil. If it were not for fear of the Authorities there would be bloodshed. . . . According to rumor the President is a decent man. But the people around him are the dregs of humanity."[65] Chaim Kaplan did not survive the destruction of the Warsaw Ghetto; miraculously, his diary did.

The leaders of the *Judenrat* possessed at least a modicum of authenticity. No such dignity can be accorded to the despised concentration camp Kapos who became all-too-willing instruments of the destructive process. Men or women who became Kapos served as tools of the concentration camp administration, and their function was to organize and intimidate the camp's inmates. These, of course, are extreme examples of how, during these times of crisis, Jewish leaders could be selected by outsiders. As outrageous as they are, they may well stimulate thoughtful analysis about the leadership selection process in more benign eras.

Any generalizations about Jewish leadership that emphasize the importance of external forces must confront an objection. It might be argued that, in a sense, every life is guided and limited by outside forces. However, what is unique in the saga of Jewish leadership is the ubiquitous presence of Jewish interstitiality. This means that contingency and powerlessness are not incidental but are the subtle, the defining, and the enduring qualities of this process. No greater evidence of the unpredictable and fragile nature of Jewish power may be sought than in the sudden reversal of fortune Jews experienced as soon as Spain became united as a Christian country. The marriage of Ferdinand and Isabella sealed the fate of Iberia's Jews. The golden age for Spain's Jews had turned into their nightmare. Within the span of a few hundred years a prosperous and creative community had been transformed into an anguished world of exiles. Their leaders were hardly to be blamed for this transition. Or were they? A failure to understand the interstitial role was always a critical factor in terms of Jewish destiny.

In summary, it is instructive to contrast patterns of Jewish leadership following the destruction of the Jerusalem Temple with those that prevailed during an earlier period of national independence. In looking backward, the fate of one of Judaism's most famous rabbis provides a dramatic illustration of a transition that occurred with almost incredible speed. As we have noted, Rabbi Akiba was one of the intellectual giants of his time. Akiba ben Joseph was regarded as both a great teacher and a charismatic political activist. He developed the ability to organize rabbinic materials in such a way that his ideas profoundly affected Judah ha-Nasi and became essential elements in the later formation of the *Mishnah* and the Talmud. Akiba studied and taught during a period of increasing oppression. He soon became a leading supporter of the Bar Kochba rebellion against Rome which broke out in 132 CE. His life, however, was destined to end tragically. He was captured by Roman soldiers and slowly tortured to death

From an interstitial point of view, Akiba's life must be seen as a transitional one. His fate, if not his entire life, is a paradigm of the interstitial changes that accompany the loss of national independence. It is tempting to suggest that Akiba's late-career interest in scholarship marked the point at which Jews turned inward toward a more contemplative and religious life. But more is involved than the mere ascendancy of rabbinic scholarship. In his times religious and political leadership could still be combined in one person. Akiba's insistence on combining study and politics, however, marked, not the beginning, but the end of an era. Akiba's doomed nationalism resulted in his execution. "Thou shalt love the Lord thy God with all thy heart, with all thy soul and with all thy might" — these were his last words. They were as prescient as they were eloquent. The days when a Jewish leader could be both a scholar and a national political hero had come to an end. With Akiba's passing, the process of Jewish dispersion sharply accelerated. Akiba's life terminates not with a defiant call to arms, but with a prayer, one that is destined to become his people's watchword and hope.

The history of Jewish life in the diaspora is one long history of promise and frustration, coupled with the constant specter of inquisition, pogrom, and exile. Invited into Poland to revitalize a stagnant economy, Jews soon found their opportunities confined to roles which ultimately made them appear as oppressors and exploiters. Invited into Alsace, to bring economic vitality to one of France's most economically deprived areas, they found themselves regarded as superfluous agents of an easily abused *rentier* program, a program in which they managed properties and extracted fees for their services, services that were invariably administrative and seldom physical. These Alsatian Jews soon found themselves among the least welcome of Jews — an embarrassment even to other French Jews. Were these Alsatians truly French or were they actually German? Were their financial activities conducted in an entirely ethical manner? These were some of the questions the Jews of Marseilles posed as they confronted their co-religionists in Strasbourg.

Jews are interstitial, and the Jewish community, even under the most benign historical conditions, plays an interstitial role. This is both a blessing and a curse. Or more correctly, all too often it has been borne as a curse. But the burden is capable of becoming a blessing. To be interstitial, to live and play and work in the midst of more clearly definable elements of society, is to exist between rich and poor, powerful and weak, oppressed and oppressors. Interstitiality may derive its definition from the presence of more easily definable forces. It may refer to the space between Protestants and Catholics, between Christians and Muslims, between rich and poor, between powerful and powerless. Interstitiality becomes a possibility whenever there are social divisions; an actuality whenever those divisions admit the third party either voluntarily or reluctantly. Interstitiality becomes dysfunctional when it leads to weakness and when it shatters the moral compass of its victims. This is the negative interstitial role. The positive interstitial role stands opposed to this model. It seeks to create a society conscious of the needs of the poor, a community dedicated to helping the needy and the powerless. This "positive interstitiality" becomes possible as the people in between become confident enough to replace selfish interests with more altruistic ones, short-term and immediate group concerns with thoughtful and long-term concerns for a society that can justifiably be called "just."

The interstitial role achieves positive concreteness whenever the third party becomes a visible and active participant in the social process. Jewish history is replete with examples of the Jewish interstitial role, with both its positive and its negative aspects. The refusal to recognize the negative aspects of this role and to understand either its tragic consequences or its fruitful potentialities has been disastrous. Historically Jewish leaders have been interstitial. They have acted within the possibilities and limitations of their roles — sometimes to the benefit and sometimes to the ultimate detriment of their people. For better or worse, they felt they were acting as individuals. What was missing was the need for the Jewish community to reorganize so that it could recognize both the limitations and the power of the people in the middle.

Chapter 7

Responses to Antisemitism

Of the analysis of antisemitism there appears to be no end. A sampling of these views can bring the interstitial problem and challenge into clearer focus. Four of the thinkers who have dealt with antisemitism within the past century and a half offer a variety of views that touch upon the complexity of this enduring social phenomenon. Theodor Herzl, the Viennese journalist and playwright, came to the problem as an assimilated Jew. Jean-Paul Sartre, the leading French existentialist, examined antisemitism through Gentile eyes at the end of the Second World War. Simon Dubnow's keen historical analysis documented patterns of Jewish success as well as the tragic consequences of their declining status. The final member of the quartet is Hannah Arendt, whose analysis of totalitarianism cast a new light on the history as well as complexity of hatred. The four thinkers also point to a definition of the interstitial role, and to the difficulties as well as the potentialities inherent in the role.

Theodor Herzl (1860–1904)

Until the revival of modern Zionism the Jewish beneficiaries of what has come to be called modernity led hyphenated lives. Not quite German and not quite French, they were always regarded as German-Jews or French-Jews. It came as a shock to French Jews, though it should hardly have been a surprise, when Napoleon asked them whether they regarded themselves as primarily Jewish or French. The question of dual loyalty has been a recurrent theme of diaspora Jewish history, annoyingly provocative on the one hand, and profoundly complex on the other.

For some Jews political liberation was never completely liberating. It presented new and difficult dilemmas. One remained a Jew despite renouncing past religious ties. Even attempts to modernize the ancient faith produced a mixed bag of social and political consequences. Thus, despite the emergence of reforming religious tendencies in nineteenth-century Germany, the only options available to most Jews remained a choice between Orthodoxy and assimilation. And, of course, even the religious reformers who first appeared at the dawn of the nineteenth

93

century could be accused of paving a path toward assimilation. The Mendelssohn family was rather the rule than the exception. The grandfather, Moses Mendelssohn, a privileged Jew in Berlin, a translator of the Bible into German, rose by the sheer force of his intellect to become the acknowledged leader of the Berlin Jewish community. The grandson Felix, baptized by his own father, the son of the pious Moses, was raised as Christian. In an act that can only be seen as a provocative renunciation of his father's values, Abraham Mendelssohn cynically insisted that his son bear the added name "Bartholdy" to distinguish him from "those Jewish Mendelssohns." The conversion to Christianity opened many doors to the young composer. It did not prevent Hitler from burning his "Jewish music."

To reaffirm one's Orthodoxy, to assimilate, or to convert to Christianity — these were the paths open to Jews in a post-Enlightenment Europe. But no matter which path one chose, antisemitism was a constant traveling companion. Would it ever be possible to escape from this unwanted companion? Zionism, reborn in the spirit of nineteenth-century nationalism, was the first modern endeavor to bring political ideas into the effort to resolve the Jewish dilemma. Reaching back to ancient Jewish promises and looking forward to a vague messianic future, Jews turned their eyes and hopes once again toward Jerusalem as an antidote to their suffering. Whether or not the fateful presence of a young Viennese reporter at the treason trial of a Jewish French army captain was crucial for the development of modern Zionism remains a moot point. What is certain is that the treason trial of Captain Alfred Dreyfus galvanized Theodor Herzl into action. Vision had encountered opportunity.

For twenty years until his untimely death in 1904, Herzl and the coalition that he created radically altered the course of Jewish history. In his own unique way, Herzl, like Moses, was an interstitial Jew. His knowledge of Judaism was minimal, and yet he came to be revered by millions of Jews all over the world, and particularly by the Jews of Eastern Europe. With equal fervor he spoke to the masses of Jews and to the royalty of Europe. His dream was of a homeland that would solve the problem of antisemitism for all time. Herzl wanted no eulogies at his funeral. He wanted to be buried in a vault beside his father and to lie there "until the day that the Jewish people transfer my remains to Palestine."[66]

Herzl's genius lay not only in his ability to galvanize political action, but in his insight that antisemitism itself had changed. No longer was it confined to the arenas of religion or finance. With the introduction of Gobineau's genetic theories it began to assume a much more ominous dimension. Herzl was not the first to dream of establishing a modern Jewish state, but it was his unique personal charisma that helped to make the dream a reality. Earlier in the nineteenth century, Moses Hess had developed a proposal for a Jewish return to Zion. He was merely echoing the dreams of millions of Jews throughout the ages. Prayers recited daily and especially on Passover reminded Jews that their faces and hearts were to be directed eastward toward the Promised Land. It remained for Herzl to connect the prayers with a political program that came to involve some of the leading personalities of his time. Herzl came to understand the painful negative side of the interstitial role as he encountered antisemitism wherever he went. He became convinced that only Jewish nationalism could save Jews from the prejudice and discrimination that had so dominated their lives.

A prosperous assimilated Jew, born in Hungary and educated in Vienna, Theodor Herzl came to Zionism only reluctantly. In Paris, as a reporter for his newspaper, *Die Neue Freie Presse*, Herzl was asked to cover the treason trial of Alfred Dreyfus. The details of the case are well known, yet they bear repeating because the whole affair had such a profound impact upon Herzl and because the consequences of the trial were so lasting. The trial remains significant as a reminder of the ways in which antisemitism can be stimulated by even perceived threats to national security as well as by challenges to the established social order. Political conservatives as well as the military establishment and most of the Catholic Church's hierarchy formed the backbone of the anti-Dreyfusard movement. Their opponents gradually coalesced into an alliance of Liberals, Jews, free thinkers, and intellectuals.

In 1894, Captain Alfred Dreyfus, a member of the French General Staff, was accused of treason. Specifically he was accused of sending secret documents to the German attaché in Paris. The prosecution insisted that there were many incriminating documents, but at the trial, it produced only one, the notorious *bordereau*, an official military memorandum written, it was claimed, in Dreyfus's handwriting. The *bordereau* was a list of military information available for sale to the German military attaché stationed in Paris. The document was a forgery, as were many other documents later created in an ever more desperate attempt to vindicate the army and to justify its role in the Dreyfus case. The actual traitor and author of the *bordereau* was a financially pressed French officer who introduced himself as Major Count Walsin-Esterhazy. Neither the culpability of Esterhazy (who was no Count) nor the innocence of Dreyfus could deter the officials of the General Staff who needed a scapegoat and in the process determined to destroy the career of the Alsatian Jew. Despite the initial paucity of documentation, Dreyfus was found guilty of treason and sentenced to spend the rest of his life confined to the notorious French penal colony on Devil's Island in French Guiana.

The matter might well have ended here. But there were growing doubts about Dreyfus's guilt. His most consistent advocates were members of his own family, his long suffering wife, Lucie, and his brother Mathieu. It was Mathieu Dreyfus, who devoted six years of his life and much of his fortune as he tirelessly sought to vindicate his brother. But despite their valiant efforts, Alfred Dreyfus might well have died a forgotten prisoner on Devil's Island had it not been for a fortuitous discovery made by a member of the French Intelligence Service.

In May of 1895, Colonel Georges Picquart, a newly appointed member of the General Staff, told his superiors that he had proof that Dreyfus was innocent and that the real traitor was Esterhazy. Pressures to review the Dreyfus conviction immediately began to build, and as they intensified, the faultlines in French society became ever more fractious. The liberal politician and newspaper editor Georges Clemenceau, who was later to become Premier of France, was an early Dreyfus advocate, as was the famous novelist Émile Zola. In 1897, Zola joined the Dreyfus defenders, issuing his famous attack on the anti-Dreyfusards, "J'Accuse," which Clemenceau published in his newspaper. Zola's fiery broadside had its painful consequences. He was arrested and accused of criminal libel. Had he not defamed the honor of the military in his defense of a dishonored Jewish traitor? As a result of his trial and subsequent conviction, Zola fled to England where he spent nine months in self-imposed exile.

Of all the Dreyfus defenders, it was Picquart who seemed the most unlikely. Picquart had been an avowed anti-Semite. He soon made it evident that he would not allow his prejudices to triumph over his integrity. Picquart began to express doubts about the guilt of Dreyfus and about the identity of the real traitor. Suddenly he found himself transferred to a dangerous post in Tunisia. He was subsequently arrested and falsely charged with forging the documents himself.

Both Picquart and Dreyfus were frequently accused of hurting their own cause because of the calm reserve with which they spoke and acted during their appearances in public. But during the trial of Emile Zola, Picquart appeared as a witness for the famous French novelist and he momentarily cast aside his customary reserve. Viewed in retrospect, his words can be read not only as a defense of Zola, and not only as a passionate affirmation of his own integrity, but also as a compelling evocation of the outrage that must have run through the mind of the absent Dreyfus. "Gentlemen of the jury,' shouted Picquart, "it has now been I don't know how much time, months that I have been heaped with insults by newspapers that are paid to spread such slander and untruth...For months, I remained in the situation most horrible for an officer, since my honor was attacked and I was unable to defend myself. Tomorrow, perhaps, I will be expelled from the Army that I love and to which I have given twenty-five years of my life. That did not stop me when I thought it my duty to pursue truth and justice."[67] Shortly after his appearance at the Zola trial, Picquart was indeed arrested, stripped of his rank, and accused of having been the actual forger of the incriminating documents.

But the Dreyfus Affair was by now much more than a question of the guilt or innocence of one man. By 1897 Picquart had raised enough questions about the innocence of Dreyfus that the case quickly turned from an issue into an "affair," one that was to expose critical fault lines within French society at large. The opponents of Dreyfus were not reticent about expressing their antisemitism, and Jewish loyalty to France was a topic they heatedly discussed — and questioned. At the end of an agonizingly bitter struggle, Dreyfus was brought back to France, tried a second time and found guilty again. But by now the evidence against him was so patently fraudulent that he was pardoned by the president of France. The infamous *bordereau* was proven to have indeed been a forgery, as were other "incriminating" documents. The real traitor, Esterhazy, had fled to England where he confessed his crime to a British journalist. In the meantime, the officer most responsible for the forgeries that sent Dreyfus to Devil's Island, Lieutenant Colonel Hubert-Joseph Henry, was discredited and proven to be a liar. Confined to a jail cell in Paris, he wrote a frantic letter to his wife before he cut his throat and died before any of the prison guards could reach him. Henry's jail cell was the same one that Picquart had occupied only a few months earlier.

Years later, after Dreyfus had been totally exonerated, the full measure of Picquart's courage was to be acknowledged. He was promoted in rank and served as minister of war in the first cabinet of Georges Clemenceau. Dreyfus, too, returned to the military. Promoted to the rank of lieutenant-colonel, soon retired for health reasons, but he volunteered again and served as an officer during the First World War. Picquart was present at the military ceremony exonerating Dreyfus. The two men never spoke again. Alfred Dreyfus died on July 12, 1935, exactly 29 years to the day after he had been official exonerated. During all those years, he never seemed to be interested in any kind of penal reform, never admitted that antisemitism had played more than an incidental role in his conviction, and even toward the end of his life never seemed to be the least bit concerned about the ominous cloud that was beginning to form on the other side of the Rhine.

When Herzl first began to cover the Dreyfus trial, in 1894, the evidence against the defendant was overwhelming, or so he thought. Herzl tells us that he personally witnessed the humiliation of Dreyfus as he was publicly stripped of his officer's insignia. The disgraced captain was generally abandoned, even by most Jews, who were uncomfortable over the publicity the affair had stimulated. For Dreyfus, as we have seen, his Jewish heritage was only an incidental part of his history. For Herzl it was critical.

As he saw Dreyfus being publicly humiliated and as anti-Jewish slogans echoed in his ears, Herzl became convinced that it was no longer possible for him to remain an indifferent Jew. The hatred he witnessed in France seemed overwhelming. Marcel Proust later reported that during the height of the affair it was not unusual to see fashionable Parisian women carrying umbrellas with the inscription "Kill a Jew." Emile Zola's trial as a result of his defense of Dreyfus only brought a fresh outburst of antisemitism. "'Death to the Jews!' 'Death to the traitors!' 'Kikes to the water!'" The shouts were accompanied by the smashing of windows at Jewish owned stores. As the venomous cries increased in volume, so did Herzl's determination to act.[68]

The Dreyfus trial was not Theodor Herzl's first encounter with antisemitism. Eleven years earlier, as a university student in Vienna, his eyes were opened at an unexpected moment. On February 13, 1883, Vienna mourned the death of Richard Wagner. Like many other Jews, Herzl loved Wagner's music, even as he detested the prejudice that seemed to affect so many Wagnerians. The national mourning that followed the death was to prove traumatic for the young Herzl. His own fraternity conducted several memorial services. Adulation for the composer was accompanied by surprisingly virulent denunciations of Jews. Herzl demanded an apology. Not only was there no apology, but Herzl was "dismissed" from his fraternity.[69]

In order to appreciate the depth of Herzl's perception of antisemitism it is important to recognize the differences as well as the similarities of his two worlds — Vienna and Paris. Herzl worked for Vienna's leading newspaper, *Die Neue Freie Presse*. In its time it was a liberal and powerful journal, and Herzl was one of its leading correspondents. But Vienna itself was facing turbulent times. Growing tensions between the lower middle classes and the aristocracy contributed to domestic unrest while growing demands for national independence frayed the Habsburg monarchy at its edges. And antisemitism became an important part of the unrest.

In the 1880s large number of Jews, seeking relief from the czarist pogroms began flooding into Vienna. Fear of competition from the new immigrants found unexpected support in the racial theories which seemed to be taking hold all over Europe. In France, Paul De Lagarde wrote a tract in which he described Jews as "vermin," and, as if to confirm his judgment, the genetic theories of Count Arthur de Gobineau were beginning to gain traction. In the meantime, Wilhelm Marr had introduced the hyphenated word antisemitism into the world's vocabulary, and suddenly hatred of the Jews appeared to be fashionable again.

At times it seemed as if Viennese Jews were living in a giddy world of their own. There were authors such as Arthur Schnitzler, Hugo von Hofmannsthal, and Stefan Zweig and musicians such as Gustav Mahler, and the young Arnold Schoenberg. There were the thousands of Jewish professionals, doctors and attorneys and countless bureaucrats who established comfortable and sometimes ostentatious homes in the Habsburg capital. And of course there was the famous Sigmund Freud whose well-publicized ambivalence toward his religion may well have been more the rule than the exception. What an amazing place fin de siècle Vienna was! Its expanding borders housed the brightest hopes and the darkest fears of Austria's expanding Jewish community.

And there were indeed ominous clouds that Herzl could not have failed to notice. In 1873, Georg von Schonerer was elected to Austria's parliament, the Reichsrat. His rabid anti-Jewish rhetoric proved to be an effective political tool. Later, in 1897, Karl Lueger, a vocal critic of the

Jewish community, succeeded in becoming the mayor of Vienna. Paradoxically, some of Lueger's closest friends were Jews. On one occasion when this was pointed out to him, Lueger is famously reported to have said: "I determine who is a Jew."

And so by the time that Herzl arrived in Paris in 1892, it was clear that the stability the Jews of Paris and Vienna had so recently achieved had been accompanied by no warranty. Complicating matters was the fact that streams of poor and unemployed refugees were fleeing from Russia and Poland as they sought refuge in Western Europe. Genetic theories began to proliferate, all of them highlighting the differences between various ethnic groups and feeding upon the fear of the poverty-stricken refugees. Overshadowing all of these tensions in the Habsburg empire was a growing demand for national independence. These demands coming from all sections of the Empire would soon mark the end of the long and troubled Habsburg domination of central Europe. In Paris, Herzl heard the nationalistic slogans coming from all parts of Europe. He began to see possibilities that he had never even dreamed of before. He also became aware of the extremes to which a nation could go in order to protect its most venerable institutions, the church and the military.

Whether the Dreyfus trial was the critical turning point in the evolution of Herzl's thought or was simply the last straw, it is clear that from the trial onward, Theodor Herzl had became a driven man. He now was convinced that antisemitism was a disease that would persist eternally unless a cure could be found. And what could cure could there be? Education? — that would take much too long. Assimilation? — that was hardly feasible. But early in his career, Herzl had actually fantasized about assimilation as a solution to the Jewish problem. "I wished to arrange for an audience with the Pope . . . and say to him: Help us against the anti-Semites and I will lead a great movement for the free and honorable conversion of Jews to Christianity. In broad daylight, on twelve o'clock of a Sunday, the exchange of faith would take place in St. Stephen's Cathedral, with solemn parade and the peal of bells...And because the Jewish leaders would remain behind, conducting the people only to the threshold of the church and themselves staying outside, it would elevate the whole performance to a display of utter sincerity." These thoughts were confined to Herzl's diary, and shared only with one of the editors of his newspaper. Nonsense — the editor exclaimed in essence. "For a hundred generations, your race has clung fast to Judaism. You are proposing now to set yourself up as the man to end this stand. This you cannot do, and have no right to do. Besides, the Pope will never receive you." The Jews, Herzl concluded, are not likely to intermarry. Another solution had to be found.[70]

Of course, Herzl was not entirely naïve about the appeal of intermarriage and conversion. The process that had begun slowly with the generation following Moses Mendelssohn assumed proportions that would have shocked the old Jew with the bent back and the brilliant mind. Moses Mendelssohn could hardly have imagined that his translation of the Bible into German would become the first act in a drama that was to witness thousands of conversions. By 1800, Rahel Varnhagen, the most brilliant hostess of her generation, was able to suggest that half of Berlin's Jews had abandoned their ancestral religion. The advantages of conversion were social and professional as well as political, as Mendelssohn's musical grandson, among many others, was sure to appreciate. Intellectual and professional doors that formerly were locked to them were now , or at least, partially, opened. The immediate economic benefits were apparent on many levels, not the least of which was that the act of conversion offered relief from special Jewish taxes as well as other communal taxes. And even after the anti-Jewish riots of 1819, Jews continued to be drawn toward Christianity in order to take advantage of the new social and professional opportunities. It was during this period that such famous names as Ludwig Borne, Karl Marx, Eduard Gans and Heinrich Heine were to be found among the list of converts.[71] But the pull of Jewish faith and tradition as well as the cohesiveness of Jewish family life served to limit the exodus from Judaism. Herzl not only recognized this reality; he used it as an argument in behalf of his own nationalistic agenda.

Like Hannah Arendt who would offer a more subtle assessment of the Jewish condition, Herzl became convinced that modern antisemitism was different from the hatred Jews experienced in other historic periods. And like Arendt, he understood that even the acts of emancipation, which accompanied Napoleon's conquests at the beginning of the nineteenth century, as welcome as they were, had not solved the Jewish problem. The apparently benign act of liberation had left Jews in a position where their fate was in greater jeopardy than ever. Herzl did not use the word "interstitial" but the idea was clearly on his mind when he warned of the dangers that accompanied the granting of civil rights: "Hence, our emancipation set us suddenly within this middle class circle where we have a double presence to sustain, from within and from without."[72]

By now, calls for national independence seemed to be coming from everywhere, from Hungary and Poland, from the Czechs and the Ukrainians. Only the Jews were without an identifiable nationality. Herzl became convinced that only the creation of a Jewish state could solve the Jewish problem. "I believe that I understand Anti-Semitism, which is a highly complex movement." Herzl wrote these words in the introduction to his most important essay, *The Jewish State*. Antisemitism, he reasoned, "is a national question, which can only be solved by making it a political world-question to be discussed and settled by the civilized nations of the world in council. We are a people — one people."[73] His call upon Jews to unite was bound to stimulate controversy among the Jews of Western Europe. But it electrified and inspired the suffering Jews of Russia and Poland.

The genesis of Herzl's nationalism provides an important key to understanding the interstitial role. Herzl came to Judaism from the outside. This tall, charismatic, bearded, and sophisticated playwright-journalist with the piercing black eyes understood that antisemitism was not the fault of the Jews, and he likewise became convinced that as long as they remained in Europe, Jews would suffer. For Herzl, Jewish life was in desperate need of "normalization," and it would not be normalized until there was a place that Jews could call their own.

The location of the Jewish state was less an issue than the creation of the state. For Herzl, self-governance was more to be desired that any particular territory. Jewish memories and centuries of prayer could be finessed by the urgent need for practical solutions. And so, initially, Herzl felt that Argentina might be as acceptable as Palestine for the future Jewish homeland. And even toward the end of his life, Herzl was willing to think of Uganda as a possible site for the future Jewish state.[74]

Herzl himself fit the role of the interstitial Jew perfectly. Like Moses, he was an outsider destined to remain aloof even as adoration for him grew among the masses of Jews he hardly knew. Like Moses, he could envision a promised land that would remain a dream rather than a reality. Herzl aroused deep passion among the suffering Jews of Russia and Poland, and at the same time he had both the credentials and enough prestige that he could approach the leading political figures of his day. Nervously, yet determinedly, he arranged meetings with the Kaiser and with the Sultan of Turkey. Even the quality of his Jewish knowledge marked the singular nature of this Jewish leader. It was possible for the zealous but impolitic Zionist, Menahem Ussishkin to remain suspicious of Herzl because of his assimilated background. "His greatest deficiency will be his most useful asset," Ussishkin was heard to remark. "He does not know the first thing about Judaism."[75]

Herzl was a leader from the periphery of Jewish life. In this he was not unusual. From ancient Moses to more modern leaders of the American Jewish community, including such names as Brandeis and Frankfurter and Bronfman, Jews have exhibited a strange fascination with those whose earliest attachments to the Children of Israel were minimal if not negligible. Herzl's initial appeal was to specific elites both Jewish and Gentile who could turn his dream into a reality. Meeting the German Kaiser in Jerusalem, the father of the future Jewish state could hardly be faulted for failing to understand the subtlety of the German ruler's support for his vision. Kaiser Wilhelm was not notoriously anti-Semitic, as Herzl biographer Amos Elon notes, but he could be cynical enough to wed his own political program for the Jews with those of his excited visitor. Herzl's proposal, he calculated, would rid Germany of "many unsympathetic elements" — a goal worthy of exploring.[76]

In seeking support for his nationalist dream, Herzl expected the wealthy Jews of Europe to be among his most enthusiastic supporters. In this he was only partly correct. As he approached wealthy Jews Herzl could be alternately angry and suppliant. To Baron de Hirsch, who was supporting projects for Jewish resettlement in the United States and Argentina, he imprudently shouted: "You are breeding *schnorrers* (beggars) . . . no people produces as much charity and so many paupers as the Jews."[77] As for the Rothschild family, Herzl spent frustrating days trying to compose an essay that would convince them to support his vision. That essay became the essence of his most important work, *The Jewish State*. Whether it was due to excessive zeal or ignorance Herzl remained unaware of the fact that by the end of the nineteenth century, Rothschild financial interests led them to be increasingly wary of all national and separatist movements. The Rothschilds had begun to invest quite heavily in the bonds of various governments, and consequently they had become quite leery of any movement that might disturb the international status quo. Was it for this reason that they had refused to become involved in the Dreyfus case, or were they merely concerned with preserving their own standing in France's aristocratic circles?

Herzl wanted to attract prominent Jews to the Zionist cause, but in the end, it was the millions of little blue boxes to be found on kitchen shelves throughout the world that helped turn his ideas into a reality. Lovingly deposited into these boxes each week were the nickels and dimes and rubles of millions of Jews who were determined not to let the dream perish.

It was of course the Dreyfus trial that acted as the catalyst for Herzl's painful confrontation with the evil of antisemitism. But was anyone at the end of the nineteenth century ready to recognize how incendiary some of the issues raised by the trial could actually become? For that matter has nationalism itself, with its constant calls for sacrifice and patriotism, been adequately understood in terms of its antisemitic history?

What made all of this so incendiary was that it touched upon a theme that can be counted upon to arouse intense and highly emotional feelings, the debate about national security. The visceral importance of national security has often been underestimated by liberal Jews, who seldom see a conflict between their patriotism and their utopian visions of one world. The extension of civil rights to Jews has often become intertwined with questions of patriotism. In 1806, for example, Napoleon convened a Sanhedrin composed of France's leading Jews. The most troubling questions were about Jewish loyalty. "Do Jews consider France their country? Are they bound to defend it?" In Germany Hitler used these very questions in a way that was ultimately to prove disastrous for millions of European Jews. And it was the trial of Captain Alfred Dreyfus that revealed just how incendiary the patriotism issue could become.

For there is a Gordian Knot that ties the issue of national security with challenges to Jewish survival. The significance of the Dreyfus trial is misunderstood unless it is viewed in terms of the putative threat it posed to the security of France. As Dreyfusards and anti-Dreyfusards developed their bitter arguments, one assumption found growing support among France's conservatives — to defend Dreyfus was to attack the integrity of the entire military establishment. It was this implicit attack upon the military that transformed the Dreyfus trial from a "mere judicial mistake" into an issue that divided all of France. The very effort to defend one man, unjustly accused of treason had the unforeseen result of creating a national debate about the integrity of the army. Were not the Dreyfusards — the liberals and intellectuals — questioning the integrity of the entire French military establishment? In response, the representatives of traditional French values — the church and the military — needed to coalesce into a movement able to assert that the security of the nation was more important than the fate of one man. Their vindication would be found in the affirmation of the guilty verdict. Thus the religion of Dreyfus, incidental at first — as Herzl himself believed — soon became transformed into a national debate about both the military preparedness of France and Jewish loyalty.

The issues raised by the Dreyfus trial had a long life. The evil genius of Hitler expressed itself in its ability to conflate two enemies — Jews and Communists — with deadly effect. As early as 1924, writing *Mein Kampf* from his cell in Landsberg prison near Munich, Hitler ferociously and repeatedly singled out the Jews and the Bolsheviks as Germany's greatest enemies. And the two evils cannot be separated. The Jews, he insisted, were the dominant element in the entire Bolshevik movement.

Questions of Jewish loyalty were to emerge as a powerful weapon in Hitler's hands. The notorious *Protocols of the Elders of Zion*, as we shall see, served to reinforce Hitler's assertion that Jews were a malignancy, but even worse, a malignancy actively working to destroy the state. It is this insidious idea that infected popular attitudes toward Captain Alfred Dreyfus as he suffered through his treason trial and subsequent imprisonment on Devil's Island. And it is this idea too that added one more rationalization to Hitler's call for a "final solution."

Theodor Herzl's view of the interstitial role was in many ways a pessimistic one. For him there was no hope of a Jewish future in Europe. With prescient vision Herzl almost seemed to be predicting the fate that was in store for the Jews of Eastern Europe. He could see no positive side of Jewish interstitiality, but his nationalistic solution was certainly a reaction to it. His vision resulted in the creation of a homeland that could be credited with saving millions of lives. Yet Herzl's answer cannot be regarded as the last word for even in Israel the interstitial dilemma has never been completely resolved. Herzl's life was dedicated to resolving one part of the interstitial dilemma. He often expressed a wish to be buried in Jerusalem, as indeed he ultimately was. But he might well have wanted to turn over in that Jerusalem grave had he lived to hear what some of the most zealous Jewish nationalists would come to say about the Zionist dream. The occasion followed upon a feeble effort of the Israeli government to dismantle a few of the illegal settlements that had been established in occupied territory. *Gush Emunim*, the bloc of the faithful, was the name adopted by an aggressive group of Jews who insisted on the right to build settlements throughout all of the land promised in the biblical book of Deuteronomy. The movement rose to prominence following the Yom Kippur War in 1973, and its members remained bitterly opposed to any proposals that might lead to the establishment of a Palestinian state. And so in 1979, when the Israeli government proposed to dismantle a few of these settlements, the response of the *Gush Emunim* leaders was immediate and bitter. Zionism has failed, declared one of their ideologues because "it tried to make the Jewish people into what it is not — that is a normal people, one people among the peoples of the world, and thereby make the land of Israel into what it is not — i.e. what every state constitutes for the people that lives in it."[78]

Herzl's solution to the Jewish problem has created a whole new series of questions and challenges related to Jewish nationalism and the "different" kind of antisemitism it seems to have engendered. Jewish life still persists in Europe, antisemitism still persists in the world, and it is clear that not all Jews are willing to cast their lot with the Jewish state. Yet the accomplishments of one man, whose years of activity were limited by his rapid physical decline, are an amazing tribute to the charismatic vision that Herzl brought to his great mission.

Herzl himself was a prototypically interstitial Jew. Emerging from a wealthy and assimilated background, he came to be regarded by masses of East European Jews as a kind of messiah figure. What marked his last years was an unshakeable faith in his own persuasive powers and in the work he was trying to accomplish. His confidence gave inspiration and strength to those who worked with him. "What if I had allowed these people to dissuade me?" Herzl posed the question and quickly offered the answer: "The world would have been poorer by an idea, and Jewry by a great movement."[79] Theodor Herzl stood between West and East, between the sophisticated world of the Paris Rothschilds and the impoverished world of the Polish *shtetl*.

The virtue of Herzl's response was that it fulfilled a millennia-old dream for a return to Zion. It also resulted in a homeland that could welcome Jews who survived the terrors of a Holocaust that not even those brooding eyes could have envisioned. Israel surely became a homeland where Jewish culture and society could thrive and feel secure. At the same time it became vulnerable to all of the liabilities that inevitably accompany nationhood. Not all of the world's Jews could live in the Jewish nation. And even Herzl was realistic enough to realize that not all Jews would want to do so.[80]

One additional problem was related to the Zionist dream. How would a Jewish state accommodate the prophetic vision of a world united by justice, rather than divided by national boundaries? It was the radical Marxist, Isaac Deutscher who expressed this criticism most caustically. Writing a mere ten years after the founding of the Jewish state, Deutscher suggested that Jewish nationalism had become unsustainable in an era that was becoming increasingly skeptical of nationalism. The decay of bourgeois Europe, he pointed out "has compelled the Jew to embrace the nation state. This is the paradoxical consummation of the Jewish tragedy. It is paradoxical because we live in an age in which the nation-state is fast becoming an anachronism, and an anachronism — not only the nation-state of Israel, but the nation-states of Russia, the United States, Great Britain, France, Germany and others. They are all anachronisms. Do you not see this yet? . . . The world has compelled the Jew to embrace the nation-state. . . . You cannot blame the Jews for this; you must blame the world."[81]

Whether Deutscher's international vision will ever be realized or not, it is clear that Israel's security needs and its territorial ambitions have come to dominate its founder's vision of a society in which Jews and Arabs would be able to live together in harmony. Israel's role in the world of real politics has come under increasing international scrutiny. The state has also stimulated sometimes painful soul-searching by Jews, both within Israel and outside of it, over its militarism and expansionist tendencies. A troubling blessing for those who live there, the State of Israel seemed to alleviate, but it certainly did not eliminate, the problem it was created to solve. The idea of a national homeland in Israel remains vulnerable on two scores. While it has failed to solve the Jewish problem in Europe, it has created a new one in the Middle East.

Simon Dubnow (1860-1941)

Like Theodor Herzl, Simon Dubnow dreamed of a restored Jewish nation. But the two dreams could not have been more dissimilar. Whereas Herzl envisioned a political state with Jews in control of a geographical entity, Dubnow's nationalism was an intellectual fabrication. A state within a state characterized by a rebirth of Jewish scholarship, this was the Zion of Dubnow's imagination. His dream was reinforced by an impressive knowledge of Jewish history coupled with an understanding that this history was much more than a series of events dominated by their heroes and villains.

"Thus the Ukrainian Jew found himself between hammer and anvil: between the pan and the *khlop*, between the Catholic and the Greek Orthodox, between the Pole and the Russian. Three classes, three religions and three nationalities, clashed on a soil which contained in its bowels terrible volcanic forces — and a catastrophe was bound to follow."[82] With these words, Simon Dubnow offered an incisive description of the interstitial situation facing the Jews in his native Russia and Poland. Dubnow did not use the word interstitial. But more clearly than anyone else he understood and documented its powerful reality. And he also was able to analyze the tragic consequences of negative interstitiality as it affected his own homeland, though he could not possibly have foreseen the even more tragic destiny that loomed on the horizon. Nor could he have predicted that he himself would become a victim. In 1941 Simon Dubnow was murdered by the Nazis near his home in Riga.

Like the German historian Heinrich Graetz whose epic *History of the Jews* began to appear in 1856, Dubnow's studies, begun a quarter century later, sought to account for the entirety of the Jewish experience. The two historians, however, approached their histories in significantly different ways. Whereas Graetz's writing was episodic, dividing history into specific and brief historical periods, Dubnow chose a more thematic approach, seeking to discern the broader patterns of Jewish history.

And it was history itself that gave purpose and meaning to Dubnow's own commitment to Judaism. The study of his people's story was for him more than a scholarly pursuit. It was an act of dedication. And it also pointed to the path that would lead to a genuine Jewish revival. Neither nationalism nor worship was congenial to Dubnow's spirit — only history. To record and interpret that history, to bring to it the insights of modern scholarship and modern sociology — this was his lifelong passion.

For Dubnow the word "nationalism" was particularly significant and also particularly troublesome. Actually, it was not the word that bothered him, but rather the uses to which his fellow Jews had put it. As his thinking matured he developed into a bitter opponent of Zionism and of any kind of Judaism that sought to define itself in geographic or political terms. Jewish nationalism needed to be understood in an entirely different sense. The true nation is a spiritual-cultural nation, he insisted, one that develops its uniqueness as completely and fully as possible. Dubnow's ideal Jewish nation was one that could be created within the framework of existing nations and did not require the establishment of a Jewish homeland.

For Dubnow, the traditional idea of the state was destined to succumb to a new vision. "Lately," he wrote, "the view has gained ground that a nation may be defined as a historical-cultural group which is conscious of itself as a nation even though it may have lost all or some of the external characteristics of nationality (state, territory or language), provided it possesses the determination to continue developing its own personality in the future."[83] "Modern scientific thought" requires us to stop thinking of nations in material terms but to understand the primacy of spiritual factors.[84]

This concept of nationalism left Dubnow in a position where he had to oppose not only Herzl's brand of Zionism, but also the cultural nationalism espoused by his old friend Ahad Ha-Am.[85] Asher Ginsberg, or Ahad Ha-am, the pen name by which he came to be known, agreed with Dubnow that the development of "Jewish culture" was of critical importance. But for Ahad Ha-Am that renaissance of culture had to take root in the new Jewish homeland in Palestine; for Dubnow it could and must take place wherever Jews lived. The conflict between the two men was bitterly aired in a letter Ahad Ha-Am sent to Dubnow in September 1907. "You seem to me to have overlooked the essential thing. In my view national work in the diaspora can be of use only as a stepping-stone to our national home in Palestine. Take away the hope of building a national home, and all we do in diaspora is a labor of Sisyphus; it cannot satisfy our national requirements or enable our national spirit to live a healthy life."[86]

In view of his emphasis upon educational and spiritual values, Dubnow's attitude toward religion may at first seem contradictory. As a proponent of *haskalah*, Jewish enlightenment, Dubnow began to oppose not only territorial concepts of nationalism but traditional forms of religious expression as well. Orthodox Judaism, he insisted, presents a barrier to the true understanding of Jewish nationalism. Jewish religious leaders are mired in a past that stifles the potentiality for real freedom and progress. Orthodoxy, he wrote, is mistaken only in the sense that it confuses the concepts of "spiritual" and "cultural" with "religious." "It is the result of a limited perspective characteristic of men who do not distinguish between fossilized tradition and living, creative development."[87]

As early as 1884 a young Dubnow delivered a scathing attack on the traditional heder, or Jewish day school. His criticism reveals the depth of his bitterness, and it also offers a devastating view of the religious life he wanted to transform: "The entire Pale is filled with thousands of children's prisons. These children are essentially tortured both in spirit and in body. Emaciated youngsters leave these institutions. They know nothing of childhood, fields, meadows or blue skies. They pass away their finest years of childhood within four walls, in sticky air, in spiritual tension that is far too much for their meager energies, under the rod of ignoramuses. An enormous Babylonian storehouse of wisdom is forcibly injected into the brains of these youngsters. They are told nothing about the real world, about nature and life, but only about the next world and death." Despite this bitter condemnation of the Jewish educational establishment, Dubnow could still proclaim his deep devotion to traditional Jewish spiritual values; "God is so near to me. He is in me, in every urge of mine to eternity, in my entire tense spiritual striving."[88]

The development of the interstitial analysis is indebted to Dubnow in many ways. More clearly than any historian who preceded him, Dubnow recognized how Jewish "usefulness to power elites" could so often lead to deadly consequences. This "usefulness" coupled with an incredible narrative of discrimination and persecution produced a people that became inured to tragedy and skeptical of success. Dubnow's insight was that Jews themselves were not entirely guiltless in this process — at least not in Russia and Poland. An antiquated educational system coupled, as we shall see later, with the complicity of some Jews in a draconian program of military conscription, contributed to Jewish vulnerability. But vulnerability does not inevitably lead to tragedy. For this we must turn to a consideration of Jews and commerce.

For it was the economy, after all, that remained their invitation to disaster. Subject to so many demeaning social limitations throughout their history, "Jews as individuals" gradually became transformed into "Jews as prototypes." Jews would be invited into a kingdom or territory with the expectation that their presence would lead to economic improvement. These Jews could be expected to bring with them their skills in language, their far flung family and business contacts, and most important of all, their familiarity with money. As a consequence of these expectations the newly imported Jews could anticipate a measure of protection, that is, as long as their economic value continued.

In his comprehensive *History of the Jews* and also in his earlier and more narrowly focused *History of the Jews of Russia and Poland*, Dubnow documents the ways in which his people both prospered and suffered as they became enmeshed in patterns of political and social behavior that they often repeated but never fully seemed to comprehend.

The spread of Jews throughout Europe marked the historical beginning of the process. Individual Jews, Dubnow points out, were to be found in many parts of Europe long before the destruction of the Temple in Jerusalem in 70 CE. They brought with them their ideas about one God and their appreciation of scholarship. All-important were family contacts which expedited their roles as traders and merchants. Following the fall of Jerusalem, many Jews were brought to Rome as captives or slaves. Jews already living in Rome felt a responsibility to ransom them — and, fortunately, they possessed the resources to do so. In the first and second centuries, the Jews of Rome lived in isolated communities which bore the Greek name *synagogue*. At that time the word described a communal area, not a house of worship. Jewish places of worship were designated *proseuche*.[89] Once redeemed, many of the former captives opted to remain in Rome.[90] They traded in commodities, even as they in turn gradually became commodities themselves, objects of use to rulers all over Europe.

The "commodification" of the Jewish community became a characteristic aspect of the interstitial process. The Jews of Europe could be regarded as valuable one moment, entirely disposable the next. The skills Jews brought with them wherever they went proved valuable to feudal lords who were interested in promoting the welfare of their own lands and in enriching themselves along the way. The pattern was not always the same, but there were striking similarities. Jews were denied entry into the guilds. They were not allowed to trade in basic commodities. Opportunity after opportunity was denied to them. But one area beckoned — the lending of money.

This history of Jewish involvement in moneylending is a complicated one and cannot be fully understood without recourse to the history of Jewish persecution and disenfranchisement. It is clear that the Bible expressed a hostile attitude toward lending money on interest. "Thou shalt not lend money on interest to thy brother." But there was an exception: "Unto a foreigner thou mayest lend on interest." (Deut. 23.20-21) It was this distinction between Jew and non-Jew that allowed the Jewish moneylender to fulfill an important social need, the need for capital. It also invited the ugly stereotypes which stigmatized Jews through the centuries.

The medieval church followed a policy of forbidding its members to lend money on interest. But funds were needed by all segments of society. They were needed to maintain the lavish life style of feudal lords, they were needed to build castles and highways, they were needed by artisans and farmers, and most of all, they were needed to maintain armies and wage war. Despite the church ban on lending on interest, it was not unusual to find an abbot or even a bishop turning to a Jewish lender for a "little bit" of financial help — and sometimes the loan was not that little.

These transactions were invariably clandestine ones. As a matter of fact it was not until the Age of Enlightenment in the seventeenth century that Jewish financial roles could be acknowledged in anything even approaching a positive context. Only as late as 1673, had it become possible in France to acknowledge the economic importance of Jews on a national level. In that year Jean-Baptiste Colbert, finance minister for Louis XIV, gave a speech in Marseilles before an audience of business people, many of whom had been advocating the wholesale expulsion of the Jews. Colbert drew a distinction between economic and religious antisemitism in which he admitted that France had a need for knowledgeable financiers. "There is nothing as advantageous for the general estate of commerce as the increase in the number of those engaging in it. What might not be of advantage to the particular inhabitants of Marseilles is of great importance to the kingdom as a whole. The establishment of the Jews has never been forbidden by commercial considerations . . . but only by religion." Ten years later, Colbert was even more forthright in his assessment of Jewish usefulness. Responding to accusations that the Jews of Bordeaux had behaved offensively toward the Catholic Church, Colbert defended them with these words: "His majesty knows it would be dangerous to punish this crime with rigor, because the general expulsion of all the Jews would be an inevitable result; since commerce is almost entirely in the hands of people like these."[91]

In earlier eras there had been few voices raised in defense of moneylending, a practice which at best was regarded as a "necessary evil." Evil or not, people of all social strata needed to borrow money. In France, and also in Germany and Italy as well, moneylending would be encouraged one moment and condemned the next. The economic historian R. H. Tawney offered an example of the moral ambiguities associated with the practice. Pointing to Florence as the financial capital of medieval Europe, Tawney noted that even in this busy financial center "the secular authorities fined bankers right and left for usury in the middle of the fourteenth century, and, fifty years later, first prohibited credit transactions altogether, and then imported Jews to conduct a business forbidden to Christians."[92]

Acutely aware of these historic ambiguities, Dubnow felt that his task was to document and understand how Jewish existence teetered perilously between the larger segments of society, between church and nobility, and in turn between the church and the masses. And for the Jews it was the need to survive that dominated all other instincts. It was this need that gradually fashioned the role that was later to assume a life of its own.

Acknowledging the dangers that beset medieval Jewish life, Dubnow argued that Jews could enjoy only limited rights, those that represented only a remnant of that aggregate of freedoms and privileges which had been usurped by the upper and middle classes of the Christian population. "This was a rather meager remnant that consisted of the right to engage in trade — without the protection of the merchant guild — and particularly money-lending."[93] The very repetitiveness of this restrictive pattern needs to be understood. Equally important to understand is a more important question: How was this interstitial role accepted with such seeming passivity?

In country after country, the compromise between the right to live and the right to live a normal and free life, characterized Jewish migration patterns. Early in the thirteenth century, Jews began to settle in Austria, and their life there parallels the destiny of so many other medieval Jewish communities. Frederick the Belligerent had recently captured the flourishing city of Vienna. As a result of his military activities he soon concluded that he needed help that only Jews could provide. In 1244, Frederick issued a decree protecting the Jews residing in his duchy of Austria. Anyone who destroyed a synagogue was to be severely punished. Jewish children were not to be kidnapped or forcefully converted. Jews were given permission to reside where they wished and travel and trade all over Austria.

In many ways, Frederick's statute was a welcome guarantee of Jewish rights. Indeed, for brief periods statutes modeled on his liberal legislation were adopted in areas as disparate as Bohemia, Hungary, Silesia, and even Poland. But the kindness of Frederick did not come without a hidden price. The Jews of Austria were to enter into the moneylending profession. A maximum interest rate was established — a mere 173 percent a year. Of course, the rates were lower for the nobility.[94]

113

This pattern was repeated with almost frightening regularity. Dubnow notes that following the Crusades, Jews in many European countries gradually became ever more dependent on the emperor, monarch or feudal prince who protected the "Jewish tributaries" to the extent that it was advantageous to their treasuries. By the twelfth and thirteenth centuries, the Jews of Germany's various monarchies had become increasingly dependent on the protection of the king. For that protection they were required to pay annual dues. And they literally became slaves of the king or *Kammerknechte* (servants of the royal chamber). When a king died, the rights of the *Kammerknechte* died too. And at the next coronation, these rights had to be renewed — always at considerable expense.

The financial skills of prosperous Jews were regularly exploited by Europe's rulers. And when their resources had been drained, the entire Jewish community could anticipate being expelled, their property confiscated. Thus a double advantage was extracted from these Jewish financiers. They would lend money, and when their usefulness had been exhausted, their funds and property would be seized by the crown. The actions of Philip Augustus in northern France were typical of this pattern. After squeezing as much as he could out of his Jewish chamber slaves, in 1181, he expelled all the Jews from his kingdom.[95] In other instances when funds were needed for a military campaign, the king would "mortgage" a Jewish community with a feudal lord or with the local bishop. That is, he would borrow money, offering as collateral the revenue the Jews would produce in the future. If the king failed to redeem the "mortgage" after the specified time, the creditor would become master of the local Jewish population.

Privilege and disability would often be combined in ways that resulted only in emphasizing the uniqueness and distinctiveness of this isolated people. On the one hand, Jews were given the unusual right to travel throughout the country: "The Jews may go wherever they wish, just like the knights," one of the rabbis boasted. On the other hand, most Jews had become painfully aware of their tenuous position. By now, it had become clear, as one of their leaders had to admit, that "Jews and all they own are the king's." In 1347, Charles IV expressed it this way: "We can do with them as we choose."[96]

Of critical importance during this entire perilous history was the attitude of the church. Neither the permanence of the limitations imposed upon Jewish communities nor the violence that resulted from the Black

Death which broke out in 1348 can be appreciated without understanding the overwhelming influence of official Church doctrine. The perpetuation of the ancient enmity between the two faiths proved increasingly disastrous for Jews. The polemics and charges of deicide, which tainted early Christian-Jewish relationships, gradually assumed concrete expression in church-inspired laws that served to drastically limit the freedom and mobility of the Jews.

The most significant worsening of Christian-Jewish relations occurred as a result of The Fourth Lateran Council. The great Council was convened by Pope Innocent III at the Lateran Church at Rome in 1215. Its ostensible purposes were twofold: to solidify support for the Crusades and to combat heresy. Its actual consequences were devastating for the Jews who found themselves under attack on many levels. "The more Christians refrain — conforming to their religion — from accepting interest in the lending of money, the more the unbelieving Jews engage in it; and within a short time they devour the Christian assets." The Fourth Lateran Council was disastrous for Jews. Not only were they condemned for their financial practices; they were also to be deprived of basic human rights. They were forbidden to appear in public three days before Easter (the way they dressed on these days was deemed a provocation). Jews were no longer to hold public office. A priest, the Council declared, may physically restrain a convert who seeks to revert to Judaism. And, perhaps most humiliating of all, Jews and Saracens were ordered to wear a distinctive garb so that there would be no chance of their being confused as Christian. The mark of Cain, the church was declaring, had to be plainly visible for all to see.[97]

At the Fourth Lateran Council a new and poisonous element was injected into Jewish-Christian relations. Prior to the convening of the Council, church antipathy toward the Jews was based upon theological issues such as the crucifixion of Jesus and the Jewish refusal to accept Jesus as the Messiah. Now a dramatic new element was added. Jews were considered to be tainted not only religiously, but morally as well. With the injection of a moral component, agitation against Jews was pushed to a new and dangerous level.

The new church decrees that required Jews to wear distinguishing clothing and to disappear from public view on certain days were more pernicious than they may have at first appeared. The process of transforming Judaism from a crime into a "disease," as Hannah Arendt was later to describe it, had begun. And so, in the middle of the fourteenth century when a pandemic arrived in the form of the Black Death, the association of the word "Jew" with the word "plague" had suddenly become entirely rational.

The violent passions unleashed by the outbreak of the Black Death in 1347 revealed how poisonous not only the wells but the entire social atmosphere had become. "The wells have been poisoned by the Jews!" That was the rumor that appeared almost simultaneously with the bubonic plague, the so-called Black Death that decimated Europe's population. The rumor that Jews were responsible for the plague, as absurd as it was, could also be made to appear reasonable. In the first place the combination of historic church hostility and the vulnerability of the Jews as a result of their financial activities made Jews easy scapegoats for any "pandemic rage." In the second place, and quickly noted by their enemies, the death rate among Jews appeared to be much lower than that of the general population. The Black Death destroyed millions of lives, one third of Europe's population, by one estimate. It also stimulated mass riots against Jews scattered across the face of Europe, as well as the seizure of Jewish property and the canceling of debts. Not incidentally, it led to the enrichment of the king, the church, and the nobility — the elites, in other words, who were fortunate enough to survive.

To be fair, official church policy toward the Jews during this period was not entirely unsympathetic. There were many instances in which prominent church leaders rose to the defense of Jews. Thus, it would be a mistake to merely recount the antisemitic acts of the medieval church without also acknowledging the protective actions of many of the prelates. Nowhere was this protection more vitally needed than in sections of Europe where it was believed that Jews actually could commit murder for religious purposes.

Charges that Jews conducted ritual murders date back to the first century when the Greek polemicist Apion first gave voice to the poisonous accusation. The myth that Jews needed the blood of a Christian child for the baking of Passover matzoh is one of those fabrications that seem to survive simply because it is so patently absurd. Absurd, perhaps, but also useful! The ritual murder charge has the poisonous ability to combine traditional political and religious antisemitism with irrational fear in a way that too often has resulted in frenzies of hatred. The revival of the ancient accusation was to carry religious passion to a new and unprecedented level and to reveal dangers for both the sponsors of discrimination and its victims.

Whereas traditional power structures could both tolerate, and even encourage, antisemitic acts when they served some ulterior purpose, uncontrolled mob violence was a different matter entirely. Mass violence could lead to the destabilization of the very social and economic structures that both church and state needed for their own security. On this score the church was particularly sensitive. The church might be able to rationalize discrimination, but it would seldom countenance violence. In this regard it is helpful to remember that even during the darkest days of the Inquisition, while the church showed little reluctance to charge its enemies with heresy, the punishment upon conviction was always left to the secular authorities.

The story of Germany's Court Jews is an essential part of the interstitial drama. It requires no stretch of the imagination to move from the *Kammerknechte* of the thirteenth and fourteenth centuries to the Court Jew of the seventeenth century. Both functioned at the pleasure of their master, and both filled economic needs that made them indispensable — at least for the moment. The Court Jew had little connection to the mass of Jews, but rather lived a privileged life as long as he remained in favor. This elite Jew was allowed to live in areas forbidden to other Jews, and he often had very little contact with them. At the same time the very prestige and wealth of the Court Jew enabled him to exert, albeit from afar, an influence on the appointment of communal rabbis and Jewish lay leaders. In a sense the Court Jew was even more valuable to his master than the *Kammerknechte*. Whereas the latter primarily provided funds to be used at the pleasure of the master, the Court Jew had the additional responsibility of providing the commodities and other supplies such as the supplies and armaments that were deemed necessary for the survival of the state. Under this new arrangement, Court Jews were no longer merely a source of revenue; now they were expected to stimulate as well as manage the commerce of growing, and often competing, German states.

The impact of the Court Jew upon his fellow co-religionists, both for good and for evil, could be profound. The story of Joseph Suess Oppenheimer (Jud Suess) is a saga of success and failure on a grand scale. In 1734 Oppenheimer became the factor of Duke Karl Alexander of Württemberg. Despite the wealth that his powerful position brought him, he frequently complained of the financial losses he incurred while serving his master. When Oppenheimer advised the duke that he might benefit by levying taxes, the duke compliantly published a law ordering every person with a steady income to pay a tax. The tax was to be paid to Joseph Suess Oppenheimer. The tax came to be known as the "Jewish groschen" or the "hell groschen." Traditional accounts have depicted Oppenheimer as the epitome of greed. Actually, his character defies any simple analysis. He tried to modernize the government of Württemberg, and to bring integrity to its procurement procedures. But in the final analysis he was a Court Jew, and his arrogance and vanity left him as isolated and alone as the royal figure he served. To the masses, he and the Court Jews as a group were nothing but the same despised people who not so many centuries before had been driven from Germany. In 1737, Oppenheimer's patron, Karl Alexander, suddenly died. Within a year, Oppenheimer was arrested, accused of high treason, and taken to be executed. On the gallows, he spoke the Hebrew words he had almost forgotten: "Hear O Israel, the Lord our God, the Lord is One."[98]

Poised between church and nobility, and simultaneously, between nobility and the masses, Jews became vulnerable in new and unsettling ways during the period of the Court Jew. The very prominence of some Jews highlighted the plight of the mass of Jews who remained strangers to both wealth and station. While their elites served the king, the masses of Jews turned inward — to the synagogue, to study, and above all to family. But there was a price extracted from them, even in their inward turning. In addition to all of their other perceived sins, they could once again be accused of clannishness. By now, the negative images others ascribed to them had seeped into their own view of themselves and tempered their behavior as well as their self-esteem. Jewish self-hatred became a recognizable feature of Jewish society. It sprang from antisemitic stereotypes so powerful that they were even able to gain acceptance among their victims.

Simon Dubnow published his comprehensive *History of the Jews* in 1929. Ten year earlier he had completed the major part of his most important work, *The Jews of Russia and Poland*. Here he undertook the task of analyzing the role of Eastern European Jews as they struggled to exist "between the parts." Precipitating his later general history, he sought to document the ways in which the ability of Jews to reside in various areas was inevitably accompanied by an assessment of their financial usefulness. His account provides a compelling picture of interstitiality as it manifested itself in a single vital Jewish community.

As early as the thirteenth century, Polish princes recognized that Jewish immigrants from Germany could bolster their country's economy. "In a land that had not yet emerged from the primitive stage of agricultural economy, and possessed only two fixed classes, owners of the soil and tillers of the soil, the Jews naturally represented the 'third estate,' acting as the pioneers of trade and finance . . . They put their capital in circulation by launching industrial undertakings, by leasing estates...and by engaging in lending money." Because these Jews were generally regarded as commercial assets, Dubnow concludes, they were not hated — at least not yet.[99]

A look at Polish Jewish life during the early years of the seventeenth century provides a picture of the opportunities as well as the perils that awaited Jews who decided to leave the ghettoes of Germany and Austria in search of a new life. These new settlers, like their co-religionists who had begun arriving as early as the thirteenth century, felt reassured by the initial welcome they received. The capital and the trade they brought contributed to Poland's growing economic strength. Wealthier Jews collected taxes on wine and other commodities and often became agents of the king. Many of them exported agrarian products to places as diverse as Austria and Turkey.

With the passage of years, as their economic opportunities became more constricted, many Jews were given the right of "*propination*," control of the liquor traffic. "*Propination*," derived from the Polish word meaning loosely, "to drink to one's health," permitted Jews to distill and sell wine and alcoholic beverages, and to collect taxes on the sale. Wealthy Jews could sell liquor and collect taxes, but most members of the community were engaged in retail trade, handicrafts and farming. The interstitial aspects of their role became apparent early in their East European experience. Supporters of the Jews were the kings and the big *Shlakhta* (the landed nobility). Their opponents were the clergy and the burghers.

In Russia and Poland, as in so much of Europe, the early granting of Jewish economic privilege was inevitably followed by economic persecution and the imposition of civic disabilities. Again it was church law, Greek and Russian Orthodox as well as Roman Catholic, that pioneered the change in attitude. In Breslau in the year 1266, canonical regulations were introduced in Poland's oldest diocese which made the position of the church toward the Jews perfectly clear: "In view of the fact that Poland is a new plantation on the soil of Christianity, there is reason to fear that her Christian population will fall an easy prey to the influence of the superstitions and evil habits of the Jews living among them. . . . For this reason we most

119

strictly enjoin that the Jews residing in the diocese of Gnessen shall not live side by side with the Christians but shall live apart, in houses adjoining each other ... The section inhabited by the Jews shall be separated from the general dwelling-place of the Christians by a hedge, wall or ditch."[100]

As a result of these regulations, Jews living near Christians were forced to sell their homes, often at a considerable loss. These earliest residential limitations were a forerunner of catastrophic residential restrictions which were to be imposed six hundred years later. They became the model for the infamous Pale of Settlement that defined the limited areas in which Russian Jews were allowed to live. Geographical confinement of Jews had begun. Yet to come were the ritual murder charges and the murderous pogroms. Yet to come was Auschwitz.

The internal structure of the Jewish community, the *shtetl*, tried to resist the pressures it felt as a result of its position between the parts of Russian and Polish society. The antagonism of the church, the exploitation of the nobility, and the anger and frustration of the peasantry all took their toll on a people whose means of survival were constantly being constricted. Simultaneously, unique patterns of communal organization gradually developed in order to deal with the pressures. In Poland every Jewish community established a *kahal* or community board. Except when there was a rabbi of unusual prominence, the *kahals* were led by laymen. The duty of the *kahal* was to supervise legal transactions among Jews, to settle disputes, to provide for the community's synagogue and school and cemetery. It was also responsible for collecting taxes for the government. Beginning in the middle of the sixteenth century, members of many *kahal* boards began to meet at regional fairs. The most significant of these meetings took place in Lublin. The fairs that were held here and at other locations gave Jews an opportunity to engage in trade, to compare notes — and to issue resolutions. The resolutions were usually devoted to approving the actions of the Polish government.[101]

It is important to remember that almost from the beginning of their history in Eastern Europe, the rights of Jews were restricted in two vital areas — their ability to live where they wanted to live and their choice of an occupation. Paradoxically, just as residential restrictions were gradually being lifted in other parts of Western Europe they were being imposed more strenuously in czarist Russia. A similar paradox can be seen in reference to military service. In Western Europe, Jewish opportunities to serve in the military generally coincided with movements toward Jewish liberation. The opposite process occurred in Russia. As Jews were forced into military service, their civic opportunities became increasingly constricted. The conscription of Jewish boys was a source of special anguish. The term of service seemed interminable, and the living conditions were incredibly harsh.

The relationship of the Jewish community to the czarist armies provides a bizarre example of the interstitial role in its most humiliating manifestation. In 1827, Czar Nicholas I issued the first of what became known as the Cantonist decrees. The canton was actually a military camp, and accordingly the new recruits came to be known as *cantonists*. As a part of the newly enacted decrees, each Jewish community was expected to supply a specified number of military recruits. But in view of the unbearable conditions that faced the future *cantonists*, there were never enough volunteers to meet the quota. And so each *kahal* hired recruiting agents who were nicknamed "hunters" or "captors." These agents could be incredibly cruel. They went around to Jewish homes, often in the middle of the night, sometimes, as Dubnow says, "snatching little children from the arms of their mothers," sometimes taking little boys no more than eight years old. These children were often sent to serve in Siberia, their families left to mourn them as if they were dead.

The young *cantonists* were immediately subjected to a new pressure. They were expected to convert to Christianity. First they were assigned to the local Greek-Orthodox priests for spiritual instruction. If that did not work, they were turned over to their sergeants and corporals who resorted to military persuasion:

"These brutal soldiers invented all kinds of tortures. A favorite procedure was to make the *cantonists* get down on their knees in the evening after all had gone to bed and to keep the sleepy children in that position for hours. Those who agreed to be baptized were sent to bed, those who refused were kept up the whole night till they dropped from exhaustion. The children who continued to hold their own were flogged, and, under the guise of gymnastic exercises, subjected to all kinds of tortures. Those who refused to eat pork or the customary cabbage soup prepared with lard were beaten and left to starve. Others were fed on salted fish and then forbidden to drink, until the little ones, tormented by thirst, agreed to embrace Christianity."[102]

The demand for new Jewish conscripts did not diminish, nor did the participation of *kahal* representatives in this cruel process. Instead of easing the lot of the general Jewish population, each new conscription call was accompanied by the imposition of new and ever harsher restrictions. For example, shortly after the military call-up of 1827, all Jews were ordered expelled from Kiev.

Historians have thoroughly analyzed the impact of the partitions of Poland which occurred at the end of the eighteenth century. Russia, Prussia and Austria — all lay claim to the ancient kingdom that lay at the divide between Eastern and Western Europe. As significant as these partitions were in terms of the general history of Europe, for the Jewish community they were cataclysmic. As a consequence of the partitions, The Pale of Settlement was established as a huge ghetto in 1791 by Catherine the Great. The word Pale means "boundary" and it was within the confines of the new clearly defined boundaries that most of Russia's Jews were forced to live. The Pale of Settlement included parts of Poland, Latvia, Lithuania, Belarus and the Ukraine. The initial goal of the new residential restriction was to expel Jews from Moscow. Catherine did not like to see so many of them in her favorite city. In practice, the establishment of the Pale resulted in further degradations by condemning 90 percent of Russia's Jews to live in an area that appeared increasingly constricting. Jews could only live outside the Pale if they received special permission. Dubnow himself settled in St. Petersburg as a young man. He was there as an illegal resident.

A look at the map reveals that the Pale of Settlement was situated in the westernmost part of imperial Russia. In its effort to "purify" its heartland and to protect its cities — most notably Moscow and St. Petersburg — millions of Jews were dislocated. They found themselves facing Russia on the East and Germany on the West. Thus another dimension was added to the pattern of their interstitiality — a geographical one. It was 1791 when the Jews of Russia were ordered to move into this crowded area on the western edges of the empire. This resettlement was to have a profound impact upon all of European Jewish life, not excluding the ultimate catastrophe that neared its tragic climax as Germany invaded Poland in 1939.

Among the limited number of occupations that were available to the Jews of Russia and Poland, two achieved a notorious distinction — selling liquor and collecting taxes. Both activities were controlled by an aristocracy that gave condescending employment to their Jewish middlemen. And both were occupations sure to sharpen negative perceptions of a people trapped between the parts. These occupations also could produce tremendous profit for the nobility and tremendous misery for the masses.

Were all Jews into collecting taxes and dumping liquor on the peasantry? Of course these professions occupied only a small proportion of east European Jewry. Other Jewish occupations seemed to have evoked little attention and less sympathy. Largely forgotten by the masses of non-Jews who formed what generously might be called "public opinion" were the struggling Tevyes and Jewish tailors. Forgotten were the academic commitments of scholarly Jews who lived in the Pale. Forgotten were the Talmudic academies and *yeshivot*, the devotion of the *Hasidim*, and the intense religious rivalries between the pious *Hasidim* and their religious rivals, the *Mitnagdim*. Never forgotten in the imagination of the gentile masses were the liquor merchants or the tax collectors who invariably turned out to be Jewish — even when they were not.

By 1809, the general condition of Russian and Polish Jews had deteriorated to the point where the government had to acknowledge its own culpability in their plight. In that year Czar Alexander I issued an advisory note to his Privy-Councilor in which he observed that "the Jews themselves on account of their destitute condition have no means which would enable them, after leaving their present abodes, to settle and found a home in their new surroundings." It is necessary, the report concluded, "to seek ways and means whereby the Jews, having been removed from their exclusive pursuit of selling wine in the villages, hamlets, inns, and public houses, may be enabled to earn a livelihood by labor."[103]

In all of his reporting, Dubnow remains keenly aware of the interstitial aspect of the Jewish position. Official records may stress Jewish participation in the "liquor traffic," but there are things (other than their scholarship and their piety) that the reports consistently ignore — namely, the roles of Jews as farmers, grain salesmen, dairymen, and merchants. The consistent policy of the government was to consciously and systematically destroy these Jewish economic endeavors.[104] The sad truth was that the helplessness of the people struggling to survive between the parts of their society was, in the final analysis, a product of official government policy. The more sinister aspect of this policy was soon to become apparent.

It revealed itself in the form of the pogroms that swept across Russia at the end of the nineteenth and the beginning of the twentieth century. Ostensibly popular riots directed against the Jews, the pogrom was more often than not a well-organized and official mechanism for preventing social change and for shifting responsibility for governmental failure. As early as the beginning of the nineteenth century, social unrest could be discerned spreading throughout Russia. The ostentatious wealth of the ruling classes, contrasted with the utter poverty of the peasantry, produced a tinderbox of social discontent. In 1881, the comparatively liberal Czar Alexander II was assassinated as part of a rebellion that was speedily quashed. But the embers of revolt were ready to be reignited at any moment.

There were pogroms in many cities of the empire — in Warsaw, Odessa, Zhitomir, Kiev, and, perhaps most notoriously, Kishineff. Invariably the police refused to help the victims — often they themselves were the instigators of the riots. More than the tacit approval of the Czar was involved. The riots were often preceded and even initiated by a message from the Czar's representative.[105] The messages became all too clear: The pogroms are a useful means of social control. Antisemitism is a tool that can be used to divert the masses away from the true sources of their oppression.

Dubnow realized too that even the ritual murder trials conducted well into the twentieth century represented the marriage of utilitarian politics with mass hysteria. In 1911, Mendel Beilis, a hapless young Jewish man in Kiev, was arrested after a Christian child had been murdered, his body found near a brick kiln owned by Beilis. There was actually no connection between Beilis and the murdered child, and the case was about to vanish from the public eye. But in September of 1911, the Russian premier Pyotr Stolypin was assassinated. The assassin had once been Jewish. When this fact became known, antisemitic groups in Kiev planned a pogrom but at the last minute the pogrom was cancelled. What is the connection between the trial of Mendel Beilis and the aborted pogrom? The Czar was scheduled to visit Kiev. A pogrom would look bad to the world. At the last minute a trial was substituted for the more potentially explosive pogrom. The Czar's visit was a glorious success. As for the unfortunate Beilis, he was publicly humiliated and was imprisoned for two years awaiting his trial. Finally acquitted, he spent his final years in the United States.[106] His memory persists, however, in a macabre way. It is still possible to turn to the internet, to spell out the six letter of Beilis's name, and to discover that, even in this enlightened age, hatred remains resistant to either logic or truth.

And anyone who doubts the tenacity of the ritual murder charge might turn to the work of the Princeton scholar Jan T. Gross who studied the antisemitic pogroms committed in Poland after Auschwitz. It was in Kielce, Poland, on July 4, 1946 that the most violent of these post-war riots occurred. The whole bloody incident started with the disappearance of a young Christian boy who later claimed that he had been held captive in the basement of a home occupied by Jewish survivors of the Holocaust. Scores of Jews were murdered in the riot which ensued. Simply, but appropriately, Gross titled his book with one word: *Fear*.

More than any major Jewish historian who preceded him, Dubnow realized that antisemitism was not merely an irony of history or a massive injustice, but that it was a rational, if cynical, means of either avoiding or solving other national or social problems. Inevitably these problems had little to do with Jews themselves; but their solutions benefitted from the accessibility of the people between the parts. In this process, the Jewish community became the interstitial tool of forces it would not or could not understand. Stalin was once reputed to have said: "A little bit of antisemitism is a useful thing." Stalin's instincts were as sound as his motives were sinister.

Of course, the usefulness of antisemitism extended well beyond the realm of the merely political, a realm all too familiar to Stalin as well as his czarist predecessors. During the Middle Ages, as we have seen, the property of Jewish victims often found its way into the hands of the feudal lord, and sometimes into the possession of church officials and even townspeople. The shocking replication of this pattern in Poland in the years following the Second World War provides a stark example of the interstitial role in a unique way. Both Jews and Poles suffered under Nazi oppression. The war ended with the liberation of the Poles. Poland's Jews who had suffered more than any other minority group were not to experience anything that even resembled liberation.

It is estimated that 200,000 Polish Jews may have survived the Holocaust. They were not welcomed home. In 1945 and 1946 there were riots in Krakow and Kielce where Jews were accused of child molestation and ritual murder. As many as 1,500 Polish Jews were murdered in the two years following the defeat of Hitler. In rural parts of Poland, when Jews returned home they were warned that it was unsafe for them to remain. "Why have you come back?" they were asked by former Polish neighbors.

"You don't belong here." Within a few years most of Poland's Jews emigrated to Palestine.

But why? Why, for example, were returning Jews, even returning resistance fighters, treated with such hostility, while liberated Poles were welcomed home as heroes? In his book *Fear*, Jan Gross looks back to the era of Nazi occupation and documents the consequences of the wartime seizure of Jewish property. The book, which evoked much controversy in Poland when it was published in 2006, confronted the pervasiveness of the post-war antisemitic attitudes held by the Polish proletariat. It also examined the silence and complicity of Polish elites as well as prominent church leaders. The prospect of seizing and retaining Jewish property remained a constant incentive to violence, both during the war and after. "During the course of the 'final solution,' as Jews were rounded up for deportation or execution in one locality after another, the Polish population grabbed as much as it could of what material goods had been left behind." "Don't break anything" shouted one pogrom organizer, "don't rip it up, all this is ours."[107] The end of the war was accompanied by the need to justify the expropriation of Jewish property. What was so easily seized was now to be regarded as legitimately owned. Woe to anyone who would try to take it back! Riots occurred. The victims of Auschwitz, those who managed to survive, were to become victims once again. For Poland's Jews there was no coming home.

The optimism of Simon Dubnow spared him from seeing all of this. He continued to hope and plan for a time when Jews would be able to realize their national dreams within European society. Yet his histories offer a well-documented picture of the interstitial life. His was not a "scapegoat" analysis of Jewish vulnerability. He fully realized the ways in which Jews had become tragically weakened, and he was also thoughtful enough to recognize how their vulnerability served the powerful forces that dominated them.

Dubnow could hardly have foreseen the events leading to his own tragic death. While he well understood the dangers inherent in the precarious position of East European Jews, particularly in view of the ways they were trapped between the various elements of Polish and Russian society, nothing could have prepared him for the totally destructive intensity of Hitler's hatred. Yet there were many insights in his histories that, in retrospect, make the rise of Hitler seem more rational than exceptional.

The publication of the infamous *Protocols of the Learned Elders of Zion* at the end of the nineteenth century was hardly noted by Dubnow, and yet it was an ominous harbinger of things to come. This infamous document bore a remote yet fascinating relationship to the Dreyfus trial in France. Forged documents were critical features of both, as was commitment to protect established power structures against the forces of liberalism. A complete forgery, *The Protocols* nevertheless exposed all of the fault lines analyzed so thoroughly in Dubnow's three-volume study of Russian and Polish Jews. *The Protocols* served a purpose. Written by members of the Okhrana or Russian secret police, the forgery purported to be the minutes of twenty-four sessions of a secret congress representing the twelve tribes of Israel and presided over by a Grand Rabbi. *The Protocols* were not merely an antisemitic tract; they were in effect an effort to take the blood libel accusation to a more sophisticated and political level. In his comprehensive study of *The Protocols*, Stephen Bronner suggests that, in this case, hatred of the Jews was part of a wider social agenda. *The Protocols* were conceived by czarist agents as part of "an explicitly anti liberal and antisocialist political project."[108] Once again the "people in between" were asked to pay the price for the preservation of an outmoded and corrupt political structure. The pernicious influence of *The Protocols* persists, particularly in Arab countries opposed to the existence of Israel.

From an interstitial point of view, the conjunction of charges that the Jews were intent on dominating the world, and the acceleration of pogrom activity become entirely rational. The sour taste following the Russian revolution of 1905 offered an opportunity for either reform or a renewed outbreak of antisemitism. It is not surprising that the Russian aristocracy chose the latter alternative. The Russian fleet had just been destroyed by the Japanese; someone had to be blamed for the disaster. Simultaneously, the Russian masses were growing restless as economic troubles mounted. What better instrument of suppression could the Russian establishment find than evidence of Jewish complicity in the rebellion? *The Protocols* served two vital purposes; it shielded the decadent czarist government from growing discontent and it provided a popular outlet for the oppressed masses. As for Czar Nicholas, he was presented as a gift, a gilt bound copy of *The Protocols of the Learned Elders of Zion*.

The Protocols were significant in a new way. No longer were Jews to be despised because of their religion or even because of some of their individual characteristics which could be regarded as stereotypical. Now the totality of the Jewish community could be reviled as a group that was not only genetically deficient but insidious as well. Was not *The Protocols* written evidence of their treachery? Suddenly, the Jews could be portrayed as a threat to the security of the nation. Left alone, they would no doubt claim dominion over the entire world.

It was this same mantra that Hitler invoked in order to stifle any internal opposition to his program of extermination. The Jews are not really Germans. Genetically they are inferior; politically they are all traitors. All of this becomes more significant when viewed in the context of Germany's reaction to its shattering defeat in 1918. Hitler's constant theme — and a theme of the Prussian military establishment — was that Germany had been betrayed at the peace conference at Versailles. Had not the principle architects of that disastrous treaty been Jews? By identifying Jews with the Communists, Hitler was able to undermine whatever efforts German liberals might have made to defend them. German propaganda had already pictured Jews as the most degraded of people. The rhetoric of extermination now needed one other component before it could become reality. And the war with Russia provided this component. For the first time, Hitler could depict Jews not only as a malignancy, but as a malignancy attacking from the outside as well as within. Jews and Bolsheviks were Germany's mortal enemies. They were not two enemies — but one. It is significant that the planned extermination of the Jews, as opposed to random killings, was not possible until 1941 when Germany finally invaded Russia. Once Germany's attack on the eastern front had begun, the few liberal voices of Christian protest could be permanently silenced. The fate of the Jews in Russia and Poland had been sealed.

Simon Dubnow could not have predicted the catastrophe that Hitler initiated. But his writings explain how perceived national needs combined with vicious propaganda can produce a deadly brew. Dubnow died near his home in Riga, Latvia in 1941. He was taken to a nearby forest and shot by the Nazis. He was killed by an angry mob outside his home. He was murdered by one of his own students. The sources do not agree upon the details of his death. They do agree that he was eighty-one years old when he was murdered.[109]

Jean-Paul Sartre (1905–1980)

With the end of World War II, French intellectual life succumbed to the lure of a revived form of Existentialism, one that combined the traditional emphasis on the priority of existence over essence with new psychological insights. The leading spokesman of this new movement was Jean-Paul Sartre. His reputation was based not only on his brilliance as a thinker and writer, but also upon his well-publicized role as a member of the French resistance. (The significance of his resistance activities, it should be noted, were later to become the subject of heated debate.) Sartre's study of antisemitism was published immediately after the war and bore the title *Reflexions sur la Question Juive*. In 1948, Schocken Books published an English translation bearing the title *Anti-Semite and Jew*.

The major thrust of Sartre's work is that hatred of Jews can be understood as an existential and psychological problem, not merely a social or historical one. Thus, for Sartre, antisemitism is not an incidental aspect of Jewish life, but rather the central and defining component of it. The psychological needs of the prejudiced elements of French society create the image of the despised Jew, and Jews, in turn, define their reality in response to the hatred.

"A Jew is simply one whom other men consider a Jew: that is the simple truth from which we must start."[110] With this provocative assertion, Sartre challenged post-war France to examine attitudes that had been ignored for centuries. Anti-Semitism, Sartre insisted, was not created by Jews. Rather it is the product of a non-Jewish society seeking to come to grips with its own inner demons. The war was winding toward its end as Sartre began to write, and Jews were beginning to trickle back to France. Or were they? How many survivors would there be, and how would France welcome them home? These questions troubled Sartre, and he felt they should trouble all of France.

Anti-Semite and Jew was a pioneering work in that it incisively analyzed the psychology of antisemitism. This study was never intended to be a historical one, nor did it confront the overt acts of antisemitism committed during the war in the name of France. Perhaps it is possible to understand this lacuna by acknowledging that the full record of Jewish suffering had not yet become available at the time Sartre began his essay on the Jews. In addition, it had become all too easy to rationalize specific acts of overt French antisemitism by arguing that they were committed in response to pressure created by the German occupation.

But the actual record of French involvement in the Holocaust is a troublesome one. The alacrity with which French officials first registered and then participated in the deportation of their Jewish citizens is difficult to condone. Distressing too is the action of the association of French publishers. Immediately after the occupation of Paris this prestigious group promised the German embassy in Paris that it would no longer publish or reprint the works of Jewish writers.[111] These are merely a few instances of French collaboration with their Nazi occupiers. The roots of antisemitism in France, of course, are deep and complex, but the indifference of so many "good Frenchmen" as the Jewish community was being decimated, troubled the conscience of many French intellectuals long before Sartre began his controversial study. In his eagerness to explore the phenomenon of antisemitism, Sartre remained uninterested in the historical forces that contributed so profoundly to its formation. Nor did he ever really confront evidences of French complicity in the Holocaust or in the events that preceded it.

In retrospect, one might have recommended that Sartre turn back the record of history only a few years and examine the pre-war French reactions to the political career of Léon Blum. Born in Paris to a family of Alsatian Jews, Blum served as France's premier during three turbulent terms. In 1936, less than a month before taking office, Blum was pulled from his car and badly beaten by an acknowledged Jew-hater. And shortly after he took office, one of the right-wing deputies, Xavier Vallat, stood up in the Chamber of Deputies and offered this bitter tirade: "For the first time, this old Gallo-Roman country is going to be governed by a Jew. . . . I hate to say out loud what the country is thinking in its heart. . . . It is better to place at the head of this peasant nation of France someone whose origins, however modest are rooted in our soil, rather than a subtle Talmudist."[112]

Blum's experiences as well as other historical patterns were neglected by Sartre, as were some of the larger forces that influenced their destiny, the rise and decline of feudalism, the birth of the nation state, the need for Jewish capital and then the subsequent evaporation of that need. These were but a few of the factors that fall outside the parameters of Sartre's study. Such omissions would not be reprehensible were they not accompanied by actual historical distortions. To claim, as Sartre does, that by and large working-class Frenchmen were immune to antisemitism is to close one's eyes to a painful reality. The Dreyfus trial, to recall but one example, developed into a class struggle as it became apparent that traditional French values were being threatened. Liberals and professionals stood on one side and the defenders of the old order on the other — the military and the church. In this contest, members of the proletariat hardly remained mute, as the proliferation of signs proclaiming "Death to the Jews" can testify.

Nor were the actions of Sartre himself totally courageous. When the Nazis marched into Paris they issued a *Statut des juif*, a law intended to drive Jews out of public life. Henri Dreyfus-Le Foyer, a Jew, was the professor of philosophy at the Lycée Condorcet but was forced to give up the position once the new statute had been enacted. His was the position that Sartre occupied from 1941 to 1944. The controversy over whether Sartre was complicit in the dismissal of the Jewish professor did not break out until 2000, twenty years after the death of the famous existentialist, and there is some evidence that there was an interim appointment before Sartre took the chair. Still it is possible to ask whether lingering guilt feelings may have stimulated Sartre's growing interest in the Jewish problem.[113]

It can be argued that this interest began long before the war and was rooted in Sartre's search for his own personal authenticity. Sartre's earliest and arguably most famous novel *Nausea* was begun in 1931. Its main character Antoine Roquentin spends his days struggling to understand the ways in which nausea has come to define his life. It is his existence and "it is not pleasant to see."[114] These early explorations ultimately led Sartre to the Jewish problem. *Anti-Semite and Jew* was written in the language of the psychologist, not the philosopher. Yet it reflects many of the same thoughts that were occupying Sartre as he wrote his chief philosophical work, *Being and Nothingness*. A constant theme, permeating both works, is the search for authenticity.

In January of 1940, while Sartre was serving in the army, he sent Simone de Beauvoir a letter that casts light on the connection between Sartre's own existential search and his interest in the Jewish question. "I read the biography of Heine (the beginning) which inspired some curious reflections. While in fact I was praising him internally for having known how to assume his condition as Jew, and I was understanding luminously that rational Jews like Pieter and Brunschwig were inauthentic in that they thought themselves men first and not Jews, the idea came to me, as a direct result, that I had to acknowledge myself a Frenchman; it was a rather spiritless idea and above all it was devoid of meaning for me, simply an inevitable and obvious conclusion. I wonder where it'll take me, and I'll explore it tomorrow."[115]

This curious letter, as Jonathan Judaken points out, is revealing on several levels. In the first place, it confirms the suspicion that Sartre's interest in antisemitism was not merely an academic one and secondly, that this interest preceded any knowledge of the terrible events of the Holocaust. Sartre had begun to feel that the key to his own authenticity lay in unraveling the secret of Jewish survival. The letter to Simone de Beauvoir is also interesting because of the concrete examples Sartre offers. Heine is a strange choice for an "authentic" Jew. In later writings Sartre slightly modified his choice in view of Heine's conversion to Lutheranism, yet he continued to admire the great poet who had the courage to reject the "asceticism" of both Judaism and Christianity. "My life seemed pretty futile next to his. . . "

Sartre, however, remained unrelenting in his criticism of Pieter (probably a Parisian Jew by the name of Pieterkowski), a man who in his "greedy, stay-at-home softness, his masturbated sensuality, his radical-socialist inauthenticity, personifies the 'bad faith' of the bourgeois."[116] Reading some of Sartre's early efforts to deal with their problems, Jews could hardly be blamed for asking the old question: "With friends like this...?"

On the day of his thirty-fifth birthday in June of 1940, Sartre was captured by the Germans. He was taken by cattle car to Stalag XII D, in Trier, Germany, dirty, unshaven and loaded with manuscripts. Even as a prisoner of war, Sartre continued to create. He wrote a Christmas play for his fellow prisoners, and he continued to wrestle with the problem of authenticity. Whether he escaped or was released remains a matter of continuing speculation. What is certain is that by March 1941, he was back in Paris. The need to resist the Nazis and identify with Jewish causes was now becoming a matter of growing urgency. Could his Jewish sympathies have been stimulated by an exhibition the Nazis mounted at the Palais Berlitz? Entitled *Les Juif et la France*, the exhibition featured articles and caricatures as well as huge sculptures, all designed to portray Jews as symbols of cultural decadence and racial mixing. "The cover of the catalog showed an old, bearded Jew clawing at the globe he sought to control."[117] It was time for Sartre to take a deeper look a Jewish authenticity — and also at the authenticity of his own countrymen.

That "deeper look" took place as Sartre began working on *Being and Nothingness*. Since *Being and Nothingness* represents the most complete expression of Sartre's phenomenology, it may helpful to examine the way in which it prefigured his concept of Jewish authenticity. Without becoming too involved in the complexity of Sartre's thesis, it is necessary only to point out that the first half of *Being and Nothingness* offers two types of reality. There is the world of the object and the world of the perceiving subject. The object world is the world "in itself" (*être-en-soi*) and the perceiving world is the "for itself" (*être-pour-soi*). It is only by negating what is "within itself" and attaining consciousness of one's humanity that authenticity can be achieved. Shall I become a slave to what others think of me? Or can I use my consciousness of myself to break the shackles that conventional society would impose upon me? These questions were the same as those that form the challenge contained in *Anti-Semite and Jew*.

It is in the last half of *Being and Nothingness* that the full thrust of Sartre's argument becomes apparent. There is a third kind of reality that shelters the hidden meaning of human freedom. Sartre calls this "being-for-others" (*être-pour-autrui*) and it is this consciousness that gives meaning to human beings and exposes the vast dimensions of human freedom. It is these themes permeating *Being and Nothingness* that occupied Sartre as he took a fresh look at the fate of France's Jews.

Anti-Semite and Jew, Sartre quickly reveals, is by no means an account of the tragedy which overtook France's Jews; rather it is a penetrating analysis of a society sated with historic prejudices. Nor is Sartre satisfied with merely examining the feelings of the perpetrators of antisemitism. He also takes a deep and sometimes disquieting look at the victims. "Today those Jews whom the Germans did not deport or murder are coming back to their homes. Many were among the first members of the Resistance; others had sons or cousins in Leclerc's army. Now all France rejoices and fraternizes in the streets; social conflict seems temporarily forgotten; the newspapers devote whole columns to stories of prisoners of war and deportees. Do we say anything about the Jews? Do we give a thought to those who died in the gas chambers of Lublin? Not a line in the newspapers. That is because we must not irritate the anti-Semites."[118]

Sartre's analysis remains an important one and his insights provide an important and often overlooked aspect of the interstitial analysis. It is his examples as much as his theories that lend force to his argument. Evoking the past, Sartre begins *Anti-Semite and Jew* by recalling some of the hate-filled statements he has heard over the years. All of them, he insists, are based on "passion" rather than reason. "The 'moderate' anti-Semite is a courteous man who will tell you quietly: 'Personally, I do not detest the

Jews. I simply find it preferable, for various reasons, that they should play a lesser part in the activity of the nation.'"[119] Sartre reports hearing people say: "You see there must be *something* about the Jews. They upset me physically." This is as rational as insisting, "There must be something about tomatoes, for I have a horror of eating them."[120]

For Sartre, antisemitism precedes any fact that may bring it forth. This is an essential feature of the interstitial discussion. Not only does antisemitism precede any rational explanation of its genesis, but it also exists independently of any explanation. As he attacks the small-minded bigots, "There are too many Jewish lawyers one is told." Sartre does not hesitate to resort to sarcasm: Are there too many Breton lawyers, too many Breton doctors? And if there were, would we not proudly declare that Brittany provides lawyers or doctors or engineers for all of France? To the anti-Semite, intelligence is another mark against the Jews — the virtue of intelligence becomes degraded, a rationale for hatred: "Thus the anti-Semite takes his stand from the start on the ground of irrationalism. He is opposed to the Jew just as sentiment is to intelligence, the particular to the universal, the past to the present. . . ."[121]

Not surprisingly, it is in areas that evoke national pride that prejudice often finds a welcome home. The French language is, of course, such an area. How it is pronounced becomes yet another excuse for hatred. The Jew speaks French, and may speak it perfectly. Never mind, says the anti-Semite; the Jew "has spoken this language for only twenty years, and I for a thousand years. The correctness of his style is abstract, acquired; my faults of French are in conformity with the genius of the language."[122] So reasons the anti-Semite.

Using both the language of the psychologist and the philosopher, Sartre created a study of antisemitism steeped in phenomenological concepts. The key element in such an approach is to recognize the mind's ability to organize and control the events of our lives. All of us are ultimately free in a sense that is unique to our own situation, but the complete human being is one who can acknowledge the realities that define our freedom and then find the courage to break through the boundaries to take charge of our own lives. Thus the authentic Jew that Sartre will encourage is one who recognizes the reality of antisemitism and nevertheless surmounts its limitations through deliberative action.

This analysis has its own problems. Shortly after the war, Sartre offered the controversial thesis that "there are no innocent victims of war." Everyone, he insists, is partly guilty. Those who sign the treaties allowing

Germany to march into Czechoslovakia, those who support the creation of a powerful army, even the soldier in the trenches who is reluctant to throw down his rifle and refuse to fight — all bear part of the guilt even as all are ultimately part of the machinery of war. This radical assertion, of course, evoked loud protests from war-weary French soldiers and civilians who felt that Sartre had demeaned their loyalty and belittled their sacrifice. How much more must it have infuriated the decimated remnants of France's Jewish community! Had these survivors not experienced incredible frustration and helplessness as their fathers and mothers disappeared, as sons and daughters were torn from their arms, never to be seen again? What power did they have to do anything?

It is faulty thinking, the philosopher maintains, that leads to society's mistakes and antisemitism itself is an aberration that stems from faulty thinking. Yet it is an aberration that involves the whole personality of the anti-Semite. The disease is not snobbery; it is fear. Those who hate Jews are afraid. They are afraid of themselves; they are cowards. "The anti-Semite is a man who wishes to be a pitiless stone, a furious torrent, a devastating thunderbolt — anything except a man."[123]

Having offered this broad generalization, Sartre feels the need to refine it. There are, he insists, two types of anti-Semites, both of which have an impact on Jewish life. But prior to introducing his readers to the two types, Sartre offers a warning to his readers. The antisemitism that concerns him is not identical with the politically motivated attitudes that had invaded French society during the nineteenth century. It is not based upon the fears of the old conservatives that the Jews stood at the heart of a liberal, socialist conspiracy poised to overthrow traditional French values. Nor is it based upon the suspicions of the left that the Jews were sapping the strength of France through their commercial dominance and exploitation. Rather for Sartre, antisemitism has to be understood in its psychological context, and it is in this context that visible prototypes emerge.

The first of these, the outright anti-Semite, is motivated by a fear that compels him to rationalize his own failures. It is his inadequacy and self-doubt that fuel his dislike of Jews. Culpable in a more subtle way is the second type of anti-Semite, the democrat who feels that since the Enlightenment, all human beings need to be treated equally. This democrat, who believes in reason, is eager to proclaim the universal rights of man but reluctant to let the Jew identify himself *qua Jew*. In this context Jews are to be guaranteed their humanity but denied their Jewishness. This type of enlightened Frenchman fears nothing more than the awakening of a Jewish consciousness.[124] Here Sartre touches upon the antisemitic implications of post-Enlightenment France in ways that had begun to mesmerize Hannah Arendt as she developed her own analysis of totalitarianism. But for Sartre what united his two types of antisemitism was the fact that both worked to dominate Jewish behavior and to invalidate Jewish autonomy.

Did Sartre weaken the subtle force of his own argument when he insisted that there was a Manichean quality to French antisemitism? Manichaeism explains the world as a struggle between good and evil. One force must triumph over the other. There can be no compromise. Any Manichean analysis will remain a stranger to Hannah Arendt's "banality of evil." Yet, in light of Hitler's fanatic vilification of the Jews, Sartre's reminder that there are indeed hatreds that accommodate no compromise struck a responsive chord in post-war Europe.

Opposed to the Manichean analysis of antisemitism is the utilitarian one. The depths of Hitler's perversion can be fully understood only when its "usefulness" is also recognized. Antisemitism, of course, crossed national and economic lines. Hatred of Jews was invariably a crutch used by those who found themselves unable to keep up with the changes that society was imposing upon them. But it was also a tool used by power structures in order to manipulate mass opinion and maintain social control. The failure to appreciate this insight explains the difficulty so many scholars continue to have as they try to cope with antisemitism. Only by understanding the "usefulness" of antisemitism can we fully grasp the complexities of Jewish history. Drawn to some new *goldene medina* one moment, rudely expelled the next, Jews never seemed able to comprehend the dimensions of their own helplessness. Whether it was the czarist retinue or the lowly Polish peasant, the Prussian Junker or the Midwestern farmer about to lose his land, the appeal of antisemitism as a rationalization for human failure has always been irresistible. The "usefulness" of antisemitism is something that Sartre fully appreciated. Only for him the utilitarian aspects of antisemitism were not political; they were psychological.

If there were no Jews the anti-Semite would create him. Sartre was clear on this point. Illustrations of this insight are not hard to find. For years, Franklin Roosevelt was reviled by his most dedicated enemies as a Jew despite his Episcopalian affiliation. And in Germany's Weimar period, the fate of Albert Grzesinksi provides an example of a different kind. Grzesinski was a metal worker and then a trade union leader. In Berlin in

136

1925, he first became Prussia's police president and then minister of the interior. He was also a dedicated anti-Nazi. In 1931 Grzesinski prepared an order expelling Hitler from Prussia but the order was blocked by the national government. Grzesinski was not Jewish but he was repeatedly denounced by the Goebbels press as a "Jew in a Jewish republic." The usefulness of antisemitism even without Jews serves as a stark reminder of how easy it is for evil to create its own sordid reality.[125]

Sartre understood that people victimized by hatreds become doubly victimized. First, they experience political and social deprivation as a consequence of the denial of rights and privileges granted to others; secondly, they endure wounds to their self-esteem, wounds that can prove disastrous. Antisemitism threatens not only the outer Jew, the Jew as a citizen and member of society, but also the inner Jew, who thinks and feels and suffers. Although Sartre was hardly the first intellectual to examine the damage that hatred inflicts upon its victim, he was a pioneer among the post-war thinkers in recognizing the pernicious power that antisemitism exercises over, not only its victim, but its perpetrator as well. Thus, antisemitism threatens the moral fiber of the French community.

Just as there are two types of Jew haters, so says Sartre, there are two types of Jews. The words "inauthentic" or "authentic" appear once again, only now Sartre invests them with a new urgency. The inauthentic Jew is perpetually dominated by his very sense of being a Jew. By simultaneously needing and shunning Jewish companionship, the inauthentic Jew is easily embarrassed by the inappropriate behavior of other Jews. "He seeks and flees his coreligionists; he affirms that he is only one man among others, and like others, yet he feels himself compromised by the demeanor of the first passer-by, if that passer-by is a Jew. He makes himself an anti-Semite in order to break all ties with the Jewish community"…and he continually "oscillates between pride and a sense of inferiority."[126] This Jew is pleased rather that embarrassed when he is told: You are not like other Jews. At the same time he does not hesitate to point with pride to the fact that Einstein was a Jew.

What does Sartre mean when he talks about the "authentic Jew?" The philosophical search that occupied Sartre in *Being and Nothingness* now finds its reification in less technical language. The authentic Jew, it would seem, is one who is able to confront the "nothingness" of reality and ultimately to understand the meaning of "being for others." The journey toward this goal may involve sacrifice and at times even martyrdom, but this may be the special challenge of an authentic Jewish life.

For Sartre, authenticity is closely related to the ability to form a clear understanding of one's social position and then to choose the appropriate course of action stemming from this understanding. "If it is agreed that man may be defined as a being having freedom within the limits of a situation, then it is easy to see that the exercise of this freedom may be considered to be *authentic or inauthentic* according to the choices made in the situation. Authenticity, it is almost needless to say, consists in having a true and lucid consciousness of the situation, in assuming the responsibilities and risks that it involves, in accepting it in pride or humiliation, sometimes in horror and hate." Authenticity is to accept fully the conditions of one's Jewishness. This is no easy task. "Jewish authenticity consists in choosing oneself as Jew — that is, in realizing one's Jewish condition. The authentic Jew abandons the myth of the universal man; he knows himself and wills himself into history as a historic and damned creature; he ceases to run away from himself and to be ashamed of his own kind … He knows that he is one who stands apart, untouchable, scorned, proscribed — and it is as such that he asserts his being."[127]

Caught between the anti-Semite and the enlightened French democrat, the Jew, says Sartre, is wholly a product of antisemitism. Not only is this antisemitism a decisive factor in the process of defining a Jew; it is also something that Jews internalize as they seek to formulate their own self-image. Thus Jews are twice interstitial. In society they are caught between the anti-Semite and the enlightened democrat. And internally most Jews were neither authentic nor inauthentic, but suspended somewhere between the two.

Once again, the effort to distinguish between authentic and inauthentic was bound to strike many Jews as arbitrary and dangerous. Who gave this French existentialist philosopher the right to pass such judgment on the Jews of France? At times it appeared to some Jews that under the guise of fighting antisemitism, Sartre was doing little more than giving currency to the old clichés. Yet by introducing the label "inauthentic," Sartre invited Jews to look at another problem, one that had grown increasingly troublesome — the problem of assimilation. The troublesome specter of assimilation confronted Jewish thinkers as diverse in their approaches as Theodor Herzl and Simon Dubnow, Hannah Arendt and Mordecai Kaplan. Alternating patterns of persecution and liberation in contemporary Jewish life guaranteed that assimilation would be an ongoing problem. Thus, the assimilated Jew was the offspring of a strange marriage; persecution was the father, liberation the mother.

And it is the problem of assimilation, wedded to anxieties about antisemitism that continues to be the most troublesome of concerns for all those dedicated to the preservation of Jewish life in the diaspora. Hebrew University professor Barry Rubin confronted the same themes that occupied Sartre. In his study *Assimilation and Its Discontents*, Rubin maintained that to merely label assimilated Jews as "inauthentic" is to miss the complexity of their motivations as well as their accomplishments. Rubin feels: "Assimilating Jews were bred for contradiction. Inconsistently taught to take pride in differences they no longer understood, yet to be ashamed at feeling superior; to sense themselves outsiders, while being permeated by the native culture. . . . Every act — whether flaunting or spurning one's successful assimilation, trying to win favor or provoke outrage — was done with an eye to how the majority would interpret it . . . Ambiguity between proving one's worthiness and seeing success as selling out one's own people produced radicalism, iconoclasm or self-conscious defensiveness."[128]

Sartre's distinction between two types of Jews remained problematic. What Sartre had begun to deal with in both *Being and Nothingness* and his essay on the Jews was a psychological application of a concept that had been slowly gaining general acceptance in the field of sociology. This was the concept of the "generalized other," developed by the American sociologist George Herbert Mead. With his book *Mind, Self and Society*, published in 1934, Mead argued that society, abstract society, forms judgments that easily become accepted as "social facts." Whether these "social facts" are true or not is irrelevant. Mead conceived of society as the "generalized other." Individuals and also groups are subject to the unspoken judgments of the generalized other whose social facts persist independently of any other fact, even if the actual truth might contradict them. More significantly, these judgments become internalized. They form what Mead called the social self.[129]

All of this is applicable not only to the Jewish situation in general, but also to the phenomenological perspective Sartre cast upon it. Throughout Jewish history "social facts" have had a reality that often bears little relationship to actual facts. What has proven to be tragic in this process is that all too often Jews are unaware of the social forces that enter into the formation of any particular "generalized other." In their eager search for recognition, they accept the definitions of others, while shunning the challenge to take control of the process by which they might define themselves. It was in rebellion against the power of the "generalized other," that Sartre sought to develop his ideas of authenticity and freedom. In this sense he was also acknowledging the insights of Karl Marx.

Entirely consistent with his own communistic sympathies, Sartre tends to minimize the power of antisemitism in working-class communities. Somewhat curiously, he argues that on those rare occasions when antisemitism does infect the laboring classes, it is invariably stimulated from the outside. Sartre was convinced that antisemitism was a middle-class phenomenon and seldom the disease of the proletariat. The bourgeoisie feel pressured from above and below. This explains the resonance of the charge that, on the one hand, Jews are all international bankers, and on the other, they are all communists.

In many ways Marx anticipated the psychological crisis that occupied Sartre's post-war writings. Marx spoke of the alienation of human beings from the products of their labor. Alienation, he noted, stems from persecution as well as from exploitation. Patterns of alienation can be discerned in the history of all kinds of minority groups, but it would be hard to find a group that experienced this form of alienation over the centuries more keenly than did the Jewish community. Studies of feminism and of racism abound with themes in which victims are separated from their true nature, by the false expectations that society places upon them. Jews came to be defined by their oppressors. It was hard to resist the tendency to assimilate the very characteristics, positive or negative, that had been assigned to them by others. Jews make good doctors! Jews are not athletic! Jews are clannish! Can I Jew you down? The stereotypes made the man — or the woman — or the child.

In view of all this, Sartre's distinction between authentic and inauthentic Jew seems superficial in a way that many Jews were quick to recognize. Despite his call for Jewish courage, Sartre pictures all Jews, whether authentic or inauthentic, as mere social objects, dominated by psychological forces beyond their control. One might say that Sartre is describing Jewish interstitiality solely in its painful psychological and negative dimensions. Thus, even his ideal Jew is hardly distinguishable from the interstitial Jew who stands apart, untouchable and courageous, but, for Sartre, ultimately "damned." Sartre goes no further than to suggest that this idealized Jew is morally courageous and committed to an ethical pattern of life.

While endorsing the "authentic Jew," Sartre tempers his approval with a pail full of cold water. He worries that the authentic Jew might turn toward nationalism, a nationalism which will ultimately prove harmful.[130]

This criticism of Zionism may have been prescient in many respects, but coming, as it did, at the end of the war, it struck many Jews as the wrong warning at the wrong time. Sartre's dismissal of Jewish nationalism, coming as it did just as Jews were emerging from Auschwitz and Treblinka, did not sit well among those who felt that the presence of a homeland might have made a life-and-death difference for so many of their friends and family.

It should be pointed out that by 1967, when Israel found itself at war with its Arab neighbors, Sartre had done an about-face, and was quite supportive of the Jewish state. In his initial opposition to Jewish nationalism Sartre seems to fall into a contradiction that reveals the vulnerability of his well-intentioned endeavor. Antisemitism is a psychological disease which infests much of French social life. Yet if only Jews behaved differently they could overcome it! If only they became "authentic." If only they avoided Zionism. After having placed antisemitism in a behavioral perdition, Sartre turns to France's Jews and in essence declares that, after all, "the fault, dear Jews, is not in the stars, but in yourselves." Of course, there is an even more unsettling aspect of Sartre's prescription. The authentic Jew is one who is willing to suffer in order to demonstrate his authenticity. Had not Jews suffered enough by the end of the war? Was martyrdom to be the perpetual proof of their authenticity?

As Sartre became increasingly anecdotal, uneasy feelings about his intentions grew, even though the anecdotes hardly seemed to be ill-intentioned. "A young woman said to me: 'I have had the most horrible experiences with furriers; they robbed me, they burned the fur I entrusted to them. Well, they are all Jews.'" Again: "In Berlin I knew a Protestant in whom sexual desire took the form of indignation. The sight of women in bathing suits aroused him to fury...The Anti-Semite is like that, and one of the elements of his hatred is a profound sexual attraction toward Jews."[131]

It is interesting to see how the personal and the sexual are mixed together with Sartre's existentialism. Sartre claims to have known the subject of this story: "A Jew goes to a house of prostitution, chooses one of the women, and goes upstairs with her. She tells him she is a Jew. He finds himself impotent, and very soon is overcome with an intolerable sense of humiliation ... It is not that sexual intercourse with a Jewess is repugnant to him – after all, Jews marry each other; it is rather the sense that he is contributing personally to the humiliation of the Jewish race in the person of the prostitute, and, consequently, in his own person."[132]

Jean-Paul Sartre began to write *Anti-Semite and Jew* in 1944, as the war was grinding to a close and as many Frenchmen, newly aware of the Holocaust, began to feel guilty about the Jewish tragedy. The reality was that many French citizens remained indifferent to the fate of those who had disappeared. Sartre's treatment of antisemitism was bound to be controversial. And it proved to be problematic not only for Jews. Many French Christians felt that they had been stereotyped and made to feel unduly guilty. As for Jews, words that at first had seemed so sympathetic came to be regarded as familiarly critical. And despite his protestations of friendship, Sartre seemed to doing little more than circulating the old stereotypes that had proven so painful.

Even in the face of these criticisms, the psychological insights that Sartre contributed to the interstitial analysis are sobering and relevant. What made Sartre's work so initially appealing was his understanding that antisemitism was the refuge of social losers. The hatreds that turned human beings "into stone," needed to be explored, and Sartre's great prestige as France's leading intellectual made it fashionable to discuss a topic that for too long had been ignored.

Sartre could well have hoped that his essay on antisemitism would sound a death knell to the type of prejudice he regarded as so irrational. But no such hope could have been expected to endure for long. Today antisemitism has experienced a rebirth in France in a way that Sartre could hardly have foreseen — despite, and perhaps in confirmation of, his forebodings about Jewish nationalism. Tensions between the Muslim and Jewish communities reveal a fault line in French society that seemingly resists all efforts at amelioration. Muslim resentment about the state of Israel can be only a partial explanation of the antagonism that often breaks into open conflict.

And how might Sartre react to the raw antisemitic humor of a popular light-skinned black comedian who entertains people in Paris by declaring that Judaism is "a scam. It's one of the worst because it's first." His full name is Diudonné M'bala M'bala, though on stage he uses only his first name, Diudonné. Until 1997, Diudonné appeared to lampoon all kinds of racism. His partner was Élie Semoun, a childhood friend — and a Jewish comic. So successful was Diudonné that he bought a leading theater in Paris. Then in December, 2003, he appeared in a television panel show wearing a black ski mask and an Orthodox Jewish hat, with artificial sidelocks. According to a report in the *New Yorker* magazine, he then "launched" into a speech that called on the audience to join 'the American

Zionist Axis — the only one . . . that offers you happiness, and the only one to give you a chance of living a little bit longer.' . . . Diudonné finished his polemic by raising his arm and crying, 'Isra-heil.' He then took off his mask and joined the panel to a standing ovation." Diudonné's antisemitic rhetoric has become increasingly hostile. Recently he called France's main Jewish organization "a mafia that controls the republic."[133]

The Holocaust was still fresh in all minds when Sartre tried to demonstrate that antisemitism was not the fault of Jews; his analysis at the time left many Jews scratching their heads in confusion over what they might have done differently. And today, the persistence of anti-Jewish sentiment in France leaves many Jews pondering not only what France might have done differently, but also what France should do differently.

Unlike Herzl, Sartre offered no real answer to the problems he so vividly analyzed. If antisemitism is not only a reality, but the defining Jewish reality in a society as sophisticated as France, then what real hope could there be for a people struggling to find its place in post-war Europe? The modest advice Sartre seemed to offer was simply: "Be good!" The words may be perfectly understandable when uttered by father at a family dinner. They hardly offer a program for survival.

Hannah Arendt (1906–1975)

Hannah Arendt loved to explore Jewish history; she was quite ambivalent about the Jews who inhabited that history. Beginning with her study of Rahel Varnhagen, and extending through her unapologetic relationship with a leading Nazi philosopher as well as her controversial coverage of the Eichmann trial, all of her Jewish commitments seem to be tempered by an attitude that proclaimed: I am part of this, but above it all.

For Arendt, Judaism was both a passion and a burden. Accused of being a "self-hating" Jew, nevertheless her whole life was absorbed in an effort to understand the fate of her people and the causes of its troubled history. Though her penchant for the flamboyant phrase led many of her readers to miss the full impact of her analysis, she was able to expose historical connections that had eluded earlier students of antisemitism. Of course, the use of the words "banality of evil" comes to mind and the appropriateness of that controversial reference to Adolf Eichmann and to his role in the catastrophe that decimated Europe's Jewish community still evokes heated debate among Holocaust scholars. Equally open to misinterpretation is her distinction between "pariah" and "*parvenu*," words she used to define segments of Jewish society.

Arendt was truly a victim of Nazism. Much of her writing, as well as her personal life, seems to represent an effort to understand and confront the trauma of her exile. Born in Hanover in 1906, Arendt studied philosophy at some of Germany's leading universities including Marburg where she met — and fell in love with — one of her teachers, Martin Heidegger. At the time she was nineteen; the great philosopher was thirty-six, married, and the father of two children. Whether the relationship between teacher and student was a physical one has been the subject of much speculation, but there is no doubt that they renewed their contact at the end of the Second World War, and even after Heidegger's morally reprehensible role as a Nazi had been exposed.

In 1933, Arendt fled to Paris, and, when the Nazis invaded France, she escaped to the United States where she became an editor at Schocken Books, wrote for publications as diverse as the *Forward* and the *New Yorker*, and taught at Berkeley, Cornell, Princeton, the University of Chicago, and ultimately, the New School for Social Research in New York.

Politics was the center of her intellectual interest, and what she called the *vita activa*, the life of activity, evoked her particular sympathy. How did this relate to her attitude toward Jewish history? Jews, she felt, had historically failed to understand the political possibilities of the "life of activity" — and this failure had left them disorganized and vulnerable. Hannah Arendt is well served by her biographer, Elisabeth Young-Bruehl and by Jerome Kohn and Ron H. Feldman who created an anthology of her Jewish writings. She became conscious of her Jewishness, both sources inform us, not through her parents, but through the antisemitic insults of her classmates at school. When she came home from school to report that she had been taunted, her mother advised her to stand up and walk out of school. She could take the rest of the day off — a "delightful" occurrence for the young child. Hannah would report these incidents to her mother, who would write a letter of protest to the school. From then on Hannah was forbidden to discuss the matter again. These childhood incidents were to have a lasting impact upon Hannah's later writing. It was not through worship or ceremony that Arendt expressed her Jewish interests, but through political life. And the effort to understand Jewish political life remained a central focus in all of her writings related to Jewish subjects.[134]

The Origins of Totalitarianism, published shortly after the end of World War II, perhaps Hannah Arendt's most enduring work, devotes its entire first section to the problem of antisemitism. Just as the "banality of evil" aroused conflicted feelings among her Jewish readers, so did her analysis of the powerlessness of the Jewish community. As profound as her ideas are, Arendt's writing can at times seem annoyingly condescending, and her detractors continue to fault not her scholarship as much as her politics. "Arendt is clever and she is formidable," suggests one such critic, "but her heart's in the wrong place."[135] Critics might also suggest that Arendt often writes as if even the most random of events is inexorably connected to the final solution. Despite these complaints her analysis is so compelling that one is almost convinced that somewhere along the line, a tremendous opportunity was missed by Jewish leaders. She seems to be saying that at some crucial moment in Jewish history, wisdom and courage might have converged in order to avert the ultimate tragedy. What she does not make clear is — whose wisdom and whose courage.

Focusing on the century and a half preceding the rise of Nazism, Arendt asserts that the period of European Enlightenment was as perilous as it was liberating for most of Europe's Jews. Liberalism, so ardently admired by Jewish intellectuals, harbored its own great dangers. As liberal ideas spread across Europe in the early years of the nineteenth century, the economic dimensions of Jewish geographical confinement were complicated by social ones: "During the 150 years when Jews truly lived amidst, and not just in the neighborhood of, Western European peoples, they always had to pay with political misery for social glory and with social insult for political success."[136] Special Jews could achieve acceptance only by separating socially from the Jewish masses. The problem was that the doors to social acceptance would be opened to them only if they became Jews, but did not behave like Jews. "The seeming paradox had a solid basis in fact. What non-Jewish society demanded was that the newcomer be as 'educated' as itself, and that, although he not behave like an 'ordinary Jew,' he be and produce something out of the ordinary, since, after all, he was a Jew."[137]

Thus, a new dilemma was created for the Jewish community. Its intellectual elites were separated from the mass of Jews. These elites ruled the Jewish community, but were not part of it. The most bizarre example of this syndrome can be found in the career of Disraeli, a more familiar one, in the history of the Rothschild family. As a result of these leadership models, so vastly different, yet similar in terms of their elitist aspects, it is easy to understand why assimilation and conversion came to be so tempting to large numbers of Jews. The goal was to separate oneself from the "vulgarity" of the Jewish masses and, simultaneously, to acquire political equality. Neither goal was to be achieved.

What are we to make of the unique success of Benjamin Disraeli, Britain's only Jewish-born prime minister? Disraeli's own attitudes toward Judaism reveal a complex mixture of chauvinism and confusion. To succeed in British politics, and even to enter Parliament, was still unthinkable for members of the Jewish faith. It is doubtful that Isaac D'Israeli had a political career in mind when he arranged for the baptism of his thirteen-year-old son. What is certain is that Benjamin Disraeli's Jewishness was inseparable from every aspect of his entire career.

Arendt is not gentle in her disdain for Queen Victoria's favorite prime minister. "Disraeli, who never denied that 'the fundamental fact about (him) was that he was a Jew,' had an admiration for all things Jewish that was matched only by his ignorance of them."[138] Disraeli's racial theories coupled with his pseudo messianism, she argues, turned him into a figure of ridicule as well as a portent of ultimate disaster. Yet it was Disraeli's very uniqueness combined with his success that makes him so relevant to the interstitial analysis.

Benjamin Disraeli was simultaneously a Jew and not a Jew. He fashioned careers for himself as a writer and a politician, but more than anything else he wanted to be a man of action. Early in his career he changed the spelling of his name from D'Israeli, removing the apostrophe from the spelling. But if the apostrophe is a mark of omission, Disraeli's name change was emblematic of his entire life. More than anything else he wanted to be accepted by the aristocracy, and he pursued this goal, first by writing novels, and second by seeking a seat in Parliament. His first work, *Vivien Grey*, astounded and then infuriated British society because it pretended to have been written by an insider. His later works, even though the central characters were Christian, were entwined with myths about Jewish chosenness and Jewish messianism. In *David Alroy*, for example (Hannah Arendt mistakenly calls this Disraeli's first novel), the hero is based upon an actual Jew who lived in the twelfth century and sought to return Jews to the Promised Land. In this, as in other of his novels, Disraeli clearly emerges as a Zionist. Fifty years before Herzl's star began to shine, Disraeli was writing about the glory of a Jewish return to Zion.

He was also promulgating, although quite innocently, the very racial theories that were later to prove so catastrophic. A central fixture in many of the Disraeli novels is a "super Jew" named Sidonia. Sidonia is young and handsome; he is brilliant and incredibly wealthy. Sidonia will not eat bacon, nor will he even contemplate marriage outside of his faith. He is an astonishingly capable horseman. His advice is sought by governments all over Europe, and his immense wealth is capable of saving or destroying even the mightiest of nations. Sidonia's father was able to spread his wealth throughout Europe. "France wanted some; Austria more; Prussia a little; Russia a few millions . . . Sidonia could furnish them all." In other words, Sidonia and his family are an idealized projection of the Rothschild family whose fortunes were later to prove so indispensable to Disraeli. He is also an innocent prefigurement of the fear and hostility that would be associated with the Rothschild name.

More, Sidonia is the epitome of the Jewish "race." Disraeli does not shirk from using the term throughout his writings. "The Hebrew is an unmixed race," Disraeli asserts, and he goes on to suggest that "the Mosaic Arabs are the most ancient, if not the only unmixed blood that dwells in cities." Disraeli could almost be accused of using race to make a case for his own political loyalty as when he has Sidonia assure a young Coningsby that "the Jews, for example . . . are a race essentially monarchical, deeply religious, and shrinking themselves from converts as from a calamity."[139] By reason of race, the Jews are Tories!

It was this racial theme proliferating throughout Disraeli's writings, coupled with his own messianic projections, that Arendt found so distressing. She regarded him as a "living embodiment of ambition," who defeated the British aristocracy at their own game "by using his rather trite and popular imagination to describe fearlessly how the Englishman 'came from a *parvenu* and hybrid race, while he himself was sprung from the purest blood in Europe.'" And Disraeli even hoped that his racial theories would preserve the very inequalities that not only had favored him so generously, but had also provided intellectual support for his entire political outlook.[140]

Arendt's profound, yet surely controversial, insight was that racial theories such as those held by Disraeli were directly related to the secularization of Jewish life. When religious and community aspects of Judaism are discarded, and one becomes Jewish by virtue only of birth, then all that is left is the feeling that one is part of an elite minority. But the "elite few" can easily become degraded, pictured as a congenital anomaly once all factors but birth are eliminated.

Hannah Arendt's analysis of Jewish history acknowledges the centrality of the interstitial role, but of course she pictures that role in a context that continually opens the door to fresh insight. The vulnerability of the Jews in the middle was regularly accentuated by the decline of traditional social structures as well as by divisions within the Jewish community itself. The fatal error of the Jewish communities of post-emancipation Europe lay in their inability to confront the real world and to recognize real, as opposed to imaginary, threats to Jewish survival. Hannah Arendt's reluctance to specify the difference between these real and imaginary threats allows room for much conjecture. Despite the vagueness of her warning, the invitation to probe these differences is a welcome one.

The complexities of anti-Jewish prejudice cannot be underestimated. In Eastern Europe antisemitism occurred as a result of social inequality. Jews were "strong in number and weak in every other respect." They "seemed to fulfill the function of a middle class because they were mostly shopkeepers and traders and because as a group they stood between the landowners and the property-less classes." But they were a middle class, Arendt notes, "without fulfilling its productive functions."

Jewish history in Western Europe is substantially different from that of any other group. Lacking a territory, and lacking a government, Jews had always been "an inter-European" element. Consequently, "whether they were welcomed or rejected it was because they were Jews." Jewish leaders have been naïve about the dangers that confront their people, and this naïveté has had disastrous consequences. Moreover, Jewish leaders have traditionally sought to affiliate the Jewish community not with the masses of people but with government and business elites. "The Jews' political ignorance, which fitted them so well for their special role and for taking roots in the state's sphere of business, and their prejudices against the people and in favor of authority, which blinded them to the political dangers of antisemitism, caused them to be oversensitive toward all forms of social discrimination."[141] This judgment regarding the nature of alliances forms a critically important part of the interstitial analysis. Do Jewish elites even today, tend to look in the wrong direction in their search for allies?

How could anything as radically evil as Nazism take root in Europe's most civilized nation? For Arendt the process which resulted in the rise of Nazism can be divided into four periods. In each of these periods the status of Jews underwent significant changes. First is the development of nation-states in the seventeenth and eighteenth centuries. Individual Jews often arose out of obscurity to become Court Jews and handle the finances of the state. This role, Arendt claims, had as little impact on the gentile masses as it did upon the Jewish people as a whole. But for the princes and nobility it was significant. Over the years, the medieval Jewish role as moneylenders had gradually become less and less significant, but by the beginning of the seventeenth century with the advent of the Thirty Years' War, a war that involved most of the countries of continental Europe, these moneylenders were again given a purpose — to provide funds needed to provision the armies of Europe. "Every feudal household needed the equivalent of the Court Jew."[142]

The French Revolution marked the beginning of a second stage, an era marked by the emergence of nation-states, and accompanied by the need for huge infusions of capital. These funds could be provided by very wealthy Jews who used their own resources plus resources that more prosperous members of the Jewish community entrusted to them. The prominence of Jewish elites and financiers, as well as a growing spirit of Enlightenment, encouraged the newly emerging nation-states to gradually allow the emancipation and enfranchisement of their Jewish populations. This pattern, so familiar in Western European nations, was not replicated in the more crowded and "backward" countries of Eastern Europe.

The relationship of Jewish financiers to governments was marked by utility rather than consistency. The Jewish financiers were drawn to power, namely, the "power" that needed their resources. It was understood that loyalty was not always to be expected. Indeed, the banks owned by the Rothschilds served many masters. "It took the French Rothschilds in 1848 hardly twenty-four hours to transfer their services from the government of Louis Philippe to the new short-lived French Republic and again to Napoleon III."[143]

Toward the end of the nineteenth century, the third stage of modern Jewish history began. It was marked, Arendt notes, by the decline of the nation-state and the rise of imperialism. During this period the need for Jewish bankers receded in the face of the imperial state's demand for huge sums of money to finance its colonial expansion. A new breed of competitive and commercially minded businessmen stood ready to help the state, and their rise was accompanied by a new and dangerous form of antisemitism. Jews could be pictured as foreign, superfluous, and even subversive. With the establishment of a regulated system of credit, Jews were no longer needed by the nobility. At the same time, the personal relationships which the Jewish bankers formerly enjoyed with political elites were now rapidly becoming irrelevant. This was a period that saw a growing political as well as financial sophistication among the bourgeoisie. The individual wealth of Jewish financiers was beginning to be seen as superfluous and even dangerous. The Dreyfus trial in Paris and the rise of virulent antisemitism in Vienna were manifestations of this growing mass awareness of a distinctive Jewish element seeking to attach itself to contemporary society.

The fourth and final stage in the process which defined the deterioration of the Jewish condition coincided with events leading to the First World War and the disintegration that followed it. In this period, Jews were deprived of their power; Jewish wealth became totally irrelevant, and Jews themselves became objects of contempt because of their useless power. The crime of being Jewish now became the "disease" of being Jewish. A crime can be punished. A disease needs to be eradicated.[144]

What is the interstitial element in Arendt's taxonomy? It can easily be discerned in her analysis of the external conditions forced upon the Jews. "Without territory and without a government of their own, the Jews had always been an inter-European element ... But even when their economic usefulness had exhausted itself, the inter-European status of the Jews remained of great national importance in times of national conflicts and wars."[145] A more subtle aspect of the middle role can be discerned in the paradoxes so characteristic of Jewish life itself. In each period of historical development the Jews emerged as both unique and problematic. As a community Jews consistently acted as if they thrived on being outside of the mainstream of European society; they rejected alliances with the masses in favor of alliances with vulnerable power structures. Then as now, so many of their leaders deluded themselves into believing that the power of the king, the nobility, the state, would protect them. They developed a bifocal political vision which led them to look inward to family and friends for psychological and moral support and outward to the non-Jewish elites for the security that was never to be totally theirs.

Did the Rothschilds and the other Jewish banking families abandon their Judaism in their effort to gain admission into the circles of the elite? Far from it! It was their Jewish connections and their commitment to family cohesiveness that contributed to their tremendous financial success. The ascendancy of Jewish banking houses in the nineteenth century is an amazing saga. As the nation-state emerged, the need for Jewish capital could no longer be regarded as a royal prerogative; it became a matter of national necessity. Whereas the old Court Jew served the personal needs of the royal families, the new banking houses met the requirements of an entire nation.

For both its promises and its disappointments, the appearance of the huge Jewish banking houses merits special attention. The promises lay in the emergence of wealthy Jewish elites who conveyed, at least for a time, a sense of dignity, almost of royalty. The threat lay in the vulnerability that adheres to wealth that is powerless, royalty that is artificial. The functions of the bankers were always contingent ones. They provided the capital, not only for the arms and military supplies that proved so vital for any national expansion, but also for the industries, utilities and railroad systems that helped define the new nation states. Arendt acknowledges the important role played by the various branches of the Rothschild family. And the story of the Rothschild involvement with Disraeli as he acted to obtain controlling interest in the Suez Canal for Queen Victoria has been well rehearsed. But the Rothschilds were only one, albeit the most lastingly successful, of these banker families. It would be a mistake to forget the importance of so many other Jewish bankers. The roster includes names such as Gerson Bleichroder and Baron Maurice de Hirsch as well as the Fruhlings, the Oppenheims, and Baron Meyer-Cohn who was the royal banker in Berlin.

Arendt pays surprisingly little attention to Bleichroder, who was, for a time, the most impressive of all the German Jewish financiers. His history deserves more than a footnote in any analysis of antisemitism. Bleichroder started his career as the Rothschild representative in Berlin and soon became the second wealthiest man in all of Germany. His experiences, though magnified, reflect those of many assimilated German Jews. For three decades Gerson Bleichroder was Otto von Bismarck's financial advisor. In his study, *Gold and Iron*, Fritz Stern documents the ways that Bleichroder's financial genius became an essential ingredient in Bismarck's success. Not only did Bleichroder guide and protect Bismarck's personal finances, but he also played a prominent and vital role in organizing and operating the finances of the new German empire. The outbreak of the Franco-Prussian war in 1870 signaled a break between Bleichroder and the French branch of the Rothschild family. Following the French defeat Bismarck wanted Bleichroder to be with him at Versailles in 1871, to help arrange reparations. With each passing year Bleichroder's financial prominence loomed larger. He purchased stocks and bonds for Bismarck and the government. He played a key role in the development of railroads all over Europe and his financial judgments had a profound effect upon German foreign policy.

Bleichroder was known as a conscientious and conservative financial advisor. He generally shunned get-rich-quick schemes, and he guarded Bismarck's interests, warning the great leader not to sink too much of his money into real estate. Yet there were many occasions when he acted more like a faithful puppy than a trusted financial advisor. Bleichroder plied Bismarck with flattering compliments and with gifts of wine and caviar as well as toys for the Bismarck children. He maintained a relationship with Bismarck not dissimilar to that which was to develop between Henry Kissinger and Richard Nixon. (Kissinger's life-long admiration of Bismarck is hardly surprising and is well documented. "Bismarck sought his opportunities in the present; he drew his inspiration from a vision of the future.")[146]

Bleichroder was like Kissinger in another way: his constant quest was for respect and honor. In this, he appeared to have achieved success. Kaiser Wilhelm bestowed on him the coveted noble title of *von* (the first German Jew to be so honored) and he was rewarded with the Iron Cross. But behind his back, German elites laughed at Baron Gerson von Bleichroder. They took sumptuous dinner at his magnificent mansion but ridiculed his dumpy wife and laughed at his pretensions. "Filthy Jew" they called him and "Jewish swine."

Bleichroder died in 1893 at the age of seventy-one, a lonely, abandoned man. He is not mentioned once in Bismarck's memoirs. After thirty years of almost daily contact, Bleichroder was to be totally ignored. The slight was not of incidental historical importance. During his last days Bleichroder reluctantly began to recognize the virulence of a new type of antisemitism. Not only was the Jewish banker rapidly becoming obsolete — as Hannah Arendt later documented — but the new hatred of Jews aroused a paranoid fear of Jewish power. Jews were suddenly looked upon as dangerous at every level — politically, financially, genetically, and, of course, morally. The new antisemitism, given expression by clergymen such as Adolf Stoecker and historian Heinrich von Treitschke, was accompanied by dire warnings that Jews were about to destroy the essence of the German character. The preconditions for Hitler were set long before the advent of Hitler.

Bleichroder's family was shown no mercy by the Nazis despite the Iron Cross and noble title. Their fate was to flee Nazi Germany or face internment. Two grandsons managed to escape to Switzerland. One of them, Curt von Bleichroder was so destitute that upon his arrival in Switzerland, the Red Cross had to help him out with the gift of an overcoat.

Hannah Arendt does not devote much attention to Bleichroder despite the important role he played in her native Germany. *The Origins of*

Totalitarianism, however, does contain one dismissive statement about him, a statement that echoes a theme that would be developed in her later writings. Bleichroder, she suggested, was either unwilling or incapable of using his wealth to enter into the political arena. "Somehow the government's reluctance to yield real power to Jews and the Jews' reluctance to engage in business with political implications coincided so well that, despite the great wealth of the Jewish group, no actual struggle for power ever developed."[147] For Arendt political action ranked among the highest of virtues, and her model was the Greek agora, where political action could be developed in its purist form. The compatibility of such a model with a large polity and a representative form of government remains problematic; Arendt's admiration of action was to remain constant.

During her many years as a teacher and writer, Arendt was often accused of being an assimilationist Jew. In reality, however, she was as critical of Jewish assimilationists as she was of those Jewish notables who had failed to recognize opportunities to organize politically and to act decisively. It is not always clear what sort of political activity she really favored. Whether or not her reluctance to define meaningful political activity was intentional, some critics would accuse her of replacing definition with slogans. Even years later when she tried to spell out what she meant by the term *vita activa*, as she did in her study of *The Human Condition*, readers were left to ponder what an "active life" really meant."[148]

Despite these charges, it is clear that Arendt regarded Jewish assimilation as an intellectual dead end. Of course, assimilation was never as simple a problem as its critics claimed. Surely assimilation represented a tempting path toward opportunity and respectability. But it is too easy to blame those Jews who chose that path while neglecting to understand the tremendous pressures that had been imposed on them. In 1816, for example, the Prussian ministry of finance issued a report affirming that only through the creation of "a shared religion" could there ever be a hope of melding a people into a "unanimous whole" capable of unified action in times of an external threat. The report went on to suggest that the conversion of Jews to Christianity be "made easier" and that it should be accompanied by the granting of civil rights. The threat for failure to convert was the stick side of the equation: "As long as the Jew remained a Jew, he must not be permitted to take up a position in the state." There was a carrot too. In Prussia converts from Judaism were encouraged to ask Friedrich Wilhelm III to be their grandfather. Each convert was entitled to a baptismal gift of ten ducats. Since communion was not required, or even knowledge of the Lord's Prayer, and since there were many poor Jews, the offer often proved to be irresistible.[149]

Hannah Arendt was quite cognizant of these external inducements which Germany's Jews had to confront, but her major concern was focused upon the internal activity of Jews as a community. "In the hands of the assimilationist," she wrote, "Jewish history was turned into a history of the injustice inflicted on us." These assimilationists "managed to smuggle the history of the Jewish people right out the back door and replace it with a history of the Jewish religion, whose purest and loftiest expression was without doubt the Reform synagogue." This in turn, Arendt insisted, allowed the assimilationists to "plunge into a world history whose 'creeping pace' temporarily made way for a paradoxical display of both fierce patriotism and slavish 'gratitude.' . . . Their own preoccupation was to prove that Jews were all sorts of things — a religion, the salt of the earth, world citizens par excellence — but not a people."[150]

The point is not to be dismissed lightly, and it deserves a fuller examination. The unique qualities of Jewish peoplehood have been debated endlessly. For Dubnow, it is Jewish history — not religious orthodoxy, not Zionism — that establishes the basis for Jewish continuity. Of course, Dubnow was responding to the traditional assertion that religion was responsible for Jewish survival. As hostile as he was to religious orthodoxy, he was equally suspicious of all those who claimed that only Zionism could guarantee Jewish survival. And, despite his own scholarly analysis of antisemitism, he struggled against defining Jewish survival as a by-product of hatred and discrimination.

This, however, was the ultimate conclusion reached by Karl Marx and his interpreters. They argued that Jews were a "class-people" and that they were defined by the evils of capitalism. Thus, Abram Leon writing from Brussels in the midst of World War II could insist that antisemitism would end only with the demise of capitalism. Despite its doctrinaire position, Leon's historical analysis of Jewish commercial activity offers an important contribution to an understanding of negative interstitiality. But Leon's total preoccupation with financial systems led him to minimize other important aspects of Jewish life, such as the role of religious faith and the ability of individuals to act, even outside the limitations of the Marxian dialectic. And both Marx and Leon minimized the possibility of any internal restructuring of Jewish social life. As for Leon, his tragic end had little to do with the capitalistic critique he had so carefully developed. For it was not capitalism, but Nazism, that did him in. Arrested and tortured, he died in Auschwitz in 1944. He was only 34 years old.[151]

During the early decades of the nineteenth century, the term Jewish Notables was used to describe an elite class of French Jewish leaders. These Jews, brilliant and successful as they were, lived as far outside the Jewish community as outside the Gentile one. The Notables wanted to rule the community but not leave it. Jewish intellectuals, in contrast, wanted to leave the community and be accepted by society at large. What they had in common was the feeling that they were "exception Jews." The Notables were distinguished from the rest of Jewry by their exceptional wealth and by their usefulness to governments. Those who were regarded as exceptions by virtue of their education soon came to regard themselves as truly unusual people and, therefore, entitled to separate themselves and their families from the masses of Jews. At the same time they sought to have their uniqueness recognized by the social circles they aspired to join. Both desires for exceptional status resulted in vulnerability as well as prestige.[152]

That a few individuals can become stereotypes for a whole people is a fundamental assumption of the interstitial analysis of Jewish history. This became a theme that Arendt frequently noted, and if any one incident could document this pattern it was the trial and conviction of one single Jewish military officer who became entrapped in a drama that enmeshed an entire people. When Alfred Dreyfus was accused of treason, the whole French Jewish community went on trial with him. But the story is not simply about the Jewish captain; it is also about those who preceded him and those who followed.

The cries of "Death to the Jews" that echoed through the streets of many French villages evoked a variety of responses. Herzl, the playwright and visionary, attended the Dreyfus trial and turned his gaze forward — envisioning the establishment of a Jewish state. Arendt, the political scientist, studied the trial and looked backward, seeking to understand the conditions that made the trial so volatile. What she discovered was the Panama Scandal. The implications of the scandal were profound and illustrate how malleable facts can become in the hands of malicious bigots.

The story begins with the building of the Suez Canal. The completion of the canal was celebrated as a huge national triumph. Its construction was a source of pride for France and of wealth for Ferdinand de Lesseps, the man who supervised the canal's construction. And now the challenge was to build a canal across the Isthmus of Panama. De Lesseps was the man to turn the challenge into a reality. Between 1880 and 1888, little progress was made on the actual work of building the canal although the Panama Company had succeeded in raising 1,335,538,454 francs in private loans. What is significant, Arendt tells us, is that these funds were raised despite the traditional financial cautiousness of the French people. By the middle of the decade, however, it was apparent the company was on the verge of bankruptcy. What did not become immediately apparent was that the bankruptcy would mark the ruin of half a million middle class Frenchmen who had put their faith in the project.

A later commission of inquiry revealed what the company wanted to keep secret — that it had been bankrupt for many years, that de Lesseps had persisted in the false and dangerous hope that a miracle would occur, and that a great deal of bribery was involved in maintaining the illusion that the company was still solvent. De Lesseps had used what little funds still available to bribe the press, to bribe half the members of Parliament and key members of the government. To pass the bribes he needed intermediaries. The intermediaries were both Jewish — Jacques Reinach and Cornelius Herz.

At one time Reinach had occupied a respected office in the government. Much less respected was Herz who ended up playing a double role in the scandal. While he was bribing members of the Parliament, he was also blackmailing Reinach, implicating him ever more deeply in the nefarious process. By the end of 1892, Reinach could stand the pressure no longer and committed suicide. But just before doing so, he did one thing that was to have profound consequences for French Jewry. He wrote a letter of confession and sent it to the editor of one of the few Paris newspapers whose staff had not been bribed, *La Libre Parole*. The editor of *La Libre Parole*, Édouard Drumont, was a man of prodigious hatreds, the one man who possessed both the intellect and the means of synthesizing the antisemitism of the conservatives and the socialists. Drumont had just written *La France juive*, a venomous 1,200-page book that combined religious, political and racial antisemitism with the crudest forms of stereotyping and gossip. The hateful quality of Drumont's book did not prevent it from becoming the best-selling political book of the nineteenth century.[153]

What prompted Reinach to send his confession to the most notoriously antisemitic newspaper of them all? The fact that its editor had not been bribed by the Panama Company remains a shallow explanation. What is clear is that Edouard Drumont used the confession to foster his hate-filled agenda. With agonizing slowness he published week by week the names of the officials who had been bribed. The circulation of his newspaper soared. The antisemitic press, says Hannah Arendt, had entered into the mainstream of French political thought.[154]

Two Jews were involved in the scandal. They were not members of the company perpetrating the scandal. They were not recipients of the bribes as were the members of the parliament and the press. They were merely the middlemen, the "bag men." But in the eyes of most Frenchmen and with the encouragement of Drumont, the roles of these two Jews came to be seen as central. By understanding the actions of Herz and Reinach, and the ways the French establishment protected itself by shifting the spotlight of publicity onto these two minor participants, much can be learned about the durability of the interstitial role and about the passions aroused only a few years later during the treason trial of that diffident Jewish officer who remained so oblivious to his own historic importance.[155]

The words "pariah" and "*parvenu*" hardly describe the totality of European Jews; most of them would undoubtedly have objected to either characterization. Yet the two terms are used so frequently in Arendt's writings that it often seems that all Jews can be neatly labeled and filed under one category or the other. While agreeing with Bernard Lazare that the average Jew is neither a *parvenu* nor a "conscious pariah," Arendt nevertheless insists that "every Jew in every generation had somehow at some time to decide whether he would remain a pariah and stay out of society altogether, or become a *parvenu*." Arendt offers a third, and not very happy choice: "to conform to society" and betray the secret of his people as well."[156]

The *parvenu* is selfish and overly concerned with financial needs. The pariah is altruistic and noble. Arendt's use of the word "pariah" neglects the negative connotations the term has historically evoked. Imported from India, the Tamil word "pariah," which literally means "drummer," was the name assigned to a member of a lowly caste in southern India. While acknowledging the great German sociologist Max Weber as the popularizer of the term, she seems to neglect the fact that Weber used "pariah" in a less than complimentary way. In Weber's words, the term pariah describes "the dubious commercial activities of marginal traders."[157] The classic pariah is someone who is alienated and isolated, not necessarily someone who is brilliant and creative.

Bernard Lazare was one of the Jewish leaders Arendt could sincerely admire. It was he who first used the word pariah in reference to the Jews of Europe. Lazare lived in Paris during the time of the Dreyfus trial and made his mark as a fiery critic of the elite Jewish Notables and particularly of the Rothschilds. Had they not been silent during Dreyfus's trial? The fate of a falsely accused Jew remained a matter of indifference to these Jewish elites. It was not a matter of indifference to Lazare. But in 1894, Lazare published *L'Antisemitisme: son histoire et ses causes* (*Antisemitism: Its History and Causes*, 1903), a work in which he maintained a view he was later to regret. Antisemitism, he suggested in that unfortunate work, could be useful after all, for an abhorrence of Jewish commercial practices could lead to the death of capitalism. Despite this early clumsy attempt to rationalize antisemitism, "The moral condition of the Jew is due partly to himself, and partly to exterior circumstances. ... Throughout the centuries he lived twice a slave; he was the bondman of the law, and the bondman of everyone. He was a pariah, but a pariah whom teachers and guides united to keep in a state of servitude more complete than the ancient bondage of Egypt."[158]

Not surprisingly Lazare's book was frequently quoted by anti-Semites. Lazare himself came to modify his view as he contemplated the hatred engendered by the Dreyfus trial. His sense of history allowed him to recognize that Jews were a group in between the parts of their society, even though he, like Arendt, persisted in using the awkward term "pariah." In contrast to Herzl, with whom he later broke, Lazare foresaw the dangers that arise when Jews disdain alliances with the masses and rely upon the good will of the rich and powerful. Arendt hailed Lazare as an ideal pariah and one of the neglected heroes of Jewish history. She agreed with his insistence that Jews should openly take pride in their role as pariahs; she applauded his conclusion which today seems so unobjectionable: "it is the duty of every human being to resist oppression." But what in retrospect seems unobjectionable has not always been a conscious part of the Jewish community's agenda — neither in Lazare's time nor in our own. Arendt's analysis of Lazare contains an afterthought, a warning directed toward even the most altruistic of modern Jewish social justice endeavors. Don't become a beggar. Don't be seduced by the desire for fame and publicity. "However bitterly they may have attacked him, it was not the hostility of the Jewish nabobs that ruined Lazare. It was the fact that when he tried to stop the pariah from being a schlemiel, when he sought to give him a political significance, he encountered only the *schnorrer*. And once the pariah becomes a *schnorrer*, he is worth nothing, not because he is poor and begs, but because he begs from those he ought to fight."[159]

For Hannah Arendt the pariah is the type of Jew that ought to be emulated. Such a Jew could well follow the path taken by Moses

Mendelssohn, the grandfather of the composer. Because of his intellectual brilliance Mendelssohn was given permission to settle in Berlin at a time when other Jews were denied residence privileges. In the 1750s Mendelssohn wrote a letter to his good friend, the playwright Gotthold Ephraim Lessing, excitedly describing his growing friendship with the publisher Friedrich Nicolai. His account, so full of enthusiasm, is as much a testimony to the rarity of such inter-religious relationships as to the depth of the bond between the two men: "I visit Herr Nicolai often in his garden. (I truly love him, my dearest friend! And I believe that our own friendship can only gain by this because I cherish in him your true friend as well.) We read poetry, Herr Nicolai recites his own compositions too, and I sit on my bench, a critical judge, complimenting, laughing, approving, finding fault, until evening comes."[160]

But Arendt was less interested in the traditional Jewish scholar, Moses Mendelssohn, than in other pariahs whose religious commitments to Judaism were not so steadfast. Like Isaac Deutscher, her radical Marxist contemporary, she singled out Jews who stood alienated from the Jewish community. Both Deutscher and Arendt were drawn to these intellectual Jews who became "non-Jewish Jews" for the former, "pariahs" for the latter. For Deutscher, the list of non-Jewish Jews was a long one and included Spinoza and Marx, Heine and Borne, as well as more contemporaneous personalities such as Freud and Marx's disciples, Rosa Luxemburg and Leon Trotsky. "Assimilationists" these Jews have been contemptuously called. And they did indeed share, in varying degrees, an antagonism toward the religion of their birth. Yet to dismiss them as "self-hating Jews" is to remain blind to both the intellectual roots of their estrangement and the magnitude of their achievements.

For Hannah Arendt, the term "pariah" served to describe both the genius and the alienation of these exceptional Jews. Early in her career she discovered that she needed to look no further than Rahel Varnhagen to find her prototypical pariah. Even in her earliest writings Arendt had tried to understand the crosscurrents that made Jewish continuity so problematic. What was it that led her to concentrate on enlightened assimilation-minded Jews rather than the mass of Jews who sought to live in "simple tranquility?" More than curiosity drew Arendt to Rahel Varnhagen and other "singular" Jews. She sought to unlock the "mysteries" hidden in these isolated but flawed lives. Arendt could sympathize with the frustration of those highly sophisticated Jews who felt themselves trapped not only between Jews and Christians, but also between Jewish intellectuals and Jewish *parvenus*. Exceptional individuals, whether on the right or the left, could easily be caricatured and turned into unpleasant stereotypes. Thus Jews could be pictured as both disloyal pacifists and self-serving warmongers; as both communists and greedy capitalists. The inability of European Jews to face the possibility of creating real power, instead of fitting into the power thirst of others, was their fatal shortcoming.

Although it was not published until after the war, the Varnhagen biography was largely completed by 1933, shortly before its author was compelled to leave Germany. It is a loving, if often painful, study of the brilliant young woman, born Rahel Levin, who, between 1790 and 1806 presided over one of Berlin's most sophisticated salons. Her dual role as a Jew and a hostess coupled with her desire to escape from poverty revealed one aspect of Rahel's personality — the temptation to become a *parvenu*. Wealth, power, and prestige were her goals, and above all, marriage to a prominent nobleman. The *parvenu* struggled with the pariah and in the end, Arendt tells us, it was her self-confessed "faults" that prevented her from becoming the true *parvenu*. She had "too much consideration" for others, too much love for freedom and truth.[161] Rahel spent her life seeking status as a *parvenu*; her return to Judaism just before her death was a redemptive act, one that guaranteed her status as a true pariah.

That the pariah inevitably remains vulnerable was something that Arendt frequently analyzed. Always present are guilt and self-doubt, conditions that often prompt the pariah to abandon the Jewish community. Yet Arendt's admiration for the Berlin hostess and for all the Jewish "rebels with a conscience" who followed her is apparent. The Jewish pariahs were "those who really did most for the spiritual dignity of their people, who were great enough to transcend the bounds of nationality and to weave the strands of their Jewish genius into the general texture of European life."

The qualities that Arendt attributes to the terms "pariah" and "*parvenu*" reveal striking distinctions that had begun to develop within Europe's Jewish community. Jewish "exceptionalism" soon transformed itself into social isolation for both the pariah and the *parvenu*. The *parvenu* could be easily caricatured as someone who utilized unscrupulous methods in order to attain wealth and prominence. The characterization of the *parvenu* easily lent itself to the familiar antisemitic stereotype such as that to be seen in the nineteenth-century cartoon, the *Generalpumpe*. That cartoon, which was widely disseminated, offers a grotesque depiction of the Rothschilds while it simultaneously lampoons Jewish greed and power. The Rothschild figure is a grossly overweight and overburdened with medals.

He is pictured as a man who is both pumping out favors to European rulers and sucking in money from all quarters. The *parvenu*, the stereotypes repeatedly asserted, were Jews who had become successful through selfishness, insolence, inhumanity toward others and pushiness. All of the attributes that society found distasteful, it seems, could be attributed to one small religious group.

The distinctions that Arendt describes did not go unnoticed even within the Jewish community. By the middle of the nineteenth century, some of the leading Jewish intellectuals found their liberal instincts fueled by their opposition, not only to reactionary regimes, but to the Jewish *parvenus* who supported them. "The 'new specimens of humanity,' if they were worth their salt, all became rebels, and, since the most reactionary governments of the period were financed by Jewish bankers, their rebellion was especially virulent against the official representatives of their own people. The anti-Jewish denunciations of Marx and Boërne cannot be properly understood except in the light of this conflict between rich Jews and Jewish intellectuals."[162]

In view of the fact that Hannah Arendt was a refugee from Hitler's Germany, it was hardly surprising that she would be concerned with antisemitism. Her training was in classical philosophy, and her knowledge of Jewish religious thought was limited. Still, as early as her biography of Rahel Varhagen, the Jewish problem had become a central focus of her writing.

The use of the word "pariah" was ultimately to prove both innovative and controversial. No less an authority than the distinguished philosopher and long-time friend Gershom Scholem was to object to its usage in connection with the release of his correspondence with Arendt about the Eichmann trial.[163] But Arendt persisted in her use of the term: "The Jew of the apologists was endowed with attributes that are indeed the privileges of pariahs, and which certain Jewish rebels living on the fringes of society did possess — humanity, kindness, freedom from prejudice, sensitiveness to injustice. The trouble was that these qualities had nothing to do with the prophets."[164] The reference to the prophets was both a criticism and a perplexing challenge.

The "scapegoat" theory of antisemitism has often seemed more seductive than the interstitial analysis. It has the advantage of simplicity, and it absolves Jews of any complicity in the circumstances that enveloped them. Arendt, of course, understood the shallowness of this explanation and dismissed it out of hand — it failed to account for the inevitable nature of the German attack against its Jews. This attack, she wrote, does not have anything to do "with the old 'ventilation' theory — that a scapegoat has to be found for national discontent — or with the explanatory theory that traces it to the 'notorious' Judaization of the press, theater, and professions. Both theories are attempts to avoid taking fascism and antisemitism seriously."[165]

In view of this background, it is not surprising that the trial and execution of Adolf Eichmann should have captured her interest. Eichmann was the Nazi bureaucrat responsible for the Nazi extermination of Europe's Jews. On May 24, 1960, Israeli intelligence agents found him hiding in Argentina and brought him back to Jerusalem to stand trial for crimes against humanity and against the Jewish people. Hannah Arendt, who had written many articles for the *New Yorker* magazine approached her editor William Shawn with a proposal that she be sent to Jerusalem to cover the trial. The subsequent trip to Jerusalem proved to be the most controversial act in Hannah's career.

Eichmann in Jerusalem: A Report on the Banality of Evil is more an analysis of the psychology of genocide than a report on the trial itself. Actually, Hannah attended only a few months of the trial and was not present during the testimony of Eichmann himself. Nevertheless, her report which appeared in the *New Yorker* prior to its publication as a book, initiated a debate which, even today, evokes intense partisanship. It is not difficult to discern the themes that antagonized some of her readers. Eichmann was not an anti-Semite but simply a bureaucrat doing his job as efficiently as possible. He met his death with great dignity. The trial was a failure in that it concentrated exclusively on the Jewish aspects of Nazi criminality rather than on the universal nature of their monstrosities. Too much of the case was based upon the suffering of the Jews and not enough on the guilt or innocence of Eichmann. Was it possible that Arendt's hostility toward Gideon Hausner, the chief Israeli prosecutor, colored her thinking? In a letter to her husband, Heinrich Blücher, she disparagingly described him as a "Galician Jew" who has a "ghetto mentality."[166]

As vulnerable as her general criticism of the trial made her appear, there were two themes in her report that hung like a mushroom cloud over the entire endeavor. The first was Arendt's insistence that Jews had been complicit in their own destruction. The second was discernable from the very onset — the introduction of the term "banal." It is hard to know which of these two ideas evoked the stronger reaction.

Hannah Arendt may well have taken it for granted that her readers would not be confused when she asserted that some Jewish leaders were complicit in the extermination process. "Some" is not "all" or even "many." Critics of her Eichmann report were not privy to these assumptions. They were enraged by statements such as this: "In Amsterdam as in Warsaw, in Berlin as in Budapest, Jewish officials could be trusted to compile the lists of persons and of their property, to secure money from the deportees to defray the expenses of their deportation, and extermination." Or statements such as this: "Wherever Jews lived there were recognized Jewish leaders, and this leadership, almost without exception, cooperated in one way or another, for one reason or another, with the Nazis."[167]

Had Arendt gone too far? Had she besmirched the entire European Jewish community? Old foes thought so — and old friends as well. The Anti-Defamation League attacked her as did Norman Podhoretz in *Commentary* magazine. More painful was the break with dear and cherished friends, Robert Weltsch, Gershom Scholem, and, most painful of all, Kurt Blumenfeld. Arendt had known Blumenfeld since the early thirties when she had done some clandestine research for the Zionists at his request. She had come to love him as a father figure, and even through their views of Zionism had diverged over the years, Arendt remained devoted to him. She could only reconcile herself to his break with her by attributing his anger to the distorted reports of hostile friends.[168]

"The banality of evil" is one of those phrases that earns eternal admiration for its author — and also eternal vilification. The subtitle of Arendt's report on the Eichmann trial introduced the famous phrase and it appeared again in the very last pages of the book. Eichmann in Jerusalem represented a dramatic shift in Hannah's thinking. No longer was the concentration camp a symbol of radical evil, as it had been in *The Origins of Totalitarianism*, but it had now been reduced to an institution entirely understandable in a society lacking the will to oppose the dominance of a corrupt bureaucracy. No pariahs here! The "banality of evil," she insisted, was appropriate to understanding Eichmann as part of the huge bureaucratic machinery required for the extermination. He was merely obeying orders, an ordinary man like millions of others, who were simply doing their jobs. Eichmann's was not an example of "radical" evil, she argued, but rather of derivative evil. His role as the administrator of the death camps was not evidence that some willful evil ruled his life. Rather, he was simply a bureaucrat, following the orders of his superiors. Beside, did not Eichmann go to the gallows with great dignity?"[169]

For the thousands of Jews who had managed to survive Hitler's death camps, Eichmann was not a symbol of the "banality of evil." He was the essence of evil. Arendt's use of the term "banality" enraged not only the survivors of the death camps, but also Jewish intellectuals who felt that this phrase trivialized the enormity of Nazi brutality. How did Hannah react to the verbal attacks that were directed toward her? Clearly she was hurt, hurt by her enemies, but most painfully by old friends. Still, she would not back down nor concede that her position was in any way hostile to the Jewish community.[170] In retrospect, the evil she described was perpetrated by one person, and her book might have seemed a bit less controversial had its author confined herself to Eichmann and allowed her book to bear a subtitle something like: the banality of an evil man. This was the criticism voiced even by J. Glenn Gray, a respected friend. Would you have used such a subtitle, he asked, "had Goebbels been in the dock?" Her old friend and mentor Karl Jaspers put the matter more succinctly. The notion is illuminating; the title is striking. "It means this man's evil is banal, not evil is banal."[171]

For Hannah Arendt, the idea that Jews existed as a unique people was a reality that did not need to invoke any qualifying adjective. The uniqueness of this people was, for her, an undisputed historical fact. And this uniqueness is an underlying assumption of the entire interstitial analysis of Jewish history. It is true that the dimensions of this unique fact remained incomprehensible to assimilating West European Jews. "Jews did not even want to be emancipated as a whole," she says at the beginning of her biography of Rahel Varnhagen, "All they wanted was to escape from Jewishness, as individuals if possible." And again she points out that German Jews during the age of Enlightenment "blamed whatever was alien in them upon their history; they saw whatever was peculiar to them as Jews merely as an obstacle to citizenship."[172] The assimilationists live under the mistaken notion that Jewish history is synchronous with the history of the nation in which they live. To defend themselves against the charge that they are unproductive, they "call Moses and the Prophets, Maimonides, Spinoza, Heine, and Marx as witnesses to the contrary." In reality, Jews belong to no society; it seemed that only the Zionists were astute enough to recognize this. And again, she tellingly observed: During the 150 years when Jews truly lived amidst, and not just in the neighborhood of, Western European peoples, they always had to pay with political misery for social glory and with social insult for political success."[173]

In her historical writings, Arendt frequently laments the failure of Jews to form alliances with the masses. Paradoxically, the heroes whom she singles out are invariably those who have remained marginal to Jewish history. Spinoza and Heine were quintessential pariahs, as surely was Rahel Varnhagen, and yet organization "within the Jewish community" was hardly among their preoccupations.

What of Zionism as a response to antisemitism? Arendt became increasingly critical of Zionism despite her early attraction to Jewish nationalism. Nevertheless, her analysis of the Jewish situation acknowledged some of the problems that Herzl had confronted. Like Herzl, she reasoned that for two thousand years Jews had been subject to domination by others. Jews are a people, "a unique people," she insisted, and one can hear echoes of Herzl in her assertion. But here she and Herzl parted ways.

As early as 1937, Arendt could be heard arguing that the Zionists had failed in a basic way. They had ignored the universal rights of Jews, and, in doing so, of mankind in general. They also had committed an unforgivable sin. They had turned to *parvenus* for their support. Zionism, she complained, is "dependent on the help of wealthy Jews — who, when it comes to material questions, don't do very well with ideals — it must appeal to their interests and keep the 'brothers in faith' in the East at a good distance from their fatherlands — which ultimately means appealing to the worst element, to those who are most clearly in conflict with the interests of Jews as a whole."[174]

What course of action should the Jewish community follow? Other than to organize politically, with all of its vague implications, Arendt never really offers a program — nor would she claim that she had an obligation to do so. Her analysis, she hoped, would perhaps help others to act. In the meantime, her writings revealed a polar opposition between assimilationists and Zionists. She was equally critical in her treatment of both. The crucial problem was that "both arise out of a shared Jewish fear of *admitting that there are and always have been divergent interests between Jews and segments of the people among whom they live.*"[175]

Hannah Arendt's own Jewish attitudes were often conflicted. And although certainly not a traditional Zionist toward the end of her life, she nevertheless continued to envision a Jewish state that was sensitive to Arab needs while maintaining its democratic character. Her insights were unique and often exciting. But as often as she touched a sensitive nerve, she was unable to prescribe a cure for the illness known as antisemitism. Like the professor walking his medical school students through a complicated surgery, describing every muscle and organ, Arendt's patient lies on the operating table writhing in a pain that yields to no palliative. Yet there are lessons to be learned here. Arendt's insights continue to trouble and to challenge.

Chapter 8

Tertius Gaudens
"The Third Party Rejoices"

The interstitial role assumes the presence of a triadic relationship. This requires the acknowledgment of two entities, external to and independent of the third. The entities necessary for the formation of a triad may take a variety of forms, yet their very presence defines and limits the third party. At various times the third party may be willful or compliant, helpful or destabilizing. In other words, the third party may play a role that can fluctuate between being creative or parasitic, useful or harmful. Thus the interstitial community may be viewed from a variety of perspectives. Its functions may seem to be positive at one time, negative the next. The truly interstitial community acts between the parts. Its role is seldom deemed to be insignificant.

The child stands in a triadic relationship to its mother and father. There are many potential consequences of this relationship. The child may unite them in common purpose, or it may become a divisive element in their relationship. Parents may compete for the affection of a child — as in the case of a divorce — but the child may also play parent against parent in order to achieve other goals.

It was the German sociologist Georg Simmel (1858–1918) who took the basic family and analyzed its triadic potential in terms of society at large. Simmel not only acknowledged the child as the basic component of the simplest triad, but also formalized our understanding of how basic family relationships develop into significant social patterns: "In the most significant of all dyads, monogamous marriage, the child or children, as the third element, often has the function of holding the whole together." For Simmel the child frequently stands alone in his or her ability to "close the circle by tying the parents to one another." The child becomes the mediating figure responsible for the stimulation of feelings which otherwise might not exist.[176] It need hardly be added that the mediating role of the child can also become a focal point for increased hostility either as a direct result of the child's own behavior or as its mediating magic evaporates in the face of family conflicts. This is what often happens when a child dies, a tragedy that prematurely removes the mediating presence. In such a situation, bitter conflicts between the grieving parents are not unusual.

In its existence outside the State of Israel, the modern Jewish community has become accustomed to playing the third-party role. Although the role remains constant, there are a variety of differing dualities that frame its potentialities. Conflicts between religious and secular forces, between Islam and Christianity, between rich and poor, powerful and powerless — these are but a few of the polarities that affect modern Jewish life. Tensions related to wealth, power, or religion are inevitably involved in the triadic formula. The subtleties of any particular manifestation of a triadic relationship are of critical importance. In nineteenth-century Russia and Poland, as Dubnow has suggested, the parameters of the triad were easy to perceive. The Jews were trapped between rich and poor, on the one hand, and between church and state, on the other. The elements of the interstitial relationship, however, are not always so immediately apparent. In the United States, Jews possessing wealth and the semblance of power could reasonably hope that the interstitial role is no more than a relic of the past. In reality, the American Jewish experience has only shown how chimerical is the belief that wealth is identical with power. In reality, wealth can only purchase power as long as real power is willing to put itself up for sale. And real power is a commodity an interstitial people can never expect to possess in perpetuity.

The third party suffers when it is deemed superfluous or when its mediating role is depicted as evil or malignant. And of course, under the direst of circumstances, the third party can be utterly eliminated, as the Jews of Germany realized only after their fate had been sealed. Seldom does the third party recognize the full extent of its vulnerability. "This can't happen here!" is heard first as an affirmation, then as a question, and finally as a prayer.

The role of the third party as a mediator is a theme that needs to be understood in any analysis of positive interstitiality. The middle role is not without its rewards as well as its pitfalls. Unable or unwilling to resolve their differences, conflicting entities often invite a third party to mediate their dispute, and the mediators, Simmel suggests, are usually those who are most intellectually disposed and thereby inclined toward impartiality. Their very impartiality, however, may result in antagonizing those who demand yes-or-no answers. Simmel archly suggests that despite all of its perils, the choice of an impartial mediator guarantees, at least, that the solution to any given problem will not remain in the hands of those who are least capable of reaching an intelligent solution. The very independence of the mediator or mediating group becomes a source of objectivity and harmony.[177]

The third party rejoices — *tertius gaudens* — when it enjoys a benefit from the role that it plays. Simmel describes the syndrome in this way: The third element "may also inversely make the interaction that takes place between the parties and between himself and them, a means for his own purposes." An attorney involved in a lawsuit or divorce case provides a simple example of this syndrome. The role of the attorney is that of a mediator and sometimes a conciliator. But an advantage to the third party, the attorney, is a foreseeable consequence of the dyadic conflict.

The concept of *tertius gaudens* becomes an essential aspect of the interstitial role especially when it is attached to moral judgments. It hardly needs pointing out that the middle position entails certain perils, particularly when it nestles between two larger and hostile powers that eye each other with increasing animosity. The powerlessness which this role entails is key to understanding the perils which Jews have encountered throughout their adventurous history. But not infrequently, being located between the parts produces advantages that accrue solely and uniquely to the weaker and intermediate party. What shall we make of these circumstances? The question of whether the *gaudens,* the rejoicing of the third party, is to be regarded as a blessing or a curse depends upon many factors, most notably the ultimate judgment of history, a judgment that is as fickle as it is unpredictable. But what is certain is that the in between position gains credence and respect when it perceived to be acting to promote altruistic as opposed to selfish motives.

The complexity of the middle role demands that its advantages as well as its liabilities be more thoroughly explored. Here too, words such as "positive" and "negative" may attach themselves to the role. In a social situation in which one party persecutes another, it is not difficult to acknowledge the gains and losses which may be involved. In a situation where one group persecutes another, the advantage in being the more powerful force may seem self-evident. But the advantage accruing to the victim of persecution is hard to conceive.

It is hard to think of antisemitism as anything but an unmitigated evil, harder yet, to imagine that anything so evil may offer its rewards even to its victims. Perhaps this was what Hannah Arendt was approaching when she described evil as "banal" and insisted upon examining the actions of those Jews who were complicit in the extermination of European Jews. As macabre as it may seem, "the rejoicing of the third party" may actually find reification in some forms of antisemitism. Thus, under certain circumstances, antisemitism may produce its own rewards, not only for the perpetrator, but for the victim as well. Such rewards at times may even stimulate a sense of group solidarity among the community of victims.

To understand the "usefulness" of antisemitism it is important to examine once again the concept as Georg Simmel developed it. The German sociologist suggests that there are two forms of the role, both of which result from what he rather opaquely calls "a rather ill-defined social passivity." In the first form of this passivity, two of the parties hold each other in check, allowing the third party to make gains that the others would have denied it. In the other form, "the *tertius* does not need to take the initiative." The mere fact that it is the third party enables it to reap rewards that would otherwise not be available. And the third party may benefit when one of the principles acts merely to spite the other, or to prevent the other from gaining an advantage.[178]

How does the role impact modern Jewish life? The structure of Jewish life in the United States offers a fruitful field of study. The Jewish community in the United States is splendidly organized — some say over-organized. There are Jewish federations that not only tend to the Jewish poor and collect funds for social services in Israel, but also provide governmentally approved help for immigrants of all faiths and for Jewish organizations that aid the poor. There are Jewish hospitals and nursing homes, employment services, and agencies that help handicapped children and provide funds for religious education and day schools. There are religious institutions that offer worship and education and represent a wide and variegated pattern of Jewish spiritual life. And there are a host of defense agencies, most of which address issues of general concern in addition to fulfilling their primary duty of protecting Jews from prejudice and discrimination.

Jewish defense agencies are regarded as essential guardians of Jewish rights, and they fulfill the ancillary role of protecting other minority groups as well. An analysis of the Jewish community must acknowledge the virtues of this complex organizational structure. Yet the reality is that antisemitism has not existed without some corollary benefits to the Jewish community. The creation of most Jewish hospitals throughout the United States occurred as a direct result of antisemitism. Jewish doctors facing discrimination when they sought positions in gentile hospitals organized their own hospitals to serve their communities and themselves as well. The creative energies that have been sparked in response to antisemitism would be difficult to deny. The creation of Brandeis University represented not only a Jewish contribution to the field of higher education, but a response, as well, to decades in which quotas and other forms of discrimination prevented Jews from attending many of the nation's most prestigious universities.

The exclusion of Jews from one field did not stifle the impulse to engage in new and creative activities. For decades Jewish participation in the leadership of major banks and insurance companies was minimal — a veritable glass ceiling limited their prospects of reaching the top. The realities of antisemitism touched almost every aspect of Jewish life. This did not prevent Jews from entering into the investment banking area, where they could pioneer in areas shunned by the more traditional banking firms. It was to relatively new areas of endeavor that Jews were drawn. Starting with the 1920s large numbers of Jews were drawn to Hollywood, where they were to take a leading role in the development of a whole new industry. Their backgrounds were Jewish. Their movies were about Catholic priests. It seems as though there existed a gentlemen's agreement among the Jewish leaders of the film industry to avoid dealing with the Holocaust. *Casablanca*, one of the greatest films of them all, was released in 1942, a year in which the ovens at Auschwitz were working full blast. Directed by Michael Curtiz, a Hungarian-born Jew who had changed his name from Kaminer, *Casablanca* deals with the victims of Nazi persecution. Not once does the film acknowledge that most of the victims were Jews. Nor does the word "Jew" ever appear.

Jewish reactions to antisemitism have sometimes resulted in distortions that create their own problems. Responses to the negative interstitial role have often overwhelmed the potentialities of the positive interstitial role. The dangers of antisemitism are often exaggerated. This exaggeration, coupled with continual evocations of the Holocaust, has assaulted traditional Jewish moral values and often made them appear to be out of focus. Antisemitism has been used to create Jewish solidarity. Antisemitism has been used to create fear in the Jewish community. Antisemitism has been used to raise money in the Jewish community. There are countless Jewish organizations that create an "anti-Semite of the month" in order to augment their programs and justify their budgets.

These are some of the more obvious examples of how the third-party role has affected contemporary Jewish life. More interesting, if more complex, is the way the role fulfills the second of Simmel's categories; that is, when the third party directly benefits from the actions of one of the two conflicting parties. The third party does not need to take the initiative in order to benefit, but simply needs to understand the realities of the conflict and to take action — action that can prove to be self-beneficial. The "contract sales" battle in Chicago provides a striking illustration of this pattern.

In Chicago in the 1960s, growing tensions between whites and African Americans over Chicago's segregated housing patterns had reached alarming proportions.[179] Large numbers of African-American families had moved north in the decades following World War II, and there was a need for affordable housing. Civil rights groups began to test the housing market to determine whether that market was truly open to all prospective buyers. As the testing proceeded, it soon became evident that black families were often politely, or not so politely, told that the house they wanted to purchase had just been sold. White testers, following immediately in their footsteps, were informed that the house was still available. Martin Luther King Jr. came to Chicago in the summer of 1966 to help respond to this pattern of housing discrimination. Protest marches, summit agreements, and, following Dr. King's assassination, riots constituted the heritage of this historic segregation.

In the meantime another classic civil rights struggle was unfolding. Lawndale, located in Chicago's near west side, was a Jewish neighborhood in transition. Following the Second World War, Jews began moving south and north and in the process abandoning what had once been a vital center of East European Jewish life. Part of the move resulted from upward mobility — a desire for a home in the suburbs. But part of it was stimulated by fear. Jews, as well as white gentiles, had been conditioned to believe that integration was unworkable, that it would result in increased crime and the degradation of property values. Into this scene stepped a small group of realtors who capitalized on the fears of the Jewish community as well as upon the hopes of African-American homeseekers. As Dubnow noted in his treatment of Polish and Russian Jews, even a small number of Jews occupying negative interstitial roles can appear to be typical of a much larger segment of the population.

"Besides 'nigger lover,' men and women who sold to blacks were called something else — Jew. Many white gentiles assumed that anyone who sold to an African-American must be a Jew. This assumption was not based on the existence of large numbers of Jewish speculators. As one non-Jewish speculator admitted: 'Though we hear the Jews are coming in and buying,' only a normal percentage are Jews." Yet, as Beryl Satter is quick to acknowledge, there was money to be made in the contract sales business. The profit was directly related to a faultline in Chicago's real estate market, a faultline that separated black home buyers from the institutions that should have served them — the banks, insurance companies, and even the realty companies themselves. As one speculator put it: "They wouldn't sell it direct. They work with every broker so as not to sell it direct, and then they blame it on the Jews."[180]

In Lawndale twelve Jewish real estate brokers determined to profit from the transition that they helped to encourage. They engaged in panic peddling. Subtle signs and not so subtle hints proclaimed: "The blacks are coming!" That was the message covertly, and sometimes overtly, carried to the Jewish homeowners of Lawndale. And the word "panic" attached to "peddling" accurately described the mood as well as the reality of what ensued.

The Lawndale realtors were truly interstitial, and their identification as Jews was not a matter that could be questioned. They themselves vociferously and publicly affirmed that their actions were entirely legal, and that any antipathy toward them was prompted by anti-Jewish prejudice. In Lawndale more was involved than mere tension between African Americans and Jews. The economic endurance of the real estate brokers was made possible by the activity or inactivity of much more powerful institutions in the city — the real estate companies and the banks. The role of these institutions, camouflaged for so many years, emerged as a key to understanding the entire battle.

Jewish homeowners fled Lawndale, often selling at fire sale prices. As a result of their panic peddling, the Lawndale realtors were quickly able to realize huge gains, sometimes by doubling the home's price and selling it to an African-American purchaser. Interest rates that had previously been low, due to the long terms of the old mortgages, suddenly soared. Loans held by the original Jewish owners, at interest rates of 4-5 percent, now ballooned to as high as 14-15 percent. Thus both price and interest rates could be inflated for purchasers whose dream of home ownership often turned into a nightmare.

And most importantly, the financial instrument used in transacting these loans was a contract, and not a mortgage. The contract offered protection to the seller but not to the buyer. The difference was of tremendous significance to the often underfunded African-American buyer. Under the terms of a mortgage, the purchaser owned the home unless he or she defaulted. Even then, the home could not be taken back by the lender unless the default was ignored, and the process itself took many months. A home purchased on contract, however, enjoyed no such protection. The contract seller rather than the purchaser retained title until the final payment had been processed. In addition if the seller missed a single payment, the home could be deemed to be in default and reclaimed by the seller. In Lawndale in the 1960s, the sellers were all Jewish. How did this happen?

Insurance companies play a vital role in shaping the housing patterns of a community. Their willingness to insure the purchase of a home is essential to the stability of a neighborhood. Their refusal to grant insurance on newly purchased homes is a guarantee that the neighborhood is in trouble, at least in the eyes of major financial institutions. Who would purchase a home that cannot be insured? This refusal, known in the insurance field as "red-lining," has been responsible for the decline of many inner city areas.

As important as was the role of insurance companies, even more critical was that of banks and lending institutions. Homes are invariably purchased on credit. If banks determine that prospective customers are not creditworthy, then they decline to make loan money available. Segregation is accelerated when both banks and insurance companies deny the use of their assets based upon race. This is what happened in Lawndale. But there was a twist.

Banks and insurance companies realized that there was a profit to be made in Lawndale. The question was how to realize it while avoiding the concomitant risks. The small group of twelve Jewish contract sellers of Lawndale provided the answer. They were creditworthy. Their track record as reliable lenders was perfect. And so the banks and insurance companies made funds and insurance available to the Jewish sellers who, in turn oversaw the speedy transition of a historic Chicago neighborhood. And then there were defaults. And after the defaults came repossessions. The "contract sales battle" had begun.

Many of Chicago's more liberal Jews were upset as they became aware of the avarice involved in the contract sales process. What was, and remains troubling, however, was the passivity of the "Jewish establishment" in the face of these malpractices. No voice of condemnation was to be heard. Instead, the Jewish federation's annual support of the one of its member Jewish organizations that supported the African-American buyers was suspended. The Jewish Council on Urban Affairs was engaging in activities that were deemed "controversial." That was the word used and the rationale for the suspension of federation support.

The concept of an "idealized generalized other" is relevant here and is worth examining in the face of many social conflicts. The idealized generalized other rests on the assumption that though an individual may not adhere to the highest principles established by a primary affiliation, the group itself possesses qualities that are independently valid. When asked to define the "ideal Jew" most Jews will respond that it is one who keeps kosher, or observes the dietary laws, or attends *shul* regularly. The answer is related to ritual, offered frequently by one whose own ritual practices are remote from the ones he has just idealized. The ideal Jew, in other words, is perceived of as a creature of ritual, not of justice. Religions proclaim themselves as the exemplars of love. Their love finds its outlet in the Agent Orange devastation in Viet Nam or the civilian casualties in Baghdad. In the middle of a baseball game hats are taken off, the audience is asked to rise, "God Bless America" is sung, and the image of ideal American soldiers is evoked. The image is far from the reality of the fifty thousand people who have come to watch the Yankees bash the Red Sox. One could call this hypocrisy were it not for the fact that the idealized generalized other transcends any moral boundary and manifests itself in the delusions that constitute human nature.

The Jewish Federation of Chicago deluded itself by believing that it was capable of uniting all Jews and that dissent was the enemy of the federation's major functions — the solicitation, collection and distribution of charitable funds. The moral question persists: why did a procedure so morally justifiable as the fight against exploitive housing practices deserve to be deemed "controversial?" Not because of any thoughtful analysis of the consequences of the contract sales. Other factors were involved, economic and social ones. There were relatives — parents, aunts and uncles, many of whom possibly were unaware of the moral issues involved, but who were receiving some of the financial rewards stemming from the sales. There were attorneys and accountants and friends of the sellers. There was money involved — and money wears the mask of power. The Chicago-based Jewish Council on Urban Affairs, allied with some elements of the Catholic parish in Lawndale, supported the African-American purchasers and opposed the sellers. Some contributors to the federation had threatened to terminate their overall support — because one of its small beneficiaries was supporting powerless African-American homeowners as they struggled to hold on to their homes. The contract sales battle entered the court system. It stayed there for years.

The sellers occupied an interstitial role between the Jews of Lawndale and African-American families who wished to live there. Their interstitiality becomes more significant when viewed within the context of the role. The Jewish sellers in Lawndale were never truly independent. They were the tools of much larger economic forces operating over a vastly wider terrain. The banks and insurance companies risked little. The sellers risked a great deal — not the least of which was the moral integrity of the Jewish community.

Have all of the implications of the role been understood? How shall the Jewish community react when the morality of the role is pictured not as totally evil but rather as ambiguous? Or how shall it react when the benefits of the role are recognized as no longer exclusively Jewish? The often heard refrain that "everyone does it" can become a shield for the most egregious of offenses whether committed by Jews or non Jews. The contract sellers of Lawndale maintained that they were operating within the law, and it is clear that their actions could simultaneously be condemned as "immoral" and defended as "legal." In such cases does the Jewish community have any compelling reason to act, or does the cover of legality take precedence over any other ethical impulse? In other words, do Jews have a right to judge other Jews whose actions are shadowy, though not necessarily illegal? And when does opposition to acts that are immoral but not illegal begin to resemble an uncomfortable form of Jewish antisemitism?

In Boston during the 1970s, the oppressive actions of a group of Jewish slum landlords proved to be a source of embarrassment to the religious community. The Boston rabbis decided to appoint a rabbinic court, a Beth Din, to examine each complaint and to confront those slum landlords whose behavior was deemed to be most offensive. The Beth Din itself represented a significant step in the direction of combining ancient Jewish tradition with modern ethical problems. The court, which traditionally dealt with matters of personal status, such as divorce and conversion, now became a significant expression of Jewish moral concern. The quasi-legal status of the rabbinic court testified to the seriousness not only of its judgments, but of its growing commitment to social justice. With their Beth Din the Boston rabbis were proclaiming that the well-being of the Jewish community requires more than observance of the letter of the law. An understanding of the interstitial role implies recognition of something that Jews often wish to ignore — like it or not, Jewish history places a special burden upon the Jewish people. The burden is a moral one. It is a unique feature of Jewish diaspora life. But this "burden" is not entirely an onerous one. The third party role may offer a whole new and exciting dimension to the challenges confronting the "chosen people."

It was Hannah Arendt who reserved special contempt for those members of the Jewish community deemed to be *parvenus*. The *nouveau riche*, the *parvenu*, the men and women whose greed overcomes their sense of social responsibility — these are Jews who ultimately affect the welfare of the entire community. To identify them by name would add little to the analysis of the interstitial role. But to ignore the harm they cause both to the Jewish community in particular and society in general would be to sanction their deeds through silence. Surely there are hedge fund managers and merger specialists, as well as casino owners, who are not Jewish, but a significant number of them are — and this remains a matter of concern.

How easy it is to connect a particular fraudulent personality with the fate of an entire community! The peculations of Bernard Madoff offer classic if bizarre testimony. Convicted of stealing billions of dollars from his clients, Madoff achieved an odious immortality by perpetrating what has been described as the biggest Ponzi scheme of all time. Inflation blesses the fraudulent — at least until they are exposed. Ponzi cheated his investors of millions; billions were involved in the Madoff case. Mr. Madoff's Jewish background quickly became a prominent part of the story. Did the fact that many of his victims were also Jewish mitigate the prominent association of Jews with financial exploitation? Jewish apologists might find consolation in this knowledge. But in the long run, the Madoff scandal merely underscored the lonely isolation characteristic of Jewish diaspora life. The discomfort of the Jewish community over the daily revelations was palpable. Even in Israel, where many charitable foundations were seriously damaged, it was not unusual to hear whispered concerns about a worldwide anti-Jewish backlash. And in the United States similar fears were muted but ubiquitous.

Jewish anxiety about the Madoff affair was not baseless. Conspiracy theories involving the connection between Jews and exploitive financial practices echoed old themes questioning Jewish loyalty. After pointing out that Madoff had once been the treasurer of Yeshiva University, one vehement blogger asked: "Does the 'Jewish tradition taught at Yeshiva U. support giant Ponzi schemes like the one run by their chairman? . . . This is exactly what the Talmud teaches, make no mistake about it…This is why so many of the financial criminals involved in the current Zionist-produced 'credit crisis' are Jewish Zionists who have been indoctrinated in such 'Jewish traditions.' The Zionist criminals involved in 9-11 and the cover-up of the truth are all tied to the Jewish Theological Seminary in New York, which is a similar Talmudic yeshiva and Zionist indoctrination center."[181] It was in Palm Beach where Madoff owned one of his many businesses, that the impact of the scandal could be observed most clearly. There are a lot of gentiles here, remarked a city historian, "who thought the Jews got what was coming to them. The gentiles think this is their place. As far as they're concerned, the Jews have Boca Raton and Miami. What are they doing in Palm Beach.?"[182]

The Madoff case vividly illustrates the conflicting impulses inherent in the interstitial analysis. The pattern is a familiar one. A strange social tango takes place. Step one, the assumption that, regardless of their religion, accused criminals will be punished for their crimes. Step two, the dawning suspicion that Jewish lawbreakers seem to be identified by their religion more frequently than lawbreakers who belong to other faiths. Step three, Jewish community leaders protest widespread publicity associating the criminal with his religion. But these feeble protests serve only to reinforce the stereotypes they originally intended to counteract.

Where is the evidence for this pattern? Responding to reports about Madoff in the *New York Times*, the leader of a major Jewish organization expresses dismay, not at horrendous nature of the alleged fraud, but at the publicity created by it. The complaint is that the *Times* insists on repeatedly reminding its readers that Mr. Madoff is Jewish, while it ignores the religion of others accused of criminal behavior. One writer protests that in Madoff's case the Jewish identification was made "not just once or twice, but at least three times … To refer to the 'Jewish T-bill', 'the clubby Jewish world' and the 'world of Jewish New York' within four paragraphs near the top of the article on Mr. Madoff was over the top."[183] The suspicion that Jewish organizations and their leaders might be more concerned with the public relations fallout from the Madoff scandal than with the moral implications of the crime itself remains a troublesome one.

The more serious problem is the association, once more, of Jews with money. Of course, Madoff's behavior was the antithesis of core Jewish ethics, but in a sense, his goals, if certainly not his techniques, were compatible with an America in which growing economic gaps between the very wealthy and the very poor are met with increased indifference. The goals of a few spectacularly successful Jews who seek to influence the electoral process also invite moral scrutiny. When an incredibly wealthy casino owner devotes an incredibly large sum of money to conservative political candidates, the myth of Jewish wealth and power is given fresh credibility. And when the donor is perceived to have associated his gift with the candidate's support for Israel, old suspicions of Jewish double loyalty become hard to suppress.

The growing disparity between the very wealthy and the middle class, not to mention the very poor, has got to be a serious social concern. The emergence of a class of elites occupied solely with the manipulation of money raises serious questions about the viability of a post-industrial economy. There is something terribly wrong with the prominent persistence of a group of people solely occupied with "slicing and dicing and repackaging money" without using that money to produce something of benefit to society. The funds they play with do not build anything. They do not grow anything. These funds feed upon the mortgaged futures of the poor, and they reward no one but the sluggards who feast on them. The huge bonuses which hedge fund managers and mortgage bankers bestow upon themselves represent not only a social injustice, but they harbor the seeds of a very worrisome harvest.

These considerations might well point to an important challenge to all religious groups and not only to Jews. Income distortions are surely not the fault of any one people. But left unaddressed, huge economic and social imbalances become a threat to all. And when these conditions congeal in social outrage, as they inevitably do, no community is more vulnerable than the interstitial people, so uniquely gifted with education and culture, and so uniquely vulnerable because this very uniqueness offers so little protection.

These negative depictions invite a more nuanced appraisal. No rehearsal of community strengths or shortcomings can fail to acknowledge the tremendous commitment of individual Jews as well as Jewish organizations to the cause of those who suffer from society's injustices. Unfortunately social judgments are not determined by the fair scales of justice, but by the skewed weight of public prejudice. And negative stereotypes of Jewish life need to be confronted by the much more realistic picture of Jewish concern for its own community and care for the needy everywhere. If the third party is to rejoice, let it rejoice not in its wealth or its power, but in its virtue.

The contract sales battle in Lawndale brought out both the negative and the positive sides of the interstitial role. It revealed how seductive the desire for financial gain can become, and it also revealed the potentialities for concerted action when the true interests of the Jewish community are correctly assessed. Of course the contract sales battle has a long tail. The painful recession that began in 2008 has its genesis in some of the same practices which made the struggle in Lawndale so significant. As contract sales faded from public consciousness they were replaced by another form of exploitation that took advantage of a new generation of would be home buyers. Sub-prime mortgages entered the real estate scene with the same seductive explanations that justified the actions of Lawndale's contract sellers. Both were based upon the legitimate desire to own a home. Both were corrupted by the venality of those whose greed was insatiable. "Come all ye buyers. Ordinarily you would not be able to afford this home. But I, Mephisto, am here to help you. Come and look at this contract! Come and look at this sub-prime mortgage! Come and enter the gates of your own paradise!"

The contract sales battle was a tremor that affected a small area of a great city. But what a great earthquake it activated.

Chapter 9

Coming of Age

Nothing illustrates the complexity of the interstitial dilemma more vividly than does the history of American immigration. Jews came to America to search for freedom. There was opportunity in America, a chance to earn a decent living, to live with dignity. For the most part they were poor, poor but proud.

By the 1830s large numbers of German Jews, spurred by economic and social unrest in their native country, began to arrive in the United States. Many of them immediately moved to cities such as New York, Philadelphia and Boston. Others turned westward toward Cleveland, Chicago, or Cincinnati and some of them moved southward to hundreds of smaller towns and hamlets. They came not only to escape an oppressive past, but to encounter an uncertain yet promising future. And when they arrived they turned to the very occupation that had sustained them in the old world. They began to sell things. They became peddlers, some operating out of a wagon, many traveling on foot, selling their fabrics and kitchen goods from farm to farm, from town to town.

The point is not to be overlooked. The new German immigrants did not come to settle the land, to build railroads or to till their fifty acres; they came to do what so many of them had done in the old country — to act as middlemen, to buy merchandise, usually on credit, and then to sell it to those whose mobility was limited to their farm chores or to their small - town occupations. They started their careers as peddlers — these immigrants from Germany and Poland — carrying a pack or a trunk, often cherishing the hope that someday they might own a store, perhaps even a department store. In 1846, Isaac M. Wise, then newly arrived in Albany, New York, described a typical encounter with one of these recent immigrants:

"One afternoon I met on the street a man with a large, old straw hat drawn far over his face. He was clad in a perspired linen coat, and carried two large tin boxes on his shoulders. He had a large clay pipe in his mouth, a pair of golden spectacles on his nose, and dragged himself along with painful effort. I looked at him closely, and recognized my friend Stein. Upon noticing my astonishment, he said smilingly: 'Most of the German and Polish Jews in America look like this, and the rest of them did till a very short time ago.' As he was going homeward I accompanied him to his house. A quarter of an hour later he emerged completely metamorphosed. He looked genteel again. He informed his wife laughingly that I had met him in his peddler's costume. He now described to me graphically the misery and drudgery of the peddler's life."[184]

The life of the peddler was but the bottom rung of the ladder. There were opportunities to be found in the growing cities along the Mississippi River and throughout the country. Yet despite the lure of a growing nation, it was New York that remained a magnet for thousands of the new immigrants. And it was New York with its growing financial center that proved an irresistible magnet to a small but tremendously successful segment of the German immigrants.

In Europe the welcome which Jews received as well as the animosity which their presence often engendered were sad indications of Jewish powerlessness. To a lesser, but nevertheless significant degree, immigration laws in America have historically reflected the tenuousness of the Jewish position. These laws were often fashioned with Jews in mind. But now the picture is complicated by vast immigrations of non-Jews. What was traditionally true of the relationships between Irish or Italian immigrants and recent Jewish arrivals now reappears with new actors and a new scenario.

Today large numbers of Hispanic and Arabic-speaking immigrants exert an increasingly significant influence upon American social and political life. The impact of these groups upon the future of the American Jewish community remains to be seen. To say that there are potential tensions is not to ignore the many areas of cooperation that surely exist. It is to assert that the fragility of the interstitial role becomes apparent whenever significant new elements are grafted upon the existing order.

American Jewish immigration to America was characterized by undulating waves of acceptance and rejection. It began with the historic confrontation in 1654, with Peter Stuyvesant, who stubbornly refused to let a boatload of refugees find refuge in Manhattan. Throughout its history, American immigrants seem to have been little troubled by the fact that every European immigrant was in fact an intruder and that the resentment of intrusion came to be an attitude not only of Native Americans but of succeeding generations as they braced themselves against the intrusion of new immigrants.

A pattern of acceptance-rejection came to characterize American attitudes toward immigrants, and it became a familiar pattern for Jews too. What is noteworthy is the duality of helplessness on the one hand, and ambivalence on the other, as they tried to decide whether it would be a good idea to bring more Jews into the melting pot that America soon became. But Jews melted much more slowly than other immigrant groups. They assimilated but they did not melt. Of course, there were many Jews who abandoned their religion entirely, but for those who remained, a vast array of organizational and social networks sprang up to preserve their identity.

The history of American immigration patterns is in itself an example of the interstitial pattern at work. As the United States expanded westward, few restrictions were placed on immigration. An open and seemingly endless frontier promised limitless opportunity and growth. But the sense of openness began to change with unanticipated speed. The year was 1912. The last two of the forty-eight contiguous states, Arizona and New Mexico, were admitted to the Union. Frederick Jackson Turner's Frontier Thesis, was regarded as the classic tribute to an America that was ever expanding and ever growing. Were there limits to expansion? The income tax amendment to the Constitution, also adopted in 1911, hinted that the admission of the final two of the contingent forty-eight states might have a dark side. The expansion of America had its limits. No longer did the move west seem inevitable. No longer could Americans feel guiltless as they contemplated the carcasses of buffalo randomly shot from railroad caboose cars. Could it be that American financial resources were beginning to come under pressure?

Just as Congress was debating the income tax amendment, a small group of elite Brahmans, headed by the Cabots and the Lodges, met in Boston to launch a new organization blatantly called the Immigration Restriction League. The restrictive immigration laws of the 1920s were the ultimate results of this early endeavor. That America awoke to the need for immigration restrictions just as its ability to expand physically and economically became problematic is no coincidence. Nor is it a coincidence that large numbers of Jewish immigrants had landed at Ellis Island in the decades immediately before the first anti-immigrant legislation had been proposed.

Jewish immigrants, of course, had turned to America since the first group of former Marranos fleeing from Recife, Brazil, had petitioned Governor Peter Stuyvesant in 1654 to allow them to settle in New

Amsterdam. The first Jews were primarily of Sephardic background, but they were soon followed by significant numbers of German Jews who came to the United States following the failed revolutions in Europe in 1848. But it was in the period between 1890 and 1910 that the major Jewish immigrations occurred. The pogroms in Eastern Europe unleashed a flood of Jewish immigration to the United States. In 1892, Ellis Island was established as the major point of entry for impoverished immigrants. A peculiar companion to the Statue of Liberty, Ellis Island welcomed millions of immigrant — the huddled masses yearning to be free — but suddenly not if they came from the wrong place or from the wrong country, and certainly not if they were ill.

The new immigration laws had a profound impact on this flow of immigrants. Other minorities, particularly those from "the Orient," were affected by the final formulation of the immigration laws adopted in the 1920s, but perhaps more than any other single group, Jews were conscious of the way they had become both target and victim. The new laws established immigration quotas based mathematically upon each ethnic group's share of the total population of the United States. The problem was that the new laws did not set quotas based upon the population census of 1920, but reverted to the figures of an earlier decade when America was more monolithic. The Emergency Quota Act of 1921 set the number of immigrants at 3 percent of the number of persons from that country living in the United States in 1910. The Immigration Act of 1924 was even more draconian in its exclusionary philosophy. It reduced the number of new immigrants to 2 percent, and instead of using the more recent 1910 census; it based its quotas on the population figures of 1890.

The new legislation had the predictable effect of curtailing the flow into the United States of those who could now be regarded as "less desirable immigrants." The "less desirable immigrants" were those coming from Asia, southern Europe, as well as Russia and Poland. British immigration was not affected. French immigration was not affected. Jewish immigration was profoundly affected.

The immigration laws of the 1920s had an immediate and also long-range impact upon the Jewish community. The flow of Jewish immigrants dropped dramatically. Stranded in Europe were millions of Jews already suffering from drastic economic changes that made their interstitial roles ever more problematic. In the post-World War I era, the commercial and artisanal functions that once had characterized Jewish activity in Eastern Europe were rapidly proving to be not only insignificant but also inimical to the new industrial society that demanded an entirely different kind of work force. Masses of Jews, long accustomed to surviving in the face of hardship, now found themselves totally impoverished. Unable to survive where they were, and now unable to leave, they could not have imagined the "solution" that lay in wait for them — the final solution.

To attribute the tightening of immigration primarily to antisemitism would be to minimize the complexity of the problems the laws sought to address. A growing aversion to Asians, particularly on the West Coast, was one key element, and this aversion was abetted by the labor movement's fear of the cheap labor that was coming from China. Thus, Samuel Gompers, founder of the American Federation of Labor and a Jewish immigrant himself, could favor the legislation, despite the fact that most Jews felt that they were its primary victims. In addition, the new laws were enacted at the same time the country was experiencing one of its periodic waves of xenophobia. In this case the national phobia was related to the recent Russian revolution and prompted by paranoia about anarchism.

The infamous Sacco and Vanzetti case remains a frightening reminder of this paranoia. Sacco and Vanzetti, two Italian immigrants who were active in anarchist circles, were convicted of complicity in an armed robbery that resulted in the death of two payroll clerks. The crime occurred in 1920, in time to make it a *prima facie* argument for the new immigration laws. The hysteria over anarchy, which putatively prompted this crime, led to the ordeal that these two immigrants had to experience. Guilty of being anarchists in their politics, but innocent of murder, Sacco and Vanzetti were nevertheless executed in 1927.

The consequences of the immigration laws were both immediate and far-reaching. No people experienced its consequences more consciously than did Jews, particularly in view of the antisemitism that was growing in Europe. In 1939, frightened refugees were forced to return to Germany aboard the ocean liner *St. Louis*. Their expectations of finding refuge in Havana had been frustrated, despite the fact that they had been promised that visas would be waiting for them. These 936 refugees were then denied permission to come ashore at Miami. The State Department remained deaf to the frantic pleas of Jewish leaders and of the refugees themselves. The immigration laws would not be stretched, even enough to grant them a temporary haven in the United States. As the *St. Louis* steamed back toward Hamburg, its passengers could hardly envision the tragic fate that awaited them.

In retrospect, it is easy to condemn restrictive immigration legislation that made the task of saving European Jews so difficult. But it is painful to ask whether Jew themselves may have lent support to such legislation. To say that Jews were complicit in the anti-immigration sentiments that resulted in the 1924 act would be to pass too harsh a judgment on the masses of Jews who had found a welcome home on American shores. Yet segments of Jewish communal leadership could be accused of accommodating if not abetting these sentiments. The reliably liberal Union of American Hebrew Congregation issued an ambivalent statement extending a "hearty welcome" to the rush of new immigrants, but at the same time it could not hide its ambivalence. "We are assured by the Paris Committee (i.e. the Alliance Israelite Universelle) that the Hebrews selected for emigration to America will be young men having a trade or profession and able to work." (Evidently women were of little concern to the policy makers who may have assumed that there would always be work for women in the garment industry). In 1886, the Board of Managers of Chicago's Jewish social service agency, the Associated Charities, adopted a resolution stating that "we condemn the transportation of paupers into this country and Canada by European societies . . . All such as are unable to maintain themselves should be forthwith returned whence they came."[185] A typical, if early, example of the ambivalence toward the new immigrants can be detected in the attitude of Jacob Schiff, already one of the acknowledged elites of New York's Jewish community. In 1892, much to his later chagrin, Schiff sent a message to Paris urging officials of the Alliance Israelite Universelle to send new immigrants directly to San Francisco rather than New York. "While there, too, the Russians are not wanted, if they come they will be taken care of."[186]

In fairness to Schiff, it needs to be pointed out that in the early decades of the twentieth century he became an ardent defender of immigration and of immigrant rights. The debate about immigrants, however, was never a simple matter. Not only were some Jews embarrassed by the newcomers from Eastern Europe, but they also let their concerns about antisemitism mute their protests against the growing anti-immigrant sentiments. As historian Naomi Cohen points out: "Sensitive to the currents of Jew-hatred particularly after 1880," many Jewish leaders "were constrained by a combination of reasons. For one thing, Jewish history had taught them the futility of combating the irrationality of Judeophobia. More important, as those who had long preached the necessity of acculturation, they believed that Jewish security in the United States depended on the minority's accommodation to American law and traditions."[187]

Nowhere, it seems, is this accommodation sought more ardently than in the area of sports. Minority groups inevitably become fixated upon their heroes — or their villains. The former are idolized as paragons of virtue; the latter a source of embarrassment. Jackie Robinson, for example, bore the whole African-American community on his shoulders as he became the first African-American to play major league baseball. In a similar vein, Hank Greenberg became a Jewish symbol of pride when he decided not to play baseball on Yom Kippur. Whether Greenberg played on Sabbath or other holidays apparently was a matter of indifference to most Jews, but the symbolism of Yom Kippur was overwhelming. The iconic stature of Greenberg is noteworthy. By his one single act of abstinence, two stereotypes that touched Jewish sensitivities were confronted — the first, that Jews were atheists; and the second, that Jews were not athletic. Thus, Greenberg's one symbolic decision to sit out a single baseball game could be elevated to mythic status in the Jewish community even as it was treated with indifference by the non-Jewish one.

The Jew who was deemed "significant" was significant, not as an "individual," but as a "representative" of an entire people. As positive as this association could occasionally be, its negative uses were much more apparent — and useful. In desperately poor areas of the inner city, if there were exploitive storeowners, they were "Jewish storeowners." In the ghetto, if there were slum landlords — they were "Jewish slum landlords." The fact that the owner was Lebanese or Pakistani was irrelevant. And, as in Russia and Poland, a "few Jews" could easily be made to appear as characteristic of all Jews. And if, more recently, the Jewish venture capitalists and hedge fund managers have replaced the slum landlord, there is still danger when members of a Jewish minority make money too easily and too fast, and at the expense of "ordinary people."

In small-town America the interstitial pattern was often played out against the background of racial tension. Martin Luther King, Jr., marching in Selma, Alabama, could depend upon the support of many rabbis who came to join him from all over the country, but not on the support of the Jews of Selma. The Jews of Selma were by and large sympathetic to the cause of integration, but even their best instincts were overpowered by fears that they would be regarded as traitors by the white power structure. They were indifferent to the white clergy that accompanied Dr. King. They were troubled by the presence of black marchers. But they were terrified by the presence of rabbis "meddling in affairs that did not concern them."

Chapter 10

The American Scene

Is the interstitial analysis still applicable to the Jewish community of the United States? The question must be asked, particularly in view of the relative sense of security that pervades American Jewish life in the twenty-first century. Overt expressions of antisemitism may seem rare, and yet an uncomfortable awareness of the uniqueness of the Jewish position in American life persists. Jewish history offers slight comfort. There have been "golden ages" aplenty in the saga of the "chosen people," but the gold has too often turned to dross.

One need not be an alarmist to remain concerned. The religious traditions of the United States, of course, differ radically from those of Europe. The great diversity of America's religious institutions gives some assurance that no one tradition will be able to impose its rules upon the others. In addition, the philosophy of a country whose constitution guarantees freedom of religion, and whose history is marked by the separation of church and state, offers much comfort. Nevertheless religious demagogues have resorted to antisemitism in the past, and growing tensions between the various religions in the United States make the interstitial people an inviting target — as well as, perhaps, a potential ally.

What pattern can be discerned in Jewish communal leadership in the United States? The leadership of this community, despite the presence of influential religious leaders, has become primarily secular. Its agenda is so totally determined by the political patterns of the United States that this fact seldom merits attention. But almost every issue that occupies Jewish leadership — whether it is religious or secular, whether it involves the delivery of a sermon at religious services or debates about immigration reform — is subtly fashioned by forces exerting pressure from the outside. In a sense, of course, this is a truism, but the reality of outside pressures upon the Jewish agenda invites a deeper analysis than has generally been offered.

The transformation of leadership from religious to secular dominance is in itself a revealing part of the story. In the nineteenth century, American Jews were led by religious leaders. These religious leaders invariably acted as mediators between their immigrant congregations and the larger Christian society that often regarded them with curious eyes. The interstitial role of the early American rabbi found its expression in the life experience of the individual rabbi as well as in his social function. The rabbi was an enlightened, generally well-educated spiritual leader who could be regarded by the gentile community as the idealized Jew. But the rabbi also had an important social function, a function that, as we shall see, later secular Jewish leaders also took for granted. This responsibility was to educate Jews, to bring them out of the ghetto, to turn them into Americans.

In his *Reminiscences*, Isaac M. Wise, the "father" of American Reform Judaism, tells of his early years in America and of his closeness to enlightened Christian ministers. Clearly he felt closer to some of these liberal clergymen than to many of the members of his own congregation. So intense was the bitterness between rabbi and lay leader, for example, that on one Rosh Hashanah, the president of Bethel congregation physically attacked Wise with clenched fist, hitting him so hard that his "cap" fell to the ground. Isaac Mayer Wise was the intellectual representative of his Jewish community in Albany, and yet he found, to his regret, that it was easier for him to function outside of his congregation than within it.

In the earliest days of the American Jewish experience, even the mere accoutrements of religious leadership were enough to guarantee authority. The very first Jewish religious leaders in the United States were not rabbis at all, but *chazzanim*, men trained in the art of conducting the Orthodox ritual. Even the well-regarded "patriot Jewish Minister of the American Revolution," Gershom Mendes Seixas, was not a rabbi, and not even a trained chazzan. His authority stemmed from the position he had volunteered to fill.[188] And Isaac Leeser of Philadelphia, a national leader of Orthodoxy and a fierce opponent of Isaac Mayer Wise, was also a chazzan, not a rabbi.

It is instructive to examine the heated debate between these two early leaders of American Judaism, Wise and Leeser. Even as they traded insults with one another, both men shared a common anxiety — American Judaism needed to be transformed in dramatic ways. In a very real sense, both wanted to deliver Judaism from the negative interstitial roles that had dominated so much of European Jewish life. Although both began with ritual changes, neither was destined to be satisfied with mere cosmetic transformations.

As early as 1830, Leeser started to deliver sermons to his Philadelphia congregation in English, always with the "permission of the congregation." His repeated theme was based upon his conviction that American Jewish life was in need of a total regeneration. The term "regeneration," borrowed from Protestant Evangelicals, was given a particularly Jewish relevance by

Leeser and his congregants. The words could be harsh: "Jews are contaminated by the iniquity of unbelief, by the boldness of open sin." They are possessed," said Leeser, "by an accursed love of money, of pleasure, and of power."[189] Leeser's call for a regeneration of Judaism led him to do more than hector his congregation. He went on to translate the Bible into English, to champion Jewish day schools, and to help create the Jewish Publication Society.

Like his antagonist, Wise, too, initiated his American rabbinic career by advocating ritual reform. He began by introducing the organ and mixed seating to his Albany congregation, but even these simple reforms brought him into conflict with the traditional elements of his congregation. Wise soon yearned for a community where he would feel as comfortable "inside" as out. And so he moved from Albany to Cincinnati. "I shall go to Cincinnati," he wrote in his *Reminiscence*, "start a new weekly journal, give Judaism a new and powerful impetus, and avenge myself for the good of humanity on the narrow religious bigots."[190] The "narrow religious bigots" in this case, were not Christians, but his fellow Jews. Following the move to Cincinnati, and in rapid succession, Wise created a "union" of American Hebrew Congregations, a college for the training of American rabbis, and a centralized conference of American rabbis. Two words stand out in all of these endeavors — *union* and *American*. A new Judaism was needed, and Wise helped to fashion it.

Both Wise and Leeser were aware that American life invited a new kind of Judaism, one that could slough off the old negative interstitial roles that had dominated their European ancestors. Though coming from different points on the Jewish religious map, they both started with ritual reforms. Both soon came to realize that much more was needed than external tinkering. Wise and Leeser could never transcend their mutual enmity. "No pious Jew" will ever use one of his (Wise's) prayer books, wrote Leeser. And Wise promptly responded: "We do not acknowledge him competent to judge in matters of Judaism on account of his profound ignorance in Jewish literature."[191]

Ritual, rather than social action was on the minds of these religious leaders. Even during the Civil War, perhaps not surprisingly, the attitude of Jewish religious leaders was determined by sectional interests rather than moral ones. In New Orleans, Bernard Illowy, invoking biblical texts, offered a heated defense of slavery, while in Chicago, passionate pleas for emancipation emanated from the pulpits of Bernhard Felsenthal and Liebmann Adler. There were exceptions of course. In New York Morris Raphall defended slavery on the basis of the Bible, while in Baltimore David Einhorn had to abandon his pulpit and flee from the city due to his anti-slavery position. But in general it was geography that prevailed. As for Isaac M. Wise, his position was equivocal. Settled, now in Cincinnati, Queen City, gateway to the West and also the South, Wise remained neutral on the subject of slavery. States' rights, he argued, should be the basis for resolving the conflict. For Wise the unity of Judaism was a more pressing concern than the unity of the nation.[192]

In the years before and just after 1900, it was the religious congregation that served as the community's social service center. Following the examples of dedicated women such as Lillian Wald in New York (who was Jewish) and Jane Addams in Chicago (who was not), many metropolitan synagogues became centers for a variety of activities aimed at helping the poor, the elderly, and the immigrant. Dedicated members of the synagogue, usually women, created and staffed centers for health and child care, sewing circles, as well as English classes for immigrants. The rabbi was the head of this endeavor, but his sermons rather than his direct involvement in social service became his most memorable asset. The rabbi's voice was powerful and compelling. The frequently heard lament following upon the passing of orators such as Emil G. Hirsch or Steven Wise or Abba Hillel Silver was this: "Where have the giants of yesterday gone?" In reality, the "giants" were not replaced by epigones, but by a society that honored charisma less than wealth and political power.

Parallel to the struggle between religious and secular leaders, a geographic contest was taking place, one that affected American Jews in more palpable ways. Where would Jews settle? The contest seemed to pit New York City against the rest of the country, and in this contest the advantage was New York's. It was in New York that Jews from Western and Eastern Europe first encountered the new republic they were to call home. Beginning in 1654, with the arrival of the first Sephardic Jews who pleaded with Peter Stuyvesant for the right to stay there, New Amsterdam was to develop into the American city that symbolized hope for millions of Jews.

With succeeding immigrations from Russia and Poland at the end of the nineteenth century, New York City became arguably the most important center of Jewish life in the entire world. Like their German predecessors, many of the newcomers from Eastern Europe scattered throughout the country, but huge numbers of them chose to remain in the city that first welcomed them. There were other ports of entry, of course, but it was New York City that most frequently offered the introduction to what became known as the "*Goldene Medina.*" The establishment of Ellis Island as an immigration check point in 1892 was both an acknowledgment of New York's significance as a center of Jewish life and an omen of immigration restrictions yet to be imposed. The dry statistics tell the story of what was happening in the city. In 1870 there were approximately 80,000 Jews living in New York City. This represented 9 percent of the total population.[193] By 1915, the number of Jews had soared to a million and a half or 28 percent of the total population.

What was it that made New York such a desirable destination for the new immigrants? An obvious answer is the freedom that the city symbolized with its diverse population and openness to new ideas. Less apparent, but not to be ignored, is the fact that New York City offered commercial and economic opportunities that staggered the imagination. And it offered models of incredible success.

Even as the liberal and sometimes outspoken rabbis during the latter half of the nineteenth and early years of the twentieth century were teaching their congregants how they could become Americans and still remain Jews, a powerful group of Jewish lay leaders was beginning to transform Jewish life. The fabulous success of this elite group was seductive. Could not every immigrant be as wealthy as Seligman, as powerful as Goldman or Sachs? Were these not Jews who had started out as peddlers? Now they or their children were providing the funding for America's new railroads and utilities. They owned copper mines and investment banks. They were the "American Rothschilds."

Names such as Kahn and Warburg, Schiff and Strauss and Guggenheim, were part of an exclusive coterie of German Jews who began to call themselves "Our Crowd." They could be extravagant; they could be generous; but they were always, at least in their own eyes, "superior." When Herbert Lehman, who was to become the governor of New York State, entered Williams College in 1895, he took his car and chauffer with him. The name "Our Crowd," as reassuring as it might have seemed to its members, actually pointed to a double alienation. These German Jews never felt completely at home — either in society at large or in their own Jewish community.

Because of their wealth the new Jewish elites were often identified with the Rothschilds in the public imagination. In the case of August Belmont the identification proved to be more than figurative. In the 1830s a young man by the name of August Schonberg began his apprenticeship with the Rothschild banking firm in Frankfurt. For some reason young Schonberg did not fit the elite image that the Rothschilds wanted to project. Schonberg was sent to Naples and then to Havana. In 1837, he arrived in New York, but now his name was no longer August Schonberg. He was now August Belmont (he's "some kind of Frenchman," people would say of him) and he was now no longer a Jew.[194] Belmont represented

Rothschild interests, loved horses (the racetrack was named in his memory), and became incredibly wealthy. He also established a pattern of sorts. The German Jews had trouble retaining their Jewish connections. And where they did, it was clear that there was a world of difference between them and the Jewish masses.

Indifference to Judaism and conversion away from it was one pattern that marked these German elites. August Belmont may have been the earliest of the German Jews to cast Judaism aside, but he was surely not the last. The children of the great German Jewish leader Louis Marshall were indifferent to Judaism, and members of the Seligman family became involved in the Ethical Culture movement. Otto Kahn seriously contemplated converting to Catholicism. And the flamboyant art collector Peggy Guggenheim infuriated her mother by choosing Yom Kippur as the day to shop for furniture.

The counterpart to this move away from Judaism was to be observed in a new, or perhaps more accurately, a renewed form of Jewish observance — philanthropy. These wealthy Jews could both preserve their Judaism and maintain their paternalistic role through their gifts. Jacob Schiff was not the only member of New York's wealthy Jewish community who believed in the importance of *tzedakah*. Schiff correctly understood that the word *tzedakah* implied justice as well as charity. Throughout his life he believed that the first one-tenth of his income must be given away. And only amounts in excess of that 10 percent could be considered philanthropy.

Born in Germany in 1847, the descendent of a family of rabbis, Jacob Schiff came to the United States at the age of eighteen. He immediately entered the field of banking, married the daughter of Solomon Loeb and became head of the investment firm, Kuhn Loeb & Co. Schiff soon became a dominating force in firms as varied as the Equitable Life Insurance Company, the Union Pacific Railroad and the New York City National Bank. But Schiff's importance must be viewed not only in terms of his financial achievements, but also in terms of his philanthropic activities. He donated huge sums of money to a widely diversified group of recipients. He supported both the Hebrew Union College and its Conservative counterpart, the Jewish Theological Seminary. He contributed to Montefiore Hospital and the Young Men's Hebrew Association, and he helped to create the American Jewish Committee. The range of his philanthropic activities was incredible by any standard. He donated large sums to Harvard University and to Tuskegee Institute, to the American Red Cross and the Boy Scouts of America, and to Lillian Wald's Henry Street Settlement which provided visiting nurses to the indigent and sick of the Lower East Side. Schiff understood the importance of Wald's work and was a major benefactor of this pioneering program until the day of his death. His philanthropy was often innovative in that he began to insist on receiving matching grants, a form of giving that has grown in popularity over the years.

Schiff's beneficence was not always greeted with enthusiasm. He arranged for two large loans that are remembered even today by antisemitic conspiracy theorists, who insist on associating him with the infamous *Protocols of the Elders of Zion*. Schiff helped arrange a loan for Japan during the Russo-Japanese War, and he also gave support to the revolutionaries in Russia as they moved to overthrow the czar. The persecution of Jews in Russia was never far from his mind, and he harbored a life-long contempt for czarist Russia.

Jacob Schiff was not alone among the German Jewish philanthropists. Otto Kahn became the great benefactor of the Metropolitan Opera. Following Schiff's example, he used the promise of the "matching gift" to solicit huge sums for the Opera. His own gift was seldom less than $100,000 a year. Another of the German elites, Adolph Lewisohn, provided the funds to build Lewisohn Stadium on the campus of the City College of New York. Before its demolition in 1973, the stadium was considered a New York landmark, famous not only for the college graduations held there, but also for performances by the Metropolitan Opera and the New York Philharmonic. Lewisohn also endowed a wing at Mount Sinai Hospital, the School of Mining at Columbia University, and an orphanage for Jewish children at Pleasantville, New York. Late in his life he became interested in prison reform, and donated large sums of money to help rehabilitate former prisoners.

The impact of these German Jews was profound, and ultimately their activities affected the organization of Jewish communities all over the country. Why was philanthropy so important to these elites? A sense of guilt was partly, but only partly, responsible for the new emphasis upon giving. The shabby condition of so many immigrants from Eastern Europe was a source of embarrassment to the wealthy Fifth Avenue Jews. To neglect these immigrants was to cast a cloud upon their own Jewish origins. But it is also certain that the guilt that prompted the earliest manifestations of philanthropy soon gave way to a sense of *lèse majesté*. To help others became the "proper" thing to do, and it came as close to fulfilling a Jewish religious obligation as many of them were willing to acknowledge. The leadership of the Jewish community was clearly becoming a philanthropic oligarchy. "The ability to give" became the prerequisite for "the ability to lead."

There was one other aspect of this heightened emphasis upon charity that is worthy of note. There soon developed a competitive component to the financial gifts. Leadership positions were often awarded to the most generous of the givers. In addition, the newly established country clubs and city clubs required proof of one's charitable contributions as a prerequisite for membership. Nor were these social clubs reticent about indicating which charity was to be supported, and they often even specified the expected amount of the gift. In addition federations and welfare funds established on the new philanthropic model began to publish glossy annual reports in which the names of donors were printed alphabetically with the size of the donation accompanying each name. If anything, these practices have been refined over the years and, in many instances, have been copied by non-Jewish organizations. The goal, it needs to be emphasized, is to raise money. There is a difference between raising money and creating a just society. As a rule, extremely wealthy people tend to like the idea of charity. Charity helps the poor and needy without addressing the root causes of poverty and need. The Rothschilds were suspicious of labor organizers and community activists who advocated structural change or tax reform. So too were the members of "our crowd," that elite group of New York Jews who did so much to shape the structure of American Jewish life.

Both in style and in substance the early German Jews were vastly different from the East European Jews who began to flee Russian pogroms and the desperate poverty that afflicted so many of them. Crowded tenements and unhealthy living conditions tell only part of their story. The new immigrants brought with them a vibrant Jewish culture and literally hundreds of small *shuls* that preserved not only their religious traditions, but also memories of the old shtetl that had once been their home. Yiddish culture expressed itself in a dynamic theater and a dynamic press. By the early decades of the twentieth century, the bifurcation of American Jewish society was hard to ignore. The leadership of community structures was still German-Jewish. The dynamism was East European.

As the twentieth century progressed, American Jewish leadership became increasingly secular. This process has often resulted in growing tension between religious and secular institutions. As the secular community-wide organizations moved toward secularization, synagogues tended to move in the opposite direction. They gradually became more diverse and individualized. Synagogues were usually locally based and supported by members who consciously decided to affiliate with a rabbi or community they thought to be congenial. Thus it was hardly unusual for congregations to fragment as a result of rabbinic personality clashes. Moreover, the congregation itself inevitably harbored a tension between religious and lay leadership. The rabbi occupied a recognizably religious role, but he or she was inevitably selected and sustained by the lay leadership of the congregation. Variety and not uniformity were characteristic of the synagogue as opposed to the federation. This does not mean that the synagogue remained immune to the influence of the federation. On the contrary, the financial burdens of congregational membership often led the synagogue to seek as its leaders the very men and women who could afford to be active in the larger arena of organized Jewish life. The ancient struggle between secular and religious leadership evokes contemporary echoes. In addition, repeated warnings about antisemitism and threats to Israel emanating from many national Jewish institutions made it difficult for even the most indifferent of Jews to remain unconcerned.

There are, of course, national bodies that purport to speak for all Jews. Indeed they play an important role in fashioning a "public" agenda even as their impact upon individual Jews remains minimal. These national bodies often dedicate themselves to lobbying for Jewish interests. Characteristically, they are led by those who have either "graduated" from leadership on the local scene yet still feel the need to serve or whose wealth has prompted them to finesse the local scene and aspire to the "honor" that membership on a national board seems to offer.

But there are serious problems associated with all of these efforts to unify a community's social services. By their very nature the centralized agencies tend to emphasize the "charity" aspects of *tzedakah*, rather than the "justice" aspects. The basic problem is that organizations seeking to speak in the name of all Jews are innately hostile to dissent. In the first place, dissent threatens fund-raising. And it is doubly threatening when the dissent touches upon some of the vital interests of the larger givers. In the second place, dissent undermines the power claims of the federations. Perhaps they don't speak for all Jews after all! Finally, dissent is messy. It presents the "wrong impression" to outsiders. A fractious Jewish community is a divided Jewish community is a weakened Jewish community — so the leaders often argue.

The over-dependence of Jewish federations upon the leadership of their wealthy patrons, their reliance on governmental funds, as well as their umbilical relationship to local elites tend to compromise their independence and to turn them into guardians of the status quo, even in those instances when the status quo works to increase the suffering of the poor and powerless. Federations and welfare funds are generally quite comfortable with "soup-kitchen" aid, a type of assistance that provides services to individuals. The federations are less comfortable when asked to identify with organizations that propose a more action-oriented agenda. They generally react with caution to groups that seek innovative answers to troubling social problems, with hostility to groups that voice outright opposition to the status quo. It is simply easier to help people out than to empower them so that they can help themselves. But what is easiest is not always wisest.

No analysis of the contemporary Jewish scene can ignore the dynamism and vitality of America's various Hasidic communities. For the most part they have remained indifferent to the secular institutions of Jewish life, preferring to exercise influence through their own political structures. Through their proselytizing activities and their high birthrate they have become a potent religious force. In a sense they remain doubly interstitial — distinctly separated by garb and choice of residence not only from general society, but from the mainline Jewish community as well.

These Hasidic and ultra-Orthodox religious branches of Judaism appeal precisely because they promise a return to tradition and authority. The strength of their agenda is that they offer a response to assimilation that many Jews find irresistible. They attract by nostalgia; they appeal to an idealized way of life many Jews have heard about but few have ever experienced. However, these fundamentalist groups envision a renascence of Judaism by advocating the very values that many generations of Jew sought to reject. Ultimately their vision is of a return to the ghetto, a world which proved so dangerous to Jews throughout the centuries. While these ultra-Orthodox groups idealize ritual and tradition, they have exhibited a troubling indifference to those moral and social problems that beset society at large.

The Hasidic community is often able to summon considerable political power. A single-minded community concentrated in a particular geographic area is capable of summoning such power. And politicians will often respond to the pressures which such a bloc creates. But this type of power is limited and ultimately self-defeating. All politics may indeed be local, but when even local politics ignores the greater good, then greater evil is poised to make its appearance.

None of this can diminish the fact that many young and assimilated Jews have discovered meaning and relevance in Hasidism that eluded them in the more traditional branches of their faith. But a theology that sets survival itself as its primary goal is a self-destructive tautology. To believe that a return to social isolation together with religious authoritarianism will engender a genuine Jewish revival is to follow a dangerous path. Ethical conduct becomes subservient to community solidarity. The poor become invisible unless they are "our poor." Unquestioning support for Israel;

unstinting support for "our" private schools — these are the issues that dominate all others. In this isolation, the negative interstitial image rushes to be reborn.

And what of the Jewish role in political life? The political arena reveals the interstitial aspect of Judaism in one of its more subtle forms. When a Jew is nominated to the Supreme Court, his or her religion invariably attaches itself to the news of the nomination. Ever since Louis D. Brandeis was appointed as the first "Jewish" justice on the Supreme Court, it has been generally assumed that there was a "Jewish seat" on the court. But the religion of the nominee invariably seemed more newsworthy when that nominee was Jewish. Names like Brandeis and Cardozo, Morgenthau and Frankfurter became famous as much because of their religious origins as their political or intellectual acumen. The fate of Justice Abe Fortas offers a variation of this pattern. When President Lyndon Johnson nominated Fortas to be chief justice of the Supreme Court, a cruel battle over his nomination resulted, and Fortas ultimately withdrew and later resigned from the court. What is significant is that the news reports invariably reminded their readers that Fortas was Jewish. Were there no other nominees rejected by the Senate? Their religion is hardly ever mentioned. The religious affiliation of failed nominees — the names Carswell and Bork immediately come to mind — was never a factor in the public discussions during their confirmation hearings.

A unique, if rather bizarre, example of the interstitial role can be followed in the unique career of Henry Kissinger. In the administration of Richard Nixon, Kissinger served first as national security advisor and then as secretary of state. Kissinger was born in Bavaria and came to the United States as a refugee from Nazi persecution. Although he was a Jew by birth, his Judaism was always problematic. Kissinger nevertheless played a prominent role in matters that vitally affected the Jewish community. In his seven-hundred-plus page study of Nixon and Kissinger, Robert Dallek touches on some of the themes that define the dimensions of Kissinger's interstitial role — hunger for acceptance in society, alienation from the Jewish community, defense of Israel in its time of travail, and service in a patently corrupt administration. Because of his roles supporting the failed war in Vietnam and the cruel bombing of Cambodia, it might be expected that his influence would diminish over the years. Yet the combination of a brilliant mind and an astute advocacy of a politically active and powerful presidency have induced administration after administration to continue seeking his advice.

President Nixon never tired of demeaning his secretary of state. Nixon's prejudice, Dallek suggests, was typical of that held by many "lower-middle-class" Americans. He believed that American Jews were more loyal to Israel than to the United States. On one occasion after Kissinger had expressed an opinion about the Middle East, Nixon pointedly asked: "Now can we get an American opinion?" The stereotypes were all in evidence. For Nixon, the Jews were too liberal. Not only were they more interested in Israel than in the United States, but they were sympathetic to the Soviet Union, and their control of the media made them a powerful and dangerous group. In protecting himself in the presence of the President, Kissinger would meekly say, "Well, Mr. President, there are Jews, and then there are Jews." In private much later he was able to say: "How can I, as a Jew who lost thirteen relatives in the Holocaust, do anything that would betray Israel?"

The relationship between Henry Kissinger and Richard Nixon was not unlike that of a Court Jew and his sovereign. Kissinger's Jewishness invariably made him feel vulnerable, and if there was anything distasteful to Kissinger, presidential advisor John Ehrlichman suggested, it was feeling vulnerable. Kissinger was Nixon's "Jew Boy." He was called that on many occasions when he was with the president. How many times it was uttered behind his back can only be a matter of unpleasant speculation.[195]

Was Nixon's contempt for his Jewish Secretary of State an unusual product of their peculiar symbiotic relationship or was it characteristic of a broader pattern? The latter seems to be case. In 1970, to evoke but one example, the Democratic political boss of Albany, New York, Daniel O'Connell was approached about endorsing a slate of candidates for statewide office. The proposed slate was dominated by Jewish office seekers, but contained the name of one black candidate, Basil Paterson, the father of the man who, years later, would become New York State's first African-American governor. Pointing to Paterson's name, O'Connell is reputed to have said: "As far as I'm concerned, he's the only white man on the ticket."[196]

Henry Kissinger's unique relationship with power exhibited many of the troublesome characteristics of the interstitial role. Biographer Jeremi Suri notes that even as a brilliant Harvard student, "Kissinger was never a Harvard man. He and other Jews of his generation lived separate lives from other students. They did not have access to the elite social clubs, and they were not fully accepted among their peers...Kissinger and other Jews rose through tradition-bound universities because their attributes as 'outsiders' were valued by specific 'insiders.' . . . For all his fame and power, Kissinger remained an outsider to mainstream American society. He and other Jews depended on personal patronage from non-Jews, and they remained targets of anti-Semitic suspicion, often from the very men who promoted them."[197]

Less clear is the hold of antisemitism upon the current political scene. In the year 2000, a major political party had courage enough to pick a Jew to run for vice president of the United States. When Al Gore selected the senator from Connecticut to be his running mate, it was regarded as a sign that America had put to rest decades of religious prejudice. Joseph Lieberman was an observant Jew, and his nomination was seen as an affirmation of religious faith and of the family values that were cherished by the Christian Right. It is questionable whether antisemitism was really the non-factor it was thought to be. Gore and Lieberman lost the election in a few key states. Anecdotal reports lead to the suspicion that many Americans may not have been ready to trust the second-highest position in the land to a Jew, especially to one who practiced his religion so religiously.

And, of course, there still is the mendacious rumor that Israel was in some way connected with the destruction of the World Trade Center in September of 2001. The rumor, unsupported by any shred of fact, maintains that Israelis had consistently stayed away on that day. The toll of the Jewish dead provides eloquent refutation to this absurd canard.

No analysis of the perils of the interstitial role in the United States can ignore the tremendous prominence of Israel in the Jewish psyche. The protective relationship that American Jews have with Israel is understandable both in terms of Jewish history and the tenuousness of Israel's position since its creation in 1948. This intense relationship, however, reveals the perseverance of the interstitial role in a unique way. The inability to separate genuine criticism of Israel from exaggerated fears of antisemitism is a persistent problem. The two may indeed be hard to distinguish. Jews are quite aware that specific criticisms of their behavior can all too easily become "global attacks." Yet there remains an important difference between criticism and malice. This distinction is not always easy to acknowledge.

And so, when two distinguished college professors, one from the University of Chicago and the other from Harvard, unite to deplore the power of the pro-Israel lobby and to suggest that Israel is no longer a useful American ally, the Jewish community, as might be anticipated, suffers a severe anxiety attack. The two professors, Stephen Walt and John Mearsheimer, had only to name their work *The Israel Lobby* to guarantee a pained outcry from Israel supporters *Washington Post*: "These academics may not follow their claims all the way to antisemitism. But this is the way it begins. This is the way it always begins."[198] Lately, college campuses have become the forum of choice for debating whether Israel-made products should be boycotted as retaliation for continued Israeli settlement expansion on the West Bank. Are such debates tinged with antisemitism or are they merely political?

Does criticism of Israel, in other words, invariably lead to antisemitism? The question remains a troubling one for the American Jewish community. Yet the moral implications of American Jewish preoccupation with Israel should remain equally troubling. "While almost all federally financed programs were denied any funding increase for the coming year, aid to Israel from the United States will increase thanks to a legislative loophole and some deft maneuvering by pro-Israel lobbyists." The *Forward*, which lays claim to being the "paper of record" of the American Jewish community, printed these words, the very first sentence in its lead story on July 11, 2008. And 2008, it will be recalled was a disastrous one for millions of Americans experiencing a painful economic recession. The article went on to report: "The move was quickly applauded by the American Israel Public Affairs Committee."[199] Why are the moral implications of this kind of legislative legerdemain so often ignored? Does either the clandestine nature of the process — "thanks to a legislative loophole" — or the absence of any open assessment of the value of this funding in the light of other social needs, accord with the ideals of a positive interstitial role? To say that all of this is typical of the political process and that Jews are merely claiming their share in this process is hardly a satisfying answer.

Israel, of course, will continue to figure prominently in the American Jewish consciousness. But the enormous energy spent by the Jewish community in associating criticisms of Israel with antisemitism can lead to dangerous distortions. One need only examine the weekly Jewish newspapers, or scan the programs of the federations as well as other Jewish agencies, to perceive these distortions at work. An understanding of the interstitial role need not diminish Jewish support for Israel; but it would insist that being pro-Israel does not require the suspension of one's critical facilities — or of one's more general ethical responsibilities.

Yet all too often Jewish elites in a variety of local federations and community organizations, together with an Israel lobby that operates with myopic singleness of purpose, stifle the aspirations of those who would act in positively interstitial ways. The power of these groups is hardly subtle, and the consequences of their caution can often prove harmful to the Jewish community as well as to the cause of justice.

Even the process of dialoguing with community groups has become subject to caution that sometimes borders on paranoia. Does the group have anyone connected to the Nation of Islam? Do not meet with it. Has any member of the group criticized Israel? Do not meet with it. A litmus test has been applied to every organization (including those whose goals in almost every respect are entirely praiseworthy) that seems to make cooperation contingent on a single and arbitrary standard. The long-term advantage of lending a helping hand, even to one's critics, is seldom acknowledged.

The crimping of Jewish outreach to African-American organizations is a pattern that finds parallels in efforts to build Muslim-Jewish relationships. The insistence on shunning critics, in this case, critics of Israel, acts to stifle opportunities for meaningful encounters between Muslins and Jews. Equally troubling is the habit of Jewish elites who initially veto contacts with mainline Muslims and then seek out and promote groups that represent the most insignificant segment of that community. "If you have never criticized Israel and if you promise to agree with us, we will talk with you." Sentiments such as these hardly offer the basis for a meaningful dialogue.

When Eric Yoffie, the president of the Union of Reform Judaism, was asked to speak to the Islamic Society of North America (ISNA), the invitation could not be accepted until the credentials of the Muslim group had been carefully examined. In justifying the decision to accept the invitation, an official spokesman for the Reform Jewish movement cautiously announced: "The FBI and the Pentagon were represented, so this answers allegations about terrorist associations." How ironic it is that a group so committed to the strict separation of church and state as is the Union of Reform Judaism should depend on the FBI to vet its religious contacts! Even after his speech, Rabbi Yoffie felt it necessary to reassure the readers of Reform Judaism: "We chose ISNA as our partner in dialogue because the society has issued a strong, unequivocal condemnation of terror, including a specific denunciation of Hezbollah and Hamas violence against Jews and Israel."[200]

Of course, any leader of a national religious organization will want to know about the agenda and composition of an unfamiliar group. But repeated and public disclaimers and assertions that the host has been thoroughly investigated appear unseemly and even insulting. They certainly do not hold much promise for a trusting dialogue. A more helpful approach might be discerned in the more nuanced advice of one Harvard religious scholar. "I am by no means advocating that the Jewish community accept and ignore Muslim criticisms of Israel and of the Jewish community. Rather, I am urging the organizational leadership to broaden the universe of potential Muslim partners by excluding at the outset only those who uphold positions it regards as immoral or untenable, rather than those whose positions do not follow Jewish consensus."[201]

Muslim political power in the United States is bound to increase as the Muslim population grows. And that growth is surely taking place. To predicate Jewish security merely upon the ability to purchase congressional influence — the AIPAC approach — is to engage in a most dangerous enterprise. A day will soon come when sheer numbers will make Muslim political influence every bit as potent as Jewish influence. This prospect makes it more important than ever that a genuine dialogue takes place — one that includes a variety of viewpoints and recognizes that there are issues other than Israel that can guide our mutual endeavors.

Over and above any single manifestation of modern antisemitism, and setting aside for a moment continuing concerns for the welfare of the state of Israel, there is one aspect of the interstitial role that never entirely disappears. It is the persistent and palpable anxiety about the Jewish condition itself. Jewish angst is a perpetual reality that is a silent part of every Jewish conversation. Am I talking to a Jew or non-Jew? Can I tell this joke or had I better save it for my Jewish friends? This anxiety is something that Sartre understood better than most Jews, even if he could not totally identify with it.

The ongoing specter of antisemitism has political ramifications as well as social ones. Striking illustrations of the anxiety are to be found in the pages of *Commentary* magazine. This journal began its career as the liberal voice of the American Jewish Committee but has developed into a steady critic of liberal Jewish endeavors. Month after month, *Commentary* reminds its readers that the dangers of antisemitism are real and present. Under the editorship of Norman Podhoretz, *Commentary* came to espouse a form of neo-conservatism that identifies Jewish interests with those of a militarily active United States. Threats to Jewish security are magnified not only by the reluctance of the nation to utilize its physical power in order to confront its true enemies, but by the inability of Jews themselves to understand the difference between their true friends and their foes.[202]

"Separation" is the quality that best characterizes the uniqueness of Jewish history. Correctly understood, the interstitial nature of the people becomes not an accident of their history, but the essence of their history. "Judaism," Karl Marx famously asserted, "has survived, not in spite of history, but because of history." But Marx's aphorism fails to account for history in its more complex manifestation, and it has the consequence of turning Judaism into nothing more than an economic anomaly. The reality is that complex social roles, economic endeavors, religious commitments all combine to create a distinctive Jewish history. The idea of a "chosen people," then, has its modern reincarnation in the realization that being a distinct third party may not be merely an accident of history. It may be the essence of Jewish history. As distinguished from either a Hegelian or Marxian form of determinism, the Jewish community can now escape from the dialectic trap and assert control over its own destiny. The interstitial people indeed have a choice — they can use their lives to bless themselves and others, or they can resign themselves to a perpetual pattern of discrimination and suffering.

A distinctive characteristic of the interstitial nature of American Judaism is so prevalent that at first it seems barely noteworthy. It is the tremendous energy devoted to preserving Jewish identity. Behind this energy is the assumption that whatever happens, Jews and Judaism must be preserved! Is this self-protective instinct so noteworthy? Do not other religious communities act out of similar pure survival instincts? When the Roman pontiff issues a call for strict conformity to the authority of the Catholic Church, is this not an act aimed at guaranteeing the survival of the church? When Southern Baptists establish a worldwide missionary program, they are similarly acting to ensure the survival of their church. How, then, are Jewish efforts at self-preservation different?

What is different is that concerns about the survival of Judaism are strikingly devoid of any idealized vision of a Jewish mission. Appeals for Jewish survival are devoid of any promise to heal Third World countries, to spread Christ's message of love, or to prepare for a second coming of the messiah. As opposed to these religious missions, organized Jewish life seems to take it for granted that survival itself is the supreme good, and that the alternative is unthinkable.

What is lost is a sense of purpose. What is lost is the awareness that survival is a matter of moral and social urgency, not merely an end in itself. There is no overarching teleology, no vision of a safer and kinder world, no sense of mission. We are to educate our children, but the goal of that education is seldom explained, seldom convincing. Is there no reason for survival more compelling than the ephemeral assertion that "survival is important"?

This problem was not overlooked by Jonathan Sarna in his study *American Judaism*, written in 2004. Describing ferment in nineteenth-century American Jewish life, Sarna could point to a continuing problem. "Fear for the survival of Judaism in the United States served, as so often it would, as a potent stimulus for change. The question of what direction change would take, however, generated substantial communal controversy. Some argued that Jews themselves needed to be 'regenerated' through greater emphasis on Jewish education and the strengthening of Jewish religious life. Others insisted that Judaism as a religion was at fault and needed to be 'reformed.' Still others felt that community and kinship, rather than rituals and faith, should form the new basis for Jewish life; they sought to unite Jews around ties of peoplehood, the 'mission of uniting Israelites in the work of promoting their highest interests, and those of humanity.'"[203]

Today the "interests of humanity" are seldom evoked as a reason for the preservation of the Jewish community. As survival becomes its overriding goal, the agenda of the Jewish community is vacuumed into this seductive catch-all. Intermarriage is a problem because it threatens Jewish survival. Jewish education is a problem because Jewish illiteracy poses a threat to Jewish survival. By that calculus even the traditional Jewish love of learning is treasured not because of its intrinsic value, but because it is a key to Jewish survival. The various branches of Judaism argue over which of them will better guarantee that survival. But any discussion that raises questions about why Judaism should survive is immediately regarded as an antisemitic attack, even if the question is raised by thoughtful Jews. Nothing defines the positive interstitial community more clearly than its ability to recognize that any program for Jewish survival that is solipsistic and devoid of any moral or socially relevant agenda is bound to ultimately be regarded as irrelevant. The people in between will remain nothing more than "the people in between," its vitality hostage to the seemingly magnetic power of its compulsion to remain nothing other than "different."

An alternative and more dynamic approach remains a possibility. That the Jewish people need to survive is hardly a matter of controversy, provided that the moral and humane virtues which it has historically struggled to preserve are nourished and cherished. In the name of a just God the prophets sought to combat exploitation and oppression. The Jewish people have known oppression and exploitation as have few others. The collective memory of this people is what makes the positive interstitial role such a promising one — and a holy one too.

The anxious awareness that Jews have not recognized their potential as a true community may therefore be taken as a challenge. If Jews have acted primarily out of a sense of defensiveness in the past, there is a corresponding awareness that another path is open before them. This path offers an opportunity for Jews to delve anew into the words and history of their tradition and at the same time to use their unique position to become symbols of a vital new social conscience. Part of this renewed emphasis upon the prophetic message would be the formation of alliances with community groups that have experienced discrimination in their own way. The word of the prophet was never a word spoken in mountaintop isolation. It recognized, as any vital Jewish endeavor must, the primacy of the people who heard and preserved and cherished the word. The main prophetic figures may have been angry rebels, the pariahs of Arendt's histories, but they never abandoned their people even on their most frustrating days — and their people never abandoned them.

History has demonstrated that general economic prosperity is congenial to Jewish well-being. And it has also revealed that massive social disparities become danger signs, marking a threat to Jewish survival. These disparities may be ignored for a while but they can be neglected only at great peril. Pogroms, as Dubnow so often pointed out, occurred in Russia at precisely those moments when mass resentment seemed on the verge of erupting into violent rebellion against the czarist power structure. In other words, when the poverty of Russian peasants had become unbearably oppressive, the czarist administration invariably recognized that the interstitial Jewish community remained a convenient safety valve. Messengers would arrive from the czarist administration, and a few days later the massacre of Jews would begin. This technique was employed all the way up to that April day in 1917 when a train arrived at the Finland Station in St. Petersburg, bearing Lenin and a new, though ultimately flawed, hope for the oppressed masses of Russian workers.

Surely, antisemitism finds its roots in a variety of factors, but no one condition is more hospitable to this form of hatred than is economic despair. This despair may lie dormant for years, but the persistence of poverty, and an accompanying indifference to its etiology, remains a sure portent of disaster. Arguing that the problem is not poverty itself, so much as the way the poor are exploited, may make rational sense. What is not rational, at least to the poor, is the hopelessness and frustration that confronts them daily.

Jews study. They teach. They strive to create lives that are happy and fulfilling. They yearn for a world that is safe and peaceful — for themselves and all peoples. Their texts are ancient and profound, their rituals inspiring and fulfilling. They need to be in charge of their own destiny.

Chapter 11

Encountering Spinoza

For those who have persisted throughout this study of the interstitial role, its seductions and its promises, its negative consequences and its positive challenges, this may seem the appropriate time to draw the curtain and to allow our analysis to breathe or suffocate on its own merit. But the life and thought of Baruch (Benedict) Spinoza (1632–1677) is worthy of a fresh examination. Here is a guide whose thoughts have been studied and rejected so often in the past that his return to our work may well be viewed with apprehension. Yet Spinoza may actually be more relevant today than when his radical thoughts first crept into print during the last quarter of the seventeenth century. He is the quintessential interstitial Jew, raised in the midst of the interstitial people, whose voice will not be silenced.

Spinoza's words are particularly relevant today when traditional religious beliefs are under attack. The onslaught comes not only from atheists and popular writers who raise questions about the entire religious endeavor, but also from sincere yet troubled lay people and even clergy who are asked to accept on faith ideas their intellects can no longer sustain.

This is hardly the place for a full or even partial examination of the reasons why religious believers are becoming increasingly and sharply divided between fundamentalist and liberal ideologies. Nor is it the place to examine the wide variety of theological systems that continually vie for new adherents. Traditional faiths such as Islam and Buddhism together with New Age spiritualism and even Kabbalistic Judaism all claim devout adherents. All clamor for recognition in a field that only recently was regarded as the exclusive domain of "the Judeo-Christian" tradition. In this enlarged arena, the particular kind of Judaism stemming from an understanding of the interstitial role deserves thoughtful examination.

The "positive interstitial" role is based upon a religious view of Judaism, not a secular one. But it is a religious view that has no place for prejudice or sectarian triumphalism. And since this view emphasizes the importance of "doing justly" coupled with a reverence for the world in which we live as the two most important responsibilities of the modern Jew, a belief system congenial to these values should be enthusiastically welcomed. Indeed, while the contemporary Jewish establishment never denies the importance of social justice, its actual programs reveal an emphasis upon other values such as loyalty to Israel, ritual fidelity, and intellectual achievement.

Rabbi Abraham Joshua Heschel (1907–72), who marched with Dr. Martin Luther King, Jr. during the turbulent civil rights struggles of the 1960s, suffered from this reality. As a refugee, Heschel was offered positions, first at the Hebrew Union College and then at the Jewish Theological Seminary in New York where he taught courses on ethics and mysticism. But because of his social activism, he never felt comfortable at either of these seminaries. Heschel, of course, had a profound impact upon many of his students, but the recognition which he earned as a civil rights and peace advocate came to be appreciated by most Jews only posthumously, and only after his courage and scholarship had come to be appreciated by non-Jews.

The need to reconcile traditional Jewish values with contemporary social concerns is challenging. Beginning with Maimonides's *Guide for the Perplexed*, the first systematic attempt to reconcile Judaism with the philosophical innovations of his age, Jewish theologians have not hesitated to confront this challenge. But no one in the course of Jewish history, not even Maimonides himself, has ever been as controversial as that brilliant Dutch Jewish heretic whose thoughts assailed the world of Western philosophy with the force of a violent earthquake. He came to be known as Benedict Spinoza; the change from his given name, Baruch, or Bento, is but a sign of the alienation which took place between him and the Jewish community in which he was raised.

Spinoza's great heresy was that he rejected traditional ideas of a transcendent supernatural deity. His perception that God is identical with the universe itself evoked vehement opposition from all of those who were devoted to sustaining traditional religious institutions as well as European monarchies. Of course, it can be maintained, as it was by his most ardent followers, that his reverent view of God as nature is a deeply religious one. His insistence that morality is the essence of the religious endeavor is sophisticated and it is also totally congenial to the interstitial analysis of Judaism.

Is it possible to reconcile Spinoza's rigid materialism with the religious tradition that first nurtured him and then rejected him? Spinoza's view that nature and God are a unity immediately collides with the traditional Jewish view of God as a creator and of a God who intercedes in human affairs. Therefore, it is not irrelevant to ask whether Spinoza and Judaism can meet in any amicable way. An affirmative answer to this question would entail a suspension of the Orthodox idea that every thought and every word of the Torah tradition must be regarded as sacred and unalterable. There is reason to maintain that precisely such a transformation, namely one that manages to reinterpret the meaning of both myth and tradition while elevating a commitment to both nature and social justice, represents a transformation that many modern Jews, as well as thoughtful people everywhere, might welcome.

This possibility was recognized by the contemporary philosopher Emmanuel Levinas, who acknowledged the modern relevance of Spinoza's thought. Spinoza has played "a positive role in the history of religious faith; for it is from out of these moral elements, whose richness Spinoza, disdainful and ignorant of the rabbinic tradition, did not accurately assess, that a philosophy will eventually spring, once the perishable destiny of Spinozist dogmatism is revealed."[204] This acknowledgment of Spinoza's modern relevance is doubly significant in view of the respected position Levinas occupied in the world of both philosophy and Judaic thought following the Second World War. While acknowledging that some areas of Spinozistic thought are no longer credible, Levinas was able nonetheless to affirm the durability of Spinoza and his philosophy.

In July of 1656, Baruch d'Espinoza was placed in *herem*, the formal excommunication that prohibited all members of Amsterdam's *Talmud Torah* congregation from having any contact with him. Spinoza's criticism of biblical mythology, his antagonism to the prophets, and his revolutionary ideas about God had by now stimulated intense and growing hostility. So violent were the anti-Spinoza sentiments, that shortly after the excommunication, a young man wielding a dagger lunged at him as he was leaving a public meeting. Spinoza was unhurt, but after the assault he felt it necessary to leave Amsterdam and eventually settle in The Hague. There he worked as a lens grinder, a profession that probably damaged his lungs and may well have led to his premature death in 1677.

Baruch Spinoza may have left Judaism, but Judaism did not leave Spinoza. His writings reveal a more than superficial knowledge of Hebrew, of the Jewish Bible, and of Jewish philosophers, particularly Maimonides and the twelfth-century exegete Rabbi Abraham ibn Ezra. Nor was young Bento, as his friends called him, a stranger to Jewish practices and traditions. As a child, he studied Jewish texts with some of the leading rabbis of his native Amsterdam, rabbis who were well respected in their time, Manasseh ben Israel and Saul Levi Morteira. During the excommunication proceedings, Manasseh ben Israel had been in England meeting with Oliver Cromwell in an effort to rescind the laws preventing Jews from living in that country. Manasseh himself had briefly been excommunicated by the synagogue in Amsterdam. An impressive orator, he welcomed the belief that the messiah would arrive when Jews were to be found in all parts of the world. This argument carried great weight with religious fundamentalists in England, many of whom believed that the emancipation of the Jews was a necessary precondition for the second coming of the messiah. There are many who credit the popularity of this conviction for Cromwell's decision to readmit the Jews.

Years before his departure for England, Manasseh had taught a young Spinoza about Jewish mysticism. And he surely acquainted Spinoza with the idea of *tzimtzum*, the doctrine that holds the view that God is in the process of withdrawing from the world. God contracts in order to provide space where human freedom can prevail. By seeming to withdraw, God remains infinite while simultaneously making room for a finite universe as well as for human free will. Because *tzimtzum* results in a conceptual idea of holy space, God is often called *Ha-Makom*, the place, the ever-present space. To point to possible elements of Kabbalistic mysticism in Spinoza's metaphysics is not to suggest that the lens grinder from Amsterdam was a Jewish mystic. But he surely was drawn to some of the same speculations that occupied the mystics. And he may well have used some of their thinking in developing his own view of a God that seemed to have withdrawn from directly interfering in individual human actions.

A close reading of the *Theological-Political Treatise* (*Tractatus Theologico-Politicus*) provides insights into some of the reasons that Amsterdam's Jews became so alienated from Spinoza. Although the treatise was not published until 1670, its ideas were certainly in circulation long before that date, and Spinoza made no effort to conceal them. In the *Tractatus*, he openly questioned not only the facts of the biblical narrative, but also the integrity of many biblical personalities. He sometimes employed ideas and even stereotypes that were certain to antagonize his Jewish contemporaries in Amsterdam. "It is as clear as the noonday light," he wrote, "that the Pentateuch was not written by Moses, but by one who lived many ages after him."[205] And more painfully, he claimed that "the patriotism of the Hebrews was not simply patriotism but piety, and this together with hatred for other nations was so fostered and nourished by their daily ritual that it inevitably became part of their nature."[206]

These passages, as provocative as they are, hardly do justice to the totality of Spinoza's approach to the Bible. The *Tractatus* reveals his search for the "true" religion as opposed to one based upon superstition, for justice as opposed to empty piety. Spinoza's heroes are Moses and Jesus — men who had direct contact with God; his scorn was reserved for those who falsely presumed to speak in the name of God. Jesus, in particular, is to be regarded with admiration, not because he was a prophet, but because his life and ideas were based upon pure reason and his goal was to create a faith emphasizing loving-kindness and justice.

Whether Spinoza's admiration for Jesus stemmed from a conscious rejection of Judaism or resulted from an awareness of the realities of Dutch political and religious life remains a matter of speculation. Spinoza certainly knew about the tragic fate that had befallen the Koerbagh brothers as a result of their radical religious attitudes. Adriaan and Johannes Koerbagh had probably met Spinoza as early as 1660 and were profoundly influenced by his ideas as well as those of Spinoza's teacher and mentor Van den Enden. The Koerbagh brothers zealously and, perhaps, heedlessly attacked the evils of the Dutch Reformed Church. They repeatedly gave voice to heretical ideas about God and, as a consequence, suffered through humiliating interrogations by church and public officials. The church, they insisted, had no right to enter into political life and had also misunderstood the true meaning of God and of creation. Shocked by these radical views, church officials abetted by community leaders, saw to it that the Koerbagh brothers were arrested and tortured. Adriaan was sentenced to ten years in prison and then to banishment from Holland. He died after only three months in prison; his brother survived him by a mere three years. The painful experience of these two friends surely prompted Spinoza to move cautiously as he prepared his *Tractatus* for publication.[207]

Yet even in the face of many dangerous precedents Spinoza continued with his revolutionary approach to the Bible. The New as well as the Old Testament, he insisted, had been edited by human beings and adopted by human councils. The greatness of both works, he argued, lay in their revelation of righteousness, not in their claims of divine authorship. Spinoza was rightly concerned that the *Tractatus* would inflame the hatred of his enemies, and it was for this reason that he delayed its publication as long as possible.

Were there factors other than theological ones that affected the relationship between Spinoza and the Jewish community of Amsterdam? Many reasons have been offered to explain the bitterness which accompanied the excommunication. Spinoza personally offended the leaders of the community. He did not pay his synagogue dues. It has even been suggested that the excommunication enabled the synagogue to insulate itself from a potentially anti-Semitic reactions to Spinoza's radicalism.

The history of Holland itself may provide another clue. The country had but recently gained its independence from Spain and many of its Jewish families, including Spinoza's, were descendants of Marranos, Spanish and Portuguese Jews. They lived in constant fear of the Inquisition and could only practice their religion in secret. Like their formerly Catholic countrymen, but perhaps even more so, these Jews found that it was easier to cast off the political Inquisition than the psychological one. Religious diversity was welcomed in Spinoza's Holland, but too much independent thought was still viewed with caution and with deep suspicion. Holland had overthrown Spanish domination; the rejection of Spanish attitudes about heresy was not as easy to overcome. For Jews and Christians alike, religious fidelity remained a sensitive issue. The charge that he was a heretic pursued Spinoza all his life and colored his relationships with Jews and gentiles alike. And so here he was — the interstitial Jew *par excellence* — wreaking havoc upon the philosophies of seventeenth-century Europe.

The sensitivities of the Jewish community were seldom far from the surface. Spinoza controversially maintained that the revelations of the Hebrew Bible were designed only for the Jewish nation, whereas the revelations contained in the New Testament were intended for all of humanity. Spinoza's insight may have been more profound than pejorative. The Jewish Bible, particularly the Pentateuch and large segments of the prophetic writings, does reveal a deep concern for the land and its governance. From the moment God promises the land to Abraham to the final vision of Moses as he looks across the Jordan River, the destiny of the future nation is of paramount concern. The people and its land are the bipolar essence of the Jewish experience. The continuing relevance of Spinoza's insight is apparent in even a superficial examination of a typical prayer book where descriptions of the rituals in the Jerusalem Temple are remembered as if the Temple still stood and the ancient nation still existed. "Shine a new light on Zion" — words found in the traditional morning *yotzer* prayer may have been regularly omitted from Reform prayer books because they were too nationalistic, but the most recent incarnation of this prayer book restores the prayer, fully conscious of its nationalistic implications. And does not every Passover *Seder* end with the words: "Next

Year in Jerusalem"? As thoughtful as Spinoza's analysis may have been, the realization that Judaism's merely local and national appeal were being unfavorably compared to Christianity's universal message surely annoyed the Jews of Amsterdam.

Spinoza seems to have been impervious to the criticisms of his contemporaries. Much evidence supports the theory that his otherwise amiable behavior concealed a stubbornness and impulsiveness that often brought him to the brink of disaster. And it is this stubbornness that surely aggravated his relationship with the Jews of Amsterdam no less than with those who found his religious views unpalatable. It is well known that Spinoza was an admirer of Johan de Witt, whose leadership of Holland encouraged liberal religious and academic thought. De Witt has come to be regarded as perhaps the greatest and wisest of Holland's seventeenth century political leaders. But by 1672, public sentiment had turned against him. The same William of Orange who sixteen years later would invade England now led Dutch conservatives in a struggle for power. The collapse of the economy as well as an unfortunate war with the French — both conspired to encourage the Orange cause and to degrade the hopes of the liberals. Johan de Witt's older brother Cornelis was arrested, falsely accused of treason and tortured. When Johan was lured to the prison in the belief that his brother was about to be freed, a bloodthirsty mob, responding, some say, to the orders of William of Orange, assaulted the prison, seized the two brothers, and brutally murdered them. When he heard the news Spinoza wanted to run to the scene of the massacre and post a sign reading "You are the greatest of the barbarians." Only the prompt action of Hendrik Van der Spijk, Spinoza's landlord, prevented the philosopher from meeting the same fate as the two brothers. He bolted the front door thereby preventing Spinoza from leaving his home.[208]

If Spinoza's usually mild behavior incorporated a steely determination, it was this combination of character traits that earned him steadfast admirers as well as unrelenting adversaries. All of his life he was to remain popular among nonconformists, suspect among traditionalists. By all accounts, however, his virtues far exceeded his vices; he lived a simple life entirely in accord with the moral principles his philosophy advocated. Ultimately, however, it was not his gentle personality but his revolutionary ideas that earned him both his staunchest defenders and his most bitter critics.

Spinoza has properly been acknowledged as the father of modern biblical criticism. If he had done nothing else, this alone would mark him as one of the pioneers of the Enlightenment movement that revolutionized the intellectual and political life of Europe. By pointing out the repetitions that proliferated in the biblical narrative, Spinoza precipitated a debate that was to continue long after he died. The Bible was the creation of human beings, not of God. The impact of this assertion was shattering and earned its author a few admirers and an army of enemies. The birth of biblical criticism was hardly an innocent event; Spinoza was quite aware that it marked the beginning of an attack on all forms of traditional religious belief. His skepticism about the Bible's authorship led him to his most enduring, and also controversial, conclusion: the world itself, with its intricate beauty and complexity, is not the object of an external craftsman, but is in itself the totality of what God is. Simultaneously, Spinoza's unrelenting attack upon the historic marriage of church and state lay the intellectual groundwork for the social and political revolutions that were to emerge in the following century.

How is it possible to reconcile Spinoza's bitter criticism of the biblical prophets with his advocacy of a religion based upon justice? What bothered him was not the moral message of the prophets but their attitude. They claim to speak the word of God — these self-anointed amateurs — and this assumption is as absurd as the pompous self-assurance with which they speak. How dare they — Spinoza seems to be delivering the rebuttal at Beth-el — how dare they maintain that their message comes directly from God, a God who manipulates them and puts words in their mouth? "They provoked rather than corrected . . . they scold and reprove."[209]

The prophetic insistence that God was the source of their ideas was not merely false, Spinoza argued; more fatally, it perpetuated an unsustainable idea of God. For all their "admonitions, warnings, chidings, and denunciations," the prophets seemed "rather to have excited than improved the people, who would have yielded and been corrected had they been addressed by their king or chiefs."[210]

But there is praise too, and with it an appreciation of the moral focus that the prophets brought to their religion. The prophets become God's instruments, for it is through them that "God seeks from human beings no other knowledge of himself but the knowledge of his divine Justice and Charity — that is, such attributes of God as human beings can imitate by a certain plan of living."[211]

What lay behind Spinoza's attitude toward the prophets? The answer to this question connects Spinoza in unanticipated ways to a modern understanding of the interstitial analysis. In his opposition to the "excessive claims" of the biblical prophets he opened the way for viewing the prophets as moral individuals rather than as puppets of an unseen deity. Their voices now seem urgent in a way that is both egalitarian and rational. For the interstitial prophet relies for inspiration not on some divine *bat kol* (voice from heaven) but rather upon a rational contemplation of a God of justice and charity.

It was his skepticism about the prophets that led Spinoza to launch another assault — this time on Judaism's most venerated philosopher. Maimonides, he felt, had betrayed his own rationality by extolling the role of the prophet and, more significantly, by insisting that the Bible could be interpreted in a way that made it totally consistent with reason. Maimonides should have exposed the Bible as the "fiction that it was." In one sense, of course, the two thinkers, separated by so many centuries, sought to achieve the same goal; they wanted to adapt Holy Scripture to a new way of thinking. Maimonides wanted to do away with biblical superstition by rationalizing it. Spinoza merely wanted to do away with it altogether.

Spinoza and Maimonides had one other thing in common. Both thinkers held elitist views. Maimonides felt that his famous *Guide* would be understood by only a few intellectuals; Spinoza was convinced that most humans were so consumed by their own passions and fears (most notably their fear of death) that they would remain unmoved by his appeal to reason. He also felt that most of the biblical myths were intended to instill fear and a respect for authority in the minds of people who were incapable of reasoning for themselves.

Spinoza believed in the separation of church and state. His skepticism toward the prophetic claim to authority becomes more understandable when it is viewed in its historical perspective. In the seventeenth century, Holland's struggle to divorce itself from Spain's religious domination was still fresh in everyone's mind. Religious leaders, many liberal thinkers believed, should not be entrusted with political power. The Inquisition had left its indelible impression. The tenacity of its grip left a residue that supported religious conformity. Many of those who sought to release that grip were consistent in their opposition to any intrusion of religion into secular life. For Spinoza, and for those who sympathized with him, the prophets, for all their rebelliousness, for all their eloquence, remained a religious intrusion.

The quintessential progenitor of the Age of Enlightenment! That is how Jonathan Israel among others has described the many ways in which

Spinoza's dramatic break with the past influenced the thinking of later Enlightenment philosophers. "Can one thinker meaningfully be said to have forged a line of thought which furnished the philosophical matrix, including the idea of evolution, of the entire radical wing of the European Enlightenment, an ideological stance subscribed to by dozens of writers and thinkers right across the continent from Ireland to Russia and from Sweden to Iberia?" "The answer," says Israel, anointing Spinoza as the most consistent of all Enlightenment thinkers, "arguably is yes."[212]

The Enlightenment, of course, meant many things to different thinkers. But the one consistent theme that the Age always epitomized was openness to all kinds of knowledge. Voltaire and Rousseau, Locke and Hume, Kant and Lessing — all welcomed the new insights of science. More important than anything else, even truth itself, as Lessing famously asserted, was nothing more or less than the "search for truth."

The opponents of the Enlightenment feared its new insights, its challenges to the authority they held so dear. The enemies were invariably the remnants of feudal authority, the military, and the established churches — the forces, in other words, that felt most threatened by the new insights which the Enlightenment advocated. They were joined by the uneducated masses who perceived a threat to their values in the new openness to knowledge.

Like Hobbes who preceded him, Spinoza advocated a strong central state. His reasons, however, had little to do with any love of nationalism. It had everything to do with his mistrust of organized religion. His own experiences with *Talmud Torah* congregation in Amsterdam certainly impressed upon him the unpleasant aspects of religious authority. Of course Spinoza was not alone in his wariness of organized religion. But is it fair to characterize leaders of the Enlightenment as anti-religious? What they did fight for — and in this they almost spoke with one voice — was the ultimate separation of the church from the state. Early in his career, Spinoza, much as Hobbes had done earlier, insisted that a strong civil government is necessary, not only to maintain peace and order, but also to guarantee the religious freedom of every citizen. For a while it seemed that his excessive mistrust of religion had grown in direct proportion to his excessive endorsement of the government.

From Hobbes, Spinoza inherited the idea that a basic impulse of all human beings was to affirm and protect their own essential being. For Spinoza, this human impulse is called *conatus*. In the *Tractatus*, he asserted that our self-interests (our *conatus*) dominate all our relationships. For

Spinoza, *conatus* was more psychological than political. Our self-interests, he reasoned, do not prompt us to act in the political arena as solitary individuals. Instead they enable us to recognize that we can subdue our passions; we can cooperate with other human beings, and use our wisdom to live *sub specie aeternitatus* — under the spell of eternity. To live under the spell of eternity is to understand our true self-interest, and to be intellectually part of nature — to be intellectually, in other words, part of God.

Spinoza famously has been branded as a pantheist — that is how the world has come to regard him — and in the popular imagination, pantheists were hardly to be distinguished from atheists. If God is in everything, what distinctive meaning does the word "God" have? Spinoza remained an atheist, not only in the eyes of his own synagogue in Amsterdam but to generations of theologians. To one respected French theologian of his time, he was "that insane and evil man"; another could label him "the most impious and the most dangerous man of the century." By 1708, a Leipzig cleric felt it necessary to arm German professors with concise Latin philosophical arguments so that they could combat the atheism of Spinoza and the thinkers sympathetic to his ideas.

Of course, there was another view of Spinoza. He was a "God-intoxicated philosopher." The poet Novalis (Friedrich von Hardenberg) described him in this way, and Bertrand Russell hailed him as the "noblest and most lovable of the great philosophers."[213] Aside from his "lovability" there is something profoundly reverent and even holy in Spinoza's approach to the divinity of the universe. In the introduction to his edition of the complete Spinoza, Michael Morgan observes that Spinoza "did not shy away from religious terminology, the vocabulary of the Judaism and Christianity with which he was so familiar. Indeed, it is a remarkable feature of his temperament that his thinking never totally rejected religious themes, beliefs and vocabulary, as much as it sought to refine and refashion them." As a matter of fact Spinoza became so ecstatic about his own concept of God that in one of his earliest writings he suggested that those who understood what he was trying to say would be utterly transformed by their new insights. When we "become aware of these excellent effects, then we may say with truth *that we have been born again.*"[214]

Philosophical dualism was the demon that was the real object of Spinoza's attack. From Plato and Aristotle and even up to Descartes, whose mechanistic view of the universe Spinoza both admired and criticized, dualistic thinking had been taken for granted. The dichotomies took a variety of names — body and soul, mind and matter, thought and extension — but they invariably assumed that the universe could not be truly understood without acknowledging the presence of two distinct but equally necessary forces. Spinoza regarded all such dual views of nature as faulty, and he was determined to puncture the fallacious thinking that had produced them. The resulting monism which was a critical part of his philosophy troubled, inspired, and challenged Enlightenment thinkers for generations.

God must be understood in terms of reason and not mere wishful thinking — that was the persistent message of our radical lens grinder. Like Descartes, Spinoza insisted that reason must be based on "clear and distinct ideas" and the clearest of these ideas is God. In this formulation there is no place for either superstition or for miracles. The happy human being is one who understands the power and the inevitable judgment of nature. To do the good is to acknowledge nature, to live rationally within its laws. To have a true idea of God, Spinoza insisted over and over again, we must understand that God is indeed nature. And as his philosophical thinking matured he became ever more convinced that the universe consisted of a magnificent unity, and that God was not separate from, but identical with, that unity. It is at this point that Spinoza's mathematical background encountered his Jewish background.

When Spinoza uses the word "Nature," does he mean the same thing we do? His identification of nature with God has enraged traditional theologians. Yet his idea of nature lies at the very center of his revolutionary philosophy. Utilizing a distinction that can be traced back to Aristotle, Spinoza invoked two Latin phrases to describe the totality of nature — *Natura naturans* and *Natura naturata*. *Natura naturans* is nature in action. It is free and unfettered. It is God, active and creative. *Natura naturata*, on the other hand, is the created universe that is in God but is not God. In reality, *Natura naturans* describes God as the necessary cause of all things, while *Natura naturata* encompasses everything that follows from this necessity, things such as human desires including love and all of the emotions and aspirations of the human mind. Again, and perhaps to oversimplify, *Natura naturans* may be described as nature "naturing" or doing what nature does, while *Natura naturata* is nature "being acted upon". It is important to understand that for Spinoza these two aspects of nature do not point to a division in nature, but rather offer an explanation of how nature works. Both are essential features of the same God. But it is

Natura naturans, nature as changing and evolving, that opens a door to wonder and even to reverence.[215]

In his speculations about the natural world, Spinoza was far ahead of his time. Ideas about the unified structure of nature that seemed so heretical in the seventeenth century have now become subjects of serious speculation by modern scientists. Of course, Spinoza had no way of knowing how Darwinian concepts of evolution would confront his own idea of a universe that created itself and was self-moving, nor could he foresee the profound impact that Einstein's physics would have upon modern views of the relationship between time and space. Yet in anticipation of both Darwin and Einstein, Spinoza's idea of *Natura naturans*, nature in its "active form," opens the door to a hylozoic concept of deity, a concept that bears important affinities with modern scientific thought. In consonance with Spinoza's naturalism, hylozoism insists that humans and animals as well as plants and other life forms, all arise from one material source. In its modern formulation, hylozoism argues that all nature as well as God participate in a process of continual development. Thus, hylozoism is comfortable with the view that God-Nature, far from being static and inert, is constantly changing and evolving.

More relevant is the claim that Spinoza's theories actually made evolutionary thinking possible; that a line might be drawn, unsteady as it may appear, between the cramped quarters of the lens grinder at The Hague and the cramped quarters of the naturalist aboard the *Beagle*. If Spinoza's view of the universe did not lead directly to Darwin it certainly created a climate hospitable to a re-examination of the relationship between human and animal life. Is not a monistic philosophy in which humans and animals are both part of God-Nature entirely compatible with Darwin's revolutionary ideas about the primitive origins of our species?

It is in his *Ethics* that Spinoza spells out his reasons for understanding God as nature. Starting with a geometric formulation, he reaches God through a process of subtraction. Relying upon what he calls reason, he subtracts those finite things which are supposed to distinguish various substances from one another. The goal of the subtraction process is to discover that which is ultimately real. In the final analysis, he concludes, everything can be reduced to one substance, a substance that is absolutely necessary. That ultimate substance is infinite. It is God. The Kabbalists subtracted God from the world; Spinoza subtracted the world from God — and found that one was meaningless without the other. The resulting monism was as revolutionary as it was unique.

Over the years there has been a noticeable thaw in relations between the Jewish community and its most notorious heretic. In 1978, for example, the Hebrew Union College-Jewish Institute of Religion commemorated the 300th anniversary of Spinoza's death by devoting a full weekend to the Dutch philosopher's ideas. Professor Eugene Mihaly acknowledged the compatibility of the Jewish idea of *tzimtzum* with Spinoza's concept of God. As evidence, Mihaly offered two commentaries, one from the Midrash and one from Spinoza himself: Why is the Holy One Blessed be He, called "Place?" Because He is the Place of the world, but the world is not His place. (Genesis Rabbah LXVIII.II) Whatever is, is in God, and without God nothing can be or be conceived. (*Ethics*, Part I, Prop.XV)[216]

Nature itself has a power, that is active and not passive, a power that is holy. The essence of Spinoza's determinism is summed up in his *Ethics* with a few sentences that are worth repeating in their entirety: "With these demonstrations," he writes, "I have explained God's nature and purposes: that he exists necessarily: that he is unique: that he is and acts from the necessity alone of his nature: that (and how) he is the free cause of all things; that all things are in God and so depend on him that without him they can neither be nor be conceived; and finally, that all things have been predetermined by God, not from freedom of the will or absolute good pleasure, but from God's absolute nature or infinite power."[217]

It is hardly surprising that Spinoza's unitary view of the universe should have come under attack. The criticisms began with Leibniz, the German philosopher, who actually felt compelled to meet Spinoza in person. Because he could not accept Spinoza's concept of nature as a unity, Leibniz introduced the idea of a plurality of substances. Every substance, except the one simple substance that represented divinity, carried a spiritual core, a "monad." Each monad, in turn, was surrounded by other subservient monads that facilitated a network of relationships with other substances. It remained for Immanuel Kant to carry the argument one step further. Nature could not possibly be understood without reference to the human mind. Since Kant it has become rare for any philosopher to think of nature as having a reality outside of the mind of the perceiver. Yet it is the monism of Spinoza, and not the dualism implicit in Kant's thinking, that seems relevant to our scientific times.

In our own age, as religious tensions continue to escalate and the chasm between religious and secular forces continues to grows, Spinoza's ideas point to a new kind of faith. This new faith offers a God who is not expected to intervene in human affairs, not expected to perform miracles, but nevertheless can be venerated as the essence of all that exists. Can men and women be expected to worship such a God? For Spinoza and for later generations made cynical by the Holocaust and by the shallow displays of religious piety, the answer may surely be an affirmative one. Spinoza's challenge is a rigorous one. His religion will "work no miracles for you; it will tender no affection; show no sign of concern about your well-being… Spinoza's God is so indifferent, in fact, that one may even ask whether it is reasonable to love it."[218] The question remains — the answer, still open to debate.

Contrary to the suspicion of many of his critics, Spinoza's naturalism was not a pessimistic doctrine. In the face of nature at its most threatening moments, and surely in the presence of impending disaster, human beings are able to come together in order to lend mutual assistance to one another. Toward the end of his *Ethics*, Spinoza points to a critical aspect of the interstitial role — the vital necessity of alliances. It is appropriate for human beings, he writes, to band together in an effort to gain freedom for all and to struggle against selfishness and oppression. Thus, as important as it is for individuals to express their own righteous convictions, it is even more laudable when these individual commitments result in a community committed to justice. "Minds are conquered not by arms," he suggests, "but by love and nobility." Therefore, "it is especially useful to men to form associations, to bind themselves by those bonds most apt to make one people of them, and also to do those things which serve to strengthen friendships."[219]

The suspicion that Spinoza's thought left little room for human freedom persisted throughout the philosopher's entire life. Does the identification of God with nature destroy free will or free speech? Nowhere is any effort to unify God with nature more troublesome than in the matter of freedom of the will. Traditional Jewish thought, of course always maintained the duality of God and man, mind and matter, body and soul. Efforts to reconcile an all-powerful deity with human freedom led the rabbis into many troubling compromises, culminating in the well-known assertion that "though all is foreseen, free will is given." (*Pirkei Avot*, 3.14) Spinoza faced a similar dilemma but handled it quite differently.

Human freedom is an inherent aspect of the world of nature. And *conatus* explains why it is so essential; the key is self-interest. Even in a deterministic world, humans act to preserve their own well-being. The natural impulse of men and women to seek their own preservation not only encourages them to seek freedom, but it also enables them to unite with one another in the quest for a better life. As tempting as it is to picture Spinoza's effort to wed human behavior and nature as a negation of free will, it should be noted that the entire twentieth chapter of his Ethical Political Treatise is devoted to a defense of both freedom of thought and freedom of speech.

But paradoxically, and somewhat controversially, freedom is linked to a strong and virtuous government. Like Hobbes, Spinoza believed that human beings sacrifice some of their rights in order to obtain the protection of a secular government. It is here that Spinoza offers two insights that are crucial to the interstitial analysis. The first is that, even at in its most powerful manifestation, government's power can control only actions; it can never dominate freedom of thought or forbid freedom of speech. At the onset of the Enlightenment the requirements of a true democracy are thus posited in language that acknowledges both the role of government and the rights of the individual.

Spinoza's second insight raises an issue that, despite its apparent straightforwardness, has become surprisingly controversial — namely the right to organize. It is acknowledged that by the end of the eighteenth century in the American Colonies, the right to assemble and to seek a "redress of grievances" were regarded as so essential that they were incorporated into the first paragraph of the Constitution's Bill of Rights. Inherent in the right to assemble is the right to organize. Does it lead us too far afield to point out that in many circles the right to assemble has faced growing challenges and that the community organizer has been subjected to increasing criticism? Disruptive and even unpatriotic — these are some of the charges aimed at the community organizer. Repeatedly and unequivocally Spinoza endorsed the idea that men and women need to come together and cooperate with one another in order to identify and protect basic social interests. Freedom is more than an individual matter; it is attained and guaranteed through individuals coming together to build a community.

It is the state, the secular government that must always be the guarantor of these freedoms. If the primary role of religion is to pursue acts of charity and justice, the primary role of the state is to guarantee that religion will always have the right to seek the just society without interference from any outside authority. The state can pursue no wiser course than to judge men and women solely by their actions and to guarantee that no test be placed on their beliefs. This view of religion has had a profound impact upon religious thinking.[220]

In the midst of modern debates about the role of religion in public life, it is helpful to keep Spinoza's ideas in mind. There are questions stimulated by Spinoza's analysis. Should religion be a private matter or should it be allowed to enter into the public sphere? May clergy endorse a particular candidate? Should the government fund the service activities of religious institutions? Should the government have the power to investigate and regulate the private lives of its citizens? Spinoza would be skeptical of outside interference that impacts upon human freedom. But he would endorse one form of religious activism. Religious groups should be advocates for the poor, the oppressed, and the powerless. Religious communities have a legitimate right to lend help to those who are helpless and give a voice to those who lack an advocate.

There is another context in which it is clear that Spinoza's definition of God was never intended to discourage religious initiatives. The very godliness of nature implies a responsibility to protect and observe the world that is identical with God. In this context it is helpful to be reminded of Abraham Joshua Heschel's oft-repeated warning that "Judaism is not a science of nature, but a science of what man ought to do with nature." Spinoza, of course would go much further. In eliminating miracles and divine intervention, he implicitly makes the protection of nature much more than simply one of many virtuous things to do. The true worship of God requires a profound reverence for nature. Acts that preserve the world in which we live are the very essence of our nature as human beings; they are part of our own godliness.

Standing in the presence of Spinoza's nature we are invited to confront two other aspects of modern life — our fears and our passions. Like the ancient Stoics, Spinoza believed that human fear lies at the root of religious superstition. We love and we hate, we are afraid one moment and filled with confidence the next. The challenge which confronts us all is to understand and to liberate — to understand the true nature of the universe and to liberate ourselves from the irrational, and often dangerous, passions that enslave us. This is precisely what we can hope to achieve when we learn to view our actions as part of God-Nature, in other words, when we learn to live *sub specie aeternitatus* — "under the aspect of eternity." What Spinoza was suggesting is that all of us can learn to surmount our prejudices, our fears and class interests, and live a life that moves toward harmony with the entire universe. To achieve this harmony with nature, we have to pursue an intellectual and ethical path — a path that leads to a true love of God — *amour dei intellectualis*. Spinoza wrote in the language of ancient Rome; his ideas, tested by time, emerge as the language of a very contemporary mind.

Is it possible to reconcile Spinoza's philosophy with any recognizable form of traditional Jewish ideas about a God? The problem, of course, is not with Spinoza's ethics but with his metaphysics. Under a religious system inspired by Spinoza's thinking, why in the world should human beings remain religious? If God and nature are one, then what meaning can be ascribed to any attempt to maintain a distinct Jewish endeavor? And ultimately, if philosophical dualism has been overcome in Spinoza's unitary theory, why should any single religious system, including Judaism, persist in vaunting its own uniqueness?

The social, not to mention the spiritual, consequences of these objections threaten to undermine Spinoza's entire rigorous appeal. The whole history of a people, including its customs and ceremonies — and even its moral values — might easily be dismissed as obsolete, relics of an archaic and useless relic. And indeed, a rigid and uncritical reading of Spinoza can lead to the feeling that one has been left to wander in a spiritual desert.

So then, how does the contemporary Spinoza advocate respond to these charges? More germane to this study, how does Spinoza's seemingly austere analysis relate to the interstitial destiny of the Jewish community? Spinoza's philosophy challenges us to take the "universal" implications of Judaism most seriously. A religious view of the universe that stresses reverence for nature, while avoiding paganism or trivialization, is long overdue. As mechanical as Spinoza's words may at first sound, they nevertheless convey a powerful assessment of the physical world around us. Here God's majestic response to Job's loss of faith comes to mind: "Where were you when I laid the foundations of the earth?" (Job 38.4) Our modern world has too often treated nature as an object to be used and misused rather than as something to be considered godly. A challenge to guard and protect nature and its human life is a necessary component of any approach to a world in which cooperation triumphs over bloody competition, conservation over mindless consumption.

It took a twentieth-century Jew steeped in atheism to recognize the ultimate compatibility of this aspect of Spinoza's philosophy with contemporary moral values. Speaking from the perspective of his radical Marxist spirit, Isaac Deutscher observed that "Spinoza's ethics were no longer the Jewish ethics, but the ethics of man at large — just as his God was no longer the Jewish God; his God merged with nature, shed his separate and distinctive divine destiny. Yet, in a way, Spinoza's God and ethics were still Jewish, except that his was Jewish monotheism carried to its logical conclusion and the Jewish universal God thought out to the end; and once thought out to the end, that God ceased to be Jewish."[221] In a rebuttal of Deutscher's critique, it can be suggested that both Spinoza's God and his ethics remain congenial to Judaism, provided the full dimensions of Jewish tradition are acknowledged. "Subdue and conquer it" says the commercial profiteer, quoting the first chapter of Genesis. "Replenish it," quotes the Spinozist, turning to the same text. Always, always "replenish it."

There is another aspect of Spinoza's thinking that is congenial to an interstitial understanding of Judaism. Surprising as it may seem, this congruence is to be found in the Dutch philosopher's deep optimism about the human condition. Human beings are capable of achieving the things that are ultimately good for them and consistent with the totality of God. To take Spinoza seriously is to confront and overcome the anxieties that characterize the human condition. And so, in addition to his view of the holiness of nature, Spinoza's calm analysis of human anxiety is increasingly relevant. He projects a world in which our fears and passions are offered, not false promises and visions of eternal salvation, but a rational assessment of our place in the world. In this world each human being is a "child of God." Spinoza would not have used that language, but in its metaphoric sense it is faithful to the logic of his thought as well as to the language of traditional Judaism. A world sated with war and hatreds based upon conflicting religious and social appeals to power would be well served by a belief system that can treat the precipitating anxieties and fears as truly dysfunctional. This goal may be easier to articulate than to achieve, but there is poetry and beauty in its appeal — more, there is also hope.

Like so many of the Enlightenment philosophers who followed him, our great lens grinder was skeptical of all mythologies. Spinoza's effort was always to distinguish between superstitious mythology and a God who could be understood only through ideas that are "clear and distinct." How clear and distinct can a language be that continually delights in extracting new meaning from even the most arcane of symbolisms? In this context, Midrash, the interpretation of the text, continues to represent both peril and opportunity. *Midrashim* may be invoked in defense of primitive and superstition-filled biblical passages; on the other hand, they may infuse these same passages with a more charitable and humane impulse.

To "reconstruct philosophy" within the Jewish community it is always necessary to respect both text and traditions. "Respect" need not lead to calcification. The text is a vital guide, not a calcified skeleton drawn from the depths of a Jewish dead sea. Yet questions arise concerning deep-seated Jewish convictions and practices. What happens to tradition in a Jewish world that takes Spinoza seriously? Shall we degrade Passover, Judaism's most popular holiday, where incredible and sometimes bloody miracles are joined to a text that annually urges us to review the contemporary meaning of freedom? Shall we nullify Rosh Hashanah and Yom Kippur with their awesome portrayal of a judgmental God combined with their compelling invitation to self-examination and self-renewal? Can the holiday invocations of God as judge or God as father retain any of their powerful imagery despite their gender insensitive and archaic theology? Much of this imagery, it must be admitted, persists in defiance of Spinoza's unsparing rationalism. But does a less than literal interpretation of these rituals really cripple the moral and spiritual rock upon which Judaism stands? And are not most thoughtful Jews ready and able to accommodate the relationship, symbiotic as it may be, that a marriage of Spinozism and Judaism would create?

In writing about the Enlightenment, Louis Dupre asserts that "people's everyday lives are rarely ruled by reason, despite their frequent appeals to it."[222] This gap between reason and behavior is one of the great obstacles confronting any attempt to bring Spinoza from the sixteenth century into the twenty-first. But in this case, the effort seems time well spent. Spinoza's ethical system, writes Louis Dupre, "shows none of the one-sidedness of rationalism. . . . . Indeed, his position displays a moral realism seldom encountered since Aristotle. His method of overcoming the disruptive power of emotions by insight, a central theme of his thought, anticipates a basic principle of modern psychotherapy. At the same time, his conception of the blessed life aims higher than any other modern system of ethics. None surpassed and only Kant equated the scope of Spinoza's moral vision.[223]

In November of 1676, just a few months before his untimely and mysterious death, Spinoza was visited by one of the inventors of calculus, the great German philosopher Gottfried Wilhelm Leibniz. Drawn to Spinoza by an attraction that would remain with him all his life, Leibniz did not allow his hostile predisposition toward the Jewish heretic to interfere with his need to see him in person. "Horrible" and "terrifying" — these were the words he had earlier used to describe Spinoza. Still he came.

Did the visit last a week or only a few hours? Even the meticulous records Leibniz kept of his daily activities provide no reliable answer. Regardless of its duration, the meeting, the visit seemed to have confounded the opinions of the guest and confirmed those of his host. Although we know little about what was actually spoken between the two philosophers, we do know that throughout the rest of his life Leibniz alternately attacked and succumbed to the ideas of the modest pipe-smoking lens grinder who had hosted him at The Hague.[224]

At the time of his death, Spinoza was living in simple rented quarters in the house of his friends, the Van der Spijks. His quarters were sparse and the paucity of his physical possessions offered stark contrast to the multiplicity of friends who were intensely loyal to him. It was a Sunday afternoon and the Van der Spijks had left home to attend Sunday afternoon church services unaware that their tenant and dear friend would no longer be alive when they returned.

Baruch Spinoza was an interstitial Jew in unique ways. Like Hannah Arendt's idealized pariah, he found himself isolated not only from the Jewish community but also from much of non-Jewish society in Holland. Yet his own humility and intellectual honesty made him an object of wide interest and of growing respect. One of his biographers lovingly noted, "Children, young men, his servants, all who stood to him in any relation of dependence, seem to have felt the charm of his affability and sweetness of temper."[225]

Chapter 12

Responding to the Challenge

Judaism is a religion that assigns paramount importance to action as opposed to meditation. This is not to deny the persistence of many mystical movements within Judaism, but rather to acknowledge a bias toward action rather than meditation. It is not what a person thinks, but what a person does that truly matters. And, for Maimonides, at least, what one does is prescribed by no less than 613 commandments. To be Jewish means that you do not bless bread at a meal without at least tasting the bread. To neglect following a prayer with appropriate action is to be guilty of uttering a *b'racha l'vatala*, a prayer recited in vain. Nevertheless, in the face of explicit ceremonial and ritual prescriptions, concern for justice and the welfare of others have persisted throughout the ages.

The intellectual fire kindled in the seventeenth and eighteenth centuries has not been quenched. Enlightenment philosophy stimulated a tremendous desire for freedom, a desire, potent enough to stimulate the revolutions that occurred in both America and France. Its impact upon religious thought continues to be profound. In particular, the radical philosophy that Spinoza so convincingly developed retains its power as a tremendous religious challenge.

What follows is an effort to re-examine Spinoza's thought and to reconcile it with modern Judaism. Such a reassessment need not entail a denial of the Jewish past; it does, however, invite a thoughtful reassessment of the Jewish future. This process inevitably evokes some troubling questions. Are venerated Jewish texts amenable to emendations or to interpretations in which the demands of reason prevail over historic assumptions of Jewish exceptionalism? Does Judaism lose its vitality once its mythology as well as many of its practices is scrutinized and re-evaluated?

There are problematic areas toward which our examination of Spinoza must lead. Can the Jewish community question its moral traditions without succumbing to one of two extremes — either seeming to confirm the ancient calumnies of anti-Semites or inviting the accusation that its self-examination is motivated by self-hating Jews? The task is a sensitive one, none more sensitive than the need to explore the troubled historic relationship between Jews and money. It is not enough to point out that many of the problems in this area stem from the oppressive restrictions historically imposed upon the Jews. Despite this history, far too many Jews, for whatever reasons, remain involved in practices that are financially questionable and morally reprehensible. What is the obligation of an interstitially positive Jewish community as it confronts the financial practices of those whose behavior remains so problematic? To this question Spinoza's life as much as his thought hints at an answer. By the accounts of his contemporaries, Spinoza led a life of quiet modesty even as he remained indifferent to anything that would lead to his own self-enrichment. His philosophy, too, suggests that wealth and welfare are umbilicaly connected.

As magisterial as Spinoza's philosophical framework is, the feeling persists that when it comes to translating his ideas into a modern context something is missing. Is it his sense of warmth? His awareness of something we might call "holy?" Or perhaps it is his seeming indifference to a community's need to respond collectively in a time of crisis? To raise these questions is not to dismiss the Dutch philosopher's powerful logic but to clear the way for a reappraisal of his major theme. Such a reappraisal must begin with an examination of his identification of God with nature. Spinoza's search for the meaning of God ought not to sound so strange to a people who daily repeat the words of the *Shema*, that powerful prayer affirming the oneness of God. Here, at least, philosopher and tradition can meet in a new assessment of both the moral and scientific implications of a world under increasing stress. It should be remembered that Spinoza titled his book about God *The Ethics*. His quest for an understanding of the passions that dominate the human experience, for the elimination of avarice and greed, for a mastery of fear, and for a world in which human beings cooperate with one another in the pursuit of the common good — all reveal a brilliant mind struggling for consistency and truth.

These admirable goals are not so easily attainable. Reason and nature, as Ernest Gellner has pointed out, were the two great deities of the Enlightenment. They were "highly complementary and indeed mutually interdependent, though also in conflict . . . so, if data alone justify our convictions, we have no right whatsoever to believe in the perpetuation of an orderly nature."[226] The problem is not the past but the future The past may be discernible, but it is not a prophet. Nature is fragile; reason is fallible — and humans treat the world as though it is a charitable foundation with unlimited resources. Any effort to deal with the Enlightenment movement's seminal thinker must begin with an acknowledgement of the inherent difficulties involved in any effort to marry reason and nature. Once the difficulty is acknowledged, the task of confronting the holiness of nature becomes much more manageable,

If God and nature are one, how can we understand the damage that human behavior has inflicted upon our world? Modern man has learned how to assault nature, and if the blows are not yet fatal, they carry the potential of becoming so. God under attack! Human beings have misused nature to foster global warming, to pollute vital natural resources, and to create weapons capable of terminating life as we know it. At the same time, the realization that we are capable of acting to protect nature, to explore the universe, and to prolong life is an indication that human activity may be benign as well as malevolent. The possibility of a relationship in which humans possess the power to penetrate nature, whether for good or for evil, is one that Spinoza failed to fully acknowledge. But Spinoza was right to warn us that any such relationship was destined to failure should it neglect to recognize the divine unity with nature. It was as he confronted both the profundity and the mystery of this unity that Spinoza declared that he had been "born again."

God and nature are one — that was the theme that Spinoza consistently maintained. But to picture either one as helplessly entwined in the arms of the other is to surrender to Spinoza's darker vision. The facts of nature reveal a reality that cannot be denied. The universe, beginning with the Big Bang which set it in motion, obediently observes the "laws of nature." And these natural laws exert their inevitable influence upon human destiny. Evolution itself reveals the scientific process at work; genetic changes do indeed occur, and atmospheric intruders such as smog, mercury and lead, possess the power to leave humans at the mercy of natural forces. In the face of inevitable natural change, the role of human activity becomes all the more important. A challenge to organized religion is to truly understand the synthesis of God and nature, to recognize that neither is the enemy of the other, and to act to make the synthesis an ever more meaningful reality.

But is not the simple admission that human activity can have an effect on nature prima facie evidence of a troublesome dichotomy, one that challenges any monistic theory advocating the unity of God and nature? Surely, to the extent that humans, as a result of either greed or fear, succeed in degrading the natural world, the idea of nature as identical with God is severely challenged. And even when human activity seeks to repair the world, the effort exposes an obvious dualism. Does not this dualism compel us to admit that human activity and divine activity may be moving in directions that are clearly distinct from one another, if not actually hostile to one another?

Acknowledgment of an active human involvement with nature leads inevitably to the problem of freedom. Despite his effort to deal with the issue of the freedom of the will, Spinoza's defense of this crucial idea leaves many questions unanswered. To insist that God and nature are identical may appear to question the possibility of freedom by aggrandizing science and diminishing man. Is it reasonable to regard humans as helpless subjects of a divine power that neither feels nor responds? The problem is an ancient one. The rabbis tried to solve it by declaring: All is foreseen, yet free will is given. In Spinoza's day, as in ours too, acknowledging the new role of science was an important antidote to the superstition which had permeated most religious systems. But despite all the assaults directed at it, religion still stubbornly claims an independent role for itself.

Spinoza would insist that human beings are in possession of the intellectuals tools needed to understand God. The importance of intelligence is that it can expose motives and actions that are selfish and destructive. In this sense alone the task of "discovering nature" becomes a sacred one. All else follows from this! Whether the task is to probe the distant stars, or deal with the plight of an unemployed steelworker, the challenge to create a synthesis between science and religion remains a daunting one. It is not enough to insist that the religious must accept the new insights that science has no offer. Nor is it satisfying to suggest that life becomes meaningful as we learn to stand in awe before the magisterial power of nature. No matter how rational we wish to become there are still things we cannot understand. There are still disasters that shatter a community. There is still terror in the face of death. There is still a need for prayer, for a community willing to raise its voice: "Choose life that thou mayest live."

Religion continues to be a vital part of human life. It stubbornly offers values that are interesting, consoling, and inspiring. These remain values that no scientific or mathematical analysis seems able to suppress. While science remains value neutral, religion is constantly challenged to render moral judgments. The challenge faced by modern religion is to simultaneously acknowledge the power of science's neutrality while confronting science with another power that is seldom neutral — the search for what is good. It is this power that Spinoza sought to explore as he sat down to write his *Ethics*. It emerges now demanding a larger role than Spinoza seemed willing to acknowledge.

Is Spinoza's philosophy devoid of spirituality or is it worth fighting for? These questions were raised by Jonathan Stewart in his brief but fascinating account of the Leibniz visit with Spinoza in the summer of 1676. The answer to both questions Stewart suggests is a resounding "no." Spinoza's religion is not devoid of spirituality. The awesome majesty of nature, the need to defend and preserve it, the holiness of nature's children — all of these topics are worthy of the most profound reverence. Spinoza's philosophy leads to a view of the world not as a universal marketplace where there are assets to be exploited and exported, but rather to a view of a universe that needs to be cherished and preserved. As to whether Spinoza's religion is worth fighting for, Spinoza himself would undoubtedly insist that religion is not an area that should be hospitable to any form of competitive conflict. Why? Because, arguments about religion are meaningless and are based upon a failure to understand the fact that God is inseparable from "all that is."

It has been observed that although history has given us its Kantians and Hegelians, there is no school of thought that bears the name of Spinoza. It is hard to understand why this is so; Spinoza spent his life fighting for many of the principles we now take for granted. Yet to really understand his thinking is to undergo a transformative experience; it is, as Spinoza himself testified, to be "born again." To perpetuate Spinoza's enthusiasm, however, is not to remain indifferent to the challenges that must still be encountered.

A modern religion based on Spinoza's thinking needs to banish prejudice and superstition, but it also needs to accommodate those impulses that have made spiritual values such a compelling influence in human history. It needs song and myth. It needs laughter. And for most people, the need for prayer persists — even when reason insists that prayer must be divorced from all promises of reward or threats of punishment. Spinoza himself was quite aware that human beings needed more than the comfort of cold logic. Toward the end of the *Tractatus,* he gave expression to a thought that is perfectly congenial with the joy of Sabbath and many of the Jewish festivals: "In my opinion no more effective means can be devised to influence men's minds, for nothing can so captivate the mind as joy, springing from devotion that is love mingled with awe."[227]

In preparation for the task of adapting Spinoza's thinking to a modern and progressive religion, two important teachers can be welcomed into the dialogue. The first is Joseph Soloveitchik, (1903–1993) a revered leader of Orthodox Jewry. From Boston and New York where he lived and taught, Soloveitchik saw his influence spread throughout the intellectual world of traditional Judaism. The second is Emmanuel Levinas (1906–1995) the French Jewish Talmudist and phenomenologist, who was an intellectual model for Jacques Derrida, the founder of philosophical deconstructionism. At first these two appear to be an unlikely pair; Soloveitchik, the epitome of Orthodox traditionalism, and Levinas, a model for many of the radical young French postmodernists. Whereas the Orthodox Soloveitchik remained sensitive to the traditional view that every word of the Bible was revealed at Mount Sinai, Levinas, the pioneering phenomenologist, found meaning in isolated passages which he characteristically divorced from their historical context. Despite their significant differences, these seminal thinkers offer insights that are compatible with many of Spinoza's radical views about the meaning of religion and ethics.

Mutually dedicated to the exploration of traditional Jewish texts; both were concerned with the ethical implications of these texts. And both recognized that Judaism's greatest moments came when its traditions demanded a look into the face of the "other," the poor, the sick, the powerless. For them Passover was not merely an annual observance replete with dietary restrictions and memories of an ancient liberation. It was, as the Haggadah insists, a constant reminder to care for those who are homeless and hungry. At Passover, the door of every observant home is opened so that the prophet Elijah may enter. Who is Elijah? He is everyone, or, perhaps, no one. The open door is the answer to the important challenge of the Passover Seder: "Let everyone who is hungry come and eat." Soloveitchik and Levinas constantly sought the meaning of that invitation.

Examples of both their writings appear as a coda to this chapter but their mutual attempts stimulate a question that lies at the heart of this study. Can any kind of mythology whether coming from right-wing Orthodox Judaism or a postmodern phenomenological philosophy, ever become compatible with a Spinoza-based attack on biblical literalism and religious authoritarianism? Is it possible, in other words, to persist in the compromise belief that religion has a legitimate claim on those convictions and feelings that defy reason? The challenge, then, for anyone who still cherishes the logic of Spinoza, is to seek new formulas, new ways to remain both logically consistent and spiritually authentic.

Moral values certainly have a right, no, a duty, to be judged in the arena of public opinion, the public sphere, but when these judgments are determined by little more than tradition and superstition, then a dangerous border has been crossed. To blur the boundary between religion and science lends legitimacy to religious extremists who would insist upon politicizing questions still open to legitimate debate (when does life begin?) and would decimate generations of research in areas where there is no longer legitimate debate (the whole field of evolution). To ignore the insights of science is to succumb to the arguments of those who would oppose stem cell research. It is to lend credence to bigots who continue to demean gays and lesbians and their efforts to legalize their relationships. To ignore the insights of science is to subject reason to emotion and to jeopardize the most sensitive areas of human freedom.

Can the ideas of the Judaism of the twenty-first century and the Baruch Spinoza of the seventeenth century be reconciled? The ten basic propositions that follow represent but one tentative effort to provide an answer.

Proposition One: The purpose and mission of modern Judaism is to help its adherents achieve meaningful and fulfilling lives and to encourage them to work toward the creation of an enduring, just and peaceful world. Whether they are religious or secular, affiliated or totally divorced from any form of institutional life, Jews are bound together in profound ways. The word "Jew" bears with it a history and a responsibility that both encumbers and challenges. The pursuit of *tzedakah*, justice, lies at the root of Judaism's historic journey.

Argument: Individuals turn to religion for many reasons including fear about death or failure, the pursuit of wisdom, and the attractions of a congenial community. Tradition and a shared history combine to provide comfort and strength as well as valuable insights about the meaning of human existence. For this reason, if for no other, Jewish survival becomes a goal in itself, a goal that is seldom analyzed, frequently assumed. The ultimate religious task is not only to understand and to comfort one's friends and family; it is to protect and preserve our world, and to make it a place where just laws prevail. Because of Jewish suffering throughout the ages, and particularly the experience of the Holocaust, the task of pursuing justice may have been overshadowed by concerns about Jewish survival. The task remains urgent. True survival requires an acknowledgement of the interstitial role and its dual potential — to protect the Jewish community and to promote the welfare of the entire world.

The historic idea of Israel as a "chosen people," has gone through many transformations. Today it should be seen as an incentive to strive for a just world rather than as an assertion of superiority or privilege. To claim the primacy of justice as the true religious mission is to fashion a new awareness of "the other." It is to affirm and defend the rights of the poor and the oppressed, working people and immigrants. It is to work toward the elimination of racial, sexual, and religious discrimination. It is to strive for programs that provide for the health of all and that protect the aged and the infirm. It is to seek not only a minimum but a living wage for all workers. And it is to recognize that the protection of the universe is the ultimate survival issue, one that transcends temporary political or fiscal considerations. In a just society individual merit would be acknowledged and appreciated, but huge income imbalances that threaten to inflame social tensions would not be tolerated.

Proposition Two: God is identical with nature, and the worship of God consists of a growing awareness of the awesomeness of nature/God and of the creatures that are part of God — that are godly. The Jewish idea of deity often acknowledges a separation between God and the divine creation. Yet the idea of God as identical with nature is not incompatible with Jewish tradition. It is this idea, the unification of God and the world that may ultimately bridge the gap between religion and science. The belief in a mysterious God who responds to human requests may be appealing to poets and children, but it is hardly the basis of a theology that can withstand the rigors of a rational universe.

Argument: The "mysteries of the universe" can be encountered in an ethical context rather than a metaphysical one once the connection between God and nature is understood. Ancient thinkers confronted aspects of life they could barely understand only by conceiving of a separation between God and the visible world, between heaven and earth. Although supernatural ideas of God suffuse the biblical narrative, all concepts of a deity who exists remote from nature (supernatural) need to be seen as ancient narratives that might have served an important purpose in their day, but are only useful as metaphors in ours.

The Bible attributes to Moses the discovery of a truth that no one before him had even imagined: *"Eh'ye asher Eh'ye* — I will be what I will be."* (Exodus 3.14) The ancient assertion is strikingly relevant. Inherent in this startling pronouncement is the affirmation of a powerful unity, the unity of God and God's creation. In this sense Spinoza and scripture are in accord. These people who believe in miracles, Spinoza wrote "figure that God does nothing whenever nature acts in its usual order, and that, on the other hand, the power of nature and natural causes are suspended whenever God does act."[228] Spinoza was bitterly criticized for his identification of God with nature, and yet the most concise statement of Jewish theology affirms this very insight. The vision that seized Moses during his lonely exile in the wilderness seemed so simple, so profoundly true that, upon realizing it, Spinoza declared that he had been "born again."

Proposition Three: Human beings are drawn together by the need to share experience and to help one another. Religious communities form out of a variety of motives and express themselves in diverse ways. Past and future, tradition and innovation are the competing forces that create a dynamic faith. Commemoration, prayer, and worship are historic and appropriate ways of expressing basic human needs and aspirations, and they help to fashion the just society. Holidays and ceremonies reliving past historic events and celebrating important lifetime occasions serve not only to comfort and inspire, but also to create a knowledgeable and cohesive community. Prayer is both individual and communal, both petition and thanksgiving. In times of personal anxiety or community crisis the need to pray can be irresistible. It is not to demean the value of the prayers to describe them as "cathartic" rather than "expectational." Through words and music as well as through a variety of art forms, individuals and communities find the comfort and strength not only to face their problems but also to give voice to their highest aspirations.

Argument: Sacred days and sacred occasions fulfill important human and social needs and provide the content which gives meaning to Judaism's special role. This is why the Sabbath, Rosh Hashanah and Yom Kippur, the Festivals as well as individual lifetime ceremonies are vital aspects of a living tradition. Especially worthy of renewed appreciation are the three harvest festivals, Succoth, Shavuot and Pesach. Their recognition of the holiness of nature coupled with their emphasis upon freedom and human responsibility add to their relevance.

Above all, the Sabbath provides an opportunity for worship and for contemplation. The mere act of gathering with a sympathetic religious community may be seen as a vivid reminder of the close connection between Judaism and the quest for ultimate meaning in human life. The

237

Sabbath is an important time for pausing, for resting, and for contemplating the past. Its invitation to alter the pace of life is also a challenge to face old problems with renewed energy and imagine a future with new possibilities.

As historically important and as psychologically urgent as it is to maintain ritual and personal and communal piety, it is equally important to divorce worship from any expectation of a supernatural response. The idea of God who is part of this world and not of any externally conceived universe removes the need for the type of prayer that relies on miracles or supernatural intervention. To reject such reliance often requires tremendous courage; human suffering may sometimes seem too difficult to bear. At such times it is understandable that old and comforting formulas are utilized. Paradoxical as it may seem, the use of such historic formulas may have a therapeutic usefulness that transcends any intellectual scrutiny. The *Kaddish* prayer, so associated with the ritual of mourning and yet totally devoted instead to the praise of God, is an example of a prayer that possesses both utility and integrity.

Human beings approach God in many and diverse ways. To acknowledge the depth and also the variety of these various and deeply personally convictions does not mitigate the importance of understanding that God and nature are a single entity. Such an understanding does not lead to a static theology. On the contrary, God-nature is a continually evolving reality.

Reverence is an attitude that ennobles human life and that has its own sustaining value. Its manifestations both in prayer and private meditation possess an undeniable power. To acknowledge that prayer and worship may persist independently of any intellectual basis is hardly grounds for denying their usefulness. To utter the words "God bless you" following a sneeze may be formulaic, but to pray with a critically ill cancer patient may have a comforting effect that persists independently of its intellectual content. While they may transcend any rational function, the traditional words of Jewish prayer, far from being inimical to Spinoza's idea of God are quite compatible with it. To thank God for the bread we are about to eat, the wine we are about to drink, the Sabbath we are about to welcome, is to acknowledge the reality of a world that is truly godly. Typically, Jewish prayer does not ask, but it thanks. In this view, prayers for peace or for an end to oppression need not be viewed as a call for a miraculous intervention, but as an invitation to create a community and a social climate committed to peace and justice.

Proposition Four: For Judaism, study, and, in particular, the study of traditional texts has always been an important responsibility. Religious myths, when properly understood, serve useful purposes provided they do not encourage superstition or lead to acts engendering hatred or oppression. However, these texts need to be regarded for what they are — myths rather than injunctions. Where reason does not sustain the myth, its meaning needs to be understood as symbolic rather than literal and eternal.

Argument: Jewish religious texts, beginning with the Bible itself combine history and myth, fact and legend. It is important to recognize, that there are *Midrashim* that promote dysfunctional ideas about God and offer primitive interpretations of obscure biblical passages. It is important to interpret these passages selectively and critically. That many of these legends, however, ignore both history and reason need not destroy their efficacy unless they are used to promote values that are cruel or bigoted. The enduring nature of the Yom Kippur *Kol Nidre* prayer is an example of how legend and reason can accommodate one another. The vast majority of modern Jews do not believe in the literal meaning of the *Kol Nidre* prayer. Its assertion that promises made under pressure may be abrogated is hardly relevant today. Yet the beauty of the *Kol Nidre* melody evokes profound feelings of reverence, feelings that transcend, but never supplant, the canons of reason. And it is still the Midrash that makes the ancient Bible both modern and meaningful. With its play on words, its stories and its explanation of obscure passages the *Midrashic* process serves to reinterpret ancient ideas and invest them with modern relevance. Mining these texts can provide elevating and even inspiring insights, insights that provide rich food for sermons as well as for intellectual debate. They also nurture the intellectual tradition that has and continues to make Judaism relevant.

Proposition Five: The basic equality of all human beings is an idea that must be reaffirmed in every age. A corollary of the idea that God and nature are one is the insistence that human beings too are part of God-nature. Therefore, distinctions which grant freedom and equality to some while denying them to others are arbitrary and immoral. The task of every living being is to realize and perfect its own unique potential. The acknowledgment of the unique importance of equality entails a commitment to oppose all forms of racial, sexual and religious discrimination.

Argument: Stereotypes and ancient prejudices have produced historic and painful patterns of discrimination. Suspicion and hatred based upon ignorance and fear are the antithesis of a godly world. All forms of discrimination, whether based upon race, religion, gender, or sexual preference need to be vigorously opposed. The acknowledgement of this goal is not to deny that some human beings fulfill their potential more successfully than others and deserve to be recognized for their achievements. But the need to combat distortions in income and social status becomes increasingly urgent. The continuing domination of the many by the few represents a growing threat to the very fabric of a just society. A corollary reaction to the struggle for social and economic justice would be thoughtful resistance to the growing adoration of "celebrity" with its concomitant cult-like veneration of fame over virtue.

Proposition Six: Study remains a vital element of the Jewish experience. *Torah*, *tefilla* and *maasim tovim* — study, worship and good deeds — have traditionally been regarded as the threefold path to the holy. The understanding of a God who is identical to all of nature invites a re-examination of these pillars of Judaism. Centuries of rabbinic literature and thought beg to be studied anew with Spinoza's critical insights in mind.

The texts and traditions of Judaism are sacred in the sense that they provide a record of Israel's ongoing search for the meaning of God. The Bible, the Talmud, as well as *Midrashic* literature, all represent efforts to bridge the gap between ancient and contemporary religious ideas. They contain insights into still troublesome moral problems.

Argument: Throughout the centuries the word "Torah" evolved into a generic term conveying the totality of study itself. The act of study remains a virtue capable of enduring independent of any particular content. This is what the *Mishnah* meant when it quoted with approval the ancient appraisal of Rabbi Meir: "He who occupies himself in the study of Torah for its own sake merits many things, and the whole world is indebted to him. He is called friend, beloved, lover of God, lover of mankind." (Avot 6.1) In this sense, Torah is the record of a people continually searching for new relevance even in the face of tremendous obstacles. Great or traumatic moments in the Jewish experience have earned a special role in the collective memory of the Jewish people. And these historic moments need to be preserved and studied. The remembrance of the Holocaust stands as a unique symbol of a particular destiny and also as a stark reminder of the depravity that unchecked hatred can produce.

The very vitality of a people in between can be attributed to its ongoing commitment to the life of the intellect. Thus, the whole corpus of *Halachah*, of Jewish law, continues to be studied on the basis of its own merit. With Spinoza in mind, it would be appropriate to question those religious claims that are based upon superstition or ignorance. Yet there are customs and patterns of behavior that survive independent of any rational explanation for their persistence. These customs find their validation in the living memory of the Jewish people. It is in this respect that Auschwitz and Theresienstadt remain critical to any understanding of contemporary Jewish thought. Despite these sad memories, Jewish history becomes diminished when it is viewed solely as a record of victimization. The challenge to fulfill the positive interstitial role remains its future rather than its past, its promises rather than its disappointments.

Proposition Seven: The State of Israel is important to the survival of the Jewish people. Its effort to define itself, however, need not produce suffering among other peoples within its borders or in adjacent territories. The establishment of Israel represents the fulfillment of a Jewish longing that has persisted through the ages. Decisions about its own internal policies, however, must be determined by its own citizens. Though their history is a shared one, Israel the people and the State of Israel are not one. Despite its special and cherished position, the Jewish state, cannot expect to avoid the moral scrutiny that the Jewish religion demands. Israel's preference for a form of governance in which religion and state are combined, a combination that historically has had such deleterious consequences, evokes special concern from those who are dedicated to the idea of freedom.

Argument: Diaspora Jews find historic justification in urging modern Israel to move toward the separation of religion and state. Such a move would safeguard freedom and equal treatment for all religious faiths and for the varieties of Judaism which proliferate in the Jewish state. Though Israel continually faces the hostility of its enemies, it is important that its legitimate security needs do not subvert ethical ones. This means that the government of Israel has the responsibility of guaranteeing that its Arab population will be treated justly, and that it is willing to undertake reasonable compromises that will result in an end to ancient conflicts in the Middle East. The ultimate goal of justice is peace — but justice and peace can never survive without one another. True support of Israel is to be found by encouraging, not its biblically based fantasies about territorial boundaries, but its reality based desire for peace. In this respect the dignity and security of both Israelis and Palestinians is a requisite for any vision of the future. The defense of Israel, as urgent as it is, should not be used by Jews elsewhere in the world as an excuse for neglecting the ethical dimensions of their tradition.

Proposition Eight: "Religious authority" as it impacts private as well as public life is an authority that should be exercised cautiously. Throughout the centuries religious authorities have invoked various levels of community control in order to insure obedience and conformity. Such goals are inimical to a faith that asserts the unity of God and humanity, and that reveres the holiness of each individual human being. In Judaism, religious authority is an anachronism implying a separation between clergy and laity. The diversity of the Jewish community invites openness to a variety of attitudes and practices. This openness should be welcomed rather than stifled.

Argument: By virtue of their training and office, religious leaders often claim the authority to define acceptable religious behavior. The power to do so should be used sparingly. In the public arena, religious voices need to be heard and respected, but they should support the separation of church and state and refrain from seeking legislation that would favor the interests of their own community at the expense of the general welfare.

The American Jewish community traditionally has not seen itself as an authoritarian institution. Yet the struggle between secular and religious leadership, the continuing emphasis upon conformity with regard to the support for Israel, the increasing divide between synagogue and federation, tensions between liberal and Orthodox forms of Judaism — all reveal significant fractures within the Jewish community. Each individual Jew should be encouraged to utilize Jewish tradition to discern his or her own path to religious faith.

Questions of personal status have traditionally been vested in the hands of religious authorities, whose actions have often seemed arbitrary. Matters such as conversion and marriage, and sometimes even the right to a Jewish burial, remain difficult to resolve. It is in these areas that a concern for individuals must be carefully balanced against the traditional rules of the *Halachah*. *Minhag*, or local custom has always been an important factor in the creation of Jewish law, and a democratic religious society would seek to create a dialogue rather than to impose rules that often seem arbitrary and oppressive.

That less than half the Jews of the United States feel the need to affiliate with a synagogue is as revealing as it is troubling. Membership in the Jewish community should depend upon commitment and not merely upon genealogy, or more egregiously, upon the ability to pay. For many Jews the reasons for non-affiliation are economic — and indeed, concern that participation in Jewish life may be confined to a group of economic elites is a growing one. At the same time, there are many Jews who do not wish to become associated with an institution that they feel has lost sight of their needs and values.

Over the centuries no problem has proven to be more intractable than the question: Who is a Jew? Traditionally, Jewish status was dependent upon the religion of one's mother. Recently the Jewish world has been roiled by efforts to insist that the Jewish faith of the father was also an adequate basis for religious authenticity. Conversion is a path taken by many men and women who seek to identify with the ideas and traditions of Judaism, and there is every reason to encourage this form of religious affirmation. In the meantime, the interstitial role still defines Jews whether they are affiliated or not. In the eyes of the world, even those who have disavowed their heritage are still Jews; they remain the people in between.

Proposition Nine: Every life is sacred. In this sense, every life belongs to God. Therefore the act of taking a life is the most un-godlike thing a human being can do, for it involves an attack upon God. This general assertion, of course, merely begins but does not conclude a consideration of the definition of life. Disagreements about abortion, assisted suicide and "just war" theories, not to mention the killing of animals for food, will continue to be subjects of intense debate. The more rational a being is, the greater the responsibility to protect life rather than to destroy or inflict pain.

Argument: "Great is peace, said Rabbi Judah, for even the Holy One, blessed be He, is called peace." (Lev. R. IX.9) A special responsibility of the people in between is to seek peace wherever there is conflict. The task of peacemaking involves much more than the resolution of military confrontations. It is clear, for example, that few social areas involve as much tension as does the debate over the ultimate meaning of life. When does it begin? When should it end? This is but one of many issues that defy any clear distinction between fact and faith.

What are the principles we need to invoke in the pursuit of peaceable conclusions? One principle may be sought in the effort to confront the meaning of pain. To cause suffering is to diminish life. The sacredness of life implies recognition of the need for all things to survive and fulfill their potential, their *conatus* as Spinoza would argue. This self-recognition evokes another response — an awareness of the need to help diminish suffering in others. The end of warfare, persecution, and slavery are the obvious goals of such a theology.

But what about suffering experienced by other forms of life? It may be argued that it is part of the natural order for some creatures to survive while others perish? Animals destroy one another, and humans destroy animals for food. In the face of this reality, it is important to insist that "the survival of the fittest" does not imply an indifference to pain. The Jewish task is to minimize pain, even the pain of the animal to be eaten. This implies a need to recognize the sentient qualities of all beings and to reduce pain wherever possible, beginning with those who are most vulnerable to it.

Proposition Ten: Immortality is the gift we leave to those who follow us. It is the memory of us that lives on with others. At the end of our lives we die, as do all creatures. As comforting as it is to picture life after death and heaven as a place of eternal rest, such concepts offer false hopes, hopes that reason fails to sustain. The desire for immortality is as much a desire to leave behind some part of us that will live as it is to live beyond what we leave behind. Promises of a future life and a future resurrection do little more than play upon the fears and superstitions of people untouched by the lessons of either experience or reason.

Argument: Throughout the ages Judaism has struggled with questions about what happens to us after we die. Do we merely "sleep with our ancestors" as the early biblical narrative seems to suggest or is there a reality that persists once we stop breathing? Is the soul immortal and will the human body experience a resurrection when the Messiah appears?

Many of these thoughts are prompted by the quite understandable fear of death. But responses to these fears based upon irrational hope and superstition have inflicted more damage upon humanity than any other single error that humans could possibly concoct. These beliefs, based upon little more than wishful thinking, have been responsible for religious schisms, heresy trials, persecutions, and millions of deaths. It was Franklin Roosevelt who famously declared in his first inaugural address that "the only thing we have to fear is fear itself." Roosevelt's words to a depressed nation are an apt diagnosis of our own unrelenting concerns about death. Death is a reality we cannot overcome; fear is a reality we can overcome. We need to face these fears rationally, realistically, courageously. But to confront these fears does not imply a corollary need to denigrate legitimate efforts to extend life and to make it more fulfilling. Immortality is within the grasp of every human being, though the form that it takes may defy conventional wisdom. It is our gift to the future, not a gift to ourselves.

It is at this point that our effort to reconcile Spinoza with modern Judaism may temporarily conclude. With his stern rationalism, Spinoza would have us face death with tranquility. But, as we have seen, it would be a mistake to conclude that Spinoza demeaned the importance of worship and meditation. To him it was the beauty and inevitability of the universe that commanded reverence. Prayer has its own power, not to reward or punish, not to offer vain promises of some future blessing, but simply to offer the quiet opportunity to seek a life that is more tranquil, more thoughtful, and more meaningful. On this point, perhaps if on little else, Joseph Soloveitchik, Emmanuel Levinas, and even Baruch Spinoza would surely concur.

To bring this attempt at reconciliation to a close, a brief look at two fragments drawn from the writings of Soloveitchik and Levinas might offer a glimpse into the type of intellectual synthesis that is possible and desirable. In his groundbreaking essay, *The Lonely Man of Faith*, Soloveitchik, unwittingly perhaps, allowed tradition to encounter Spinoza. Discerning in Genesis two distinct accounts of human creation, Soloveitchik recognized the same perplexing repetitions that troubled Spinoza three centuries earlier. But instead of analyzing the repetitions in order to remove doubts about the Bible's unitary authorship, Soloveitchik employed the Midrashic techniques of the rabbis in order to offer a radical view of social justice.

In chapter one of Genesis, the human called Adam is created. This Adam is the producer, the manufacturer, the user. Adam the first, says Soloveitchik, is aggressive, bold, and goal-oriented. Arendt would call him a *parvenu*, though Soloveitchik would hardly use such a judgmental term. "Subdue it and have dominion over it, be fruitful and multiply" — these are tasks assigned to this initial Adam. In trying to fulfill the mandate of his maker, this Adam is worldly minded. He is the explorer of outer space, but he is also the collector whose aim is to own and accumulate as much as he can. But there is a different Adam, one who makes his appearance in the

245

second chapter of Genesis. This second Adam is the generous provider, the one who has learned how to share. His task is not to subdue and conquer, but rather to tend the garden, to water it and to preserve it. This Adam is a giver. He is even willing to sacrifice his own rib in order to give life to another human being. His giving is what enables society to exist. This Adam represents Soloveitchik's "lonely man of faith."

"God summoned Adam the first to advance steadily, Adam the second to retreat. Adam the first He told to exercise mastery and to 'fill the earth and subdue it,' Adam the second, to serve. He was placed in the Garden of Eden 'to cultivate it and to keep it.'"[229]

Adam the second is eternally lonely. He is lonely the minute he discovers that he stands alienated from the brutal external world. He is lonely as soon as he realizes that he has failed to ally himself with the new intelligent beings of the world into which he has entered. Adam the first is basically utilitarian and egotistic and this rules out sacrificial actions. Adam the second, however, through his thoughts and deeds, commits himself to the welfare of others. He gives up his own rib in order to create another life. He is the positively interstitial Jew.

Spinoza and Soloveitchik held radically different ideas about God. Both, however, would surely welcome this positively interstitial Jew, living not in fear but in hope, identifying not with taking and accumulating, but with giving and helping. The lonely man of faith needs to grow beyond loneliness into a vast community of faithful men and women, a community that transcends gender distinctions as well as racial ones and becomes a symbol of compassion — a symbol, in other words, of Judaism.

Surely Soloveitchik had such a goal in mind as he sat with students in Boston or New York, praying that they would become faithful teachers of teachers. His own greatness was dependent not only upon his scholarship but also upon the moral authority and commitment he brought to the study of the ancient text. A similar magnetism can be found in the life of Emmanuel Levinas. It was this wellrespected French scholar who had once predicted that any future reconstruction of philosophy would stem from "a fresh examination of Spinoza's thinking." Levinas was known as the "philosopher of the other," and his searching analysis of *alterity* stimulated profound questions about our responsibility to one another. Here is but one example of Levinas's thinking, an analysis based on the story of Jacob's deception of his father. Jacob deceives his blind father by donning the clothes of Esau. "Doesn't Jacob, in putting on the violent Esau's clothes, take on his brother's responsibilities? How to preserve oneself from evil? By each taking upon himself the responsibility of the others. . . . I can be responsible for that which I did not do and take upon myself a distress that is not mine."[230] The awareness of the "other," the consciousness of what it means to be a stranger, the constant search for the moral life — these are themes that permeate the thought of this important French philosopher. They are also themes that emerge throughout Jewish history and haunt Jewish scholarship.

In an age in which nationalism has produced rivalries that are increasingly disastrous, in which the world-wide potential for terrorism excites its perpetrators and terrorizes its victims, in which the very fate of human life seems to have become a question and not a certainty, an awesome faith based on justice and dedicated to its realization, may be not only timely but absolutely necessary.

Conclusion

The essential Jewish prayer is the *Shema*. To listen is to hear the word. And the word that needs to be heard is to be found in the call to justice. In the twenty-first century, the need for a community built on justice is more than a moral admonition. It is the key to Jewish survival. In the seventh volume of the *Mishneh Torah*, his remarkable compendium of Jewish law, Moses Maimonides famously argued that the best way to help those who are unfortunate is to empower them to help themselves. Maimonides's formula has been rightly praised, but it is seldom quoted in its entirety. "There are eight levels of *tzedakah*, each one greater than the other. The greatest level, above which there is no other, is to strengthen another Jew by giving him a present or loan, or forming a partnership with him, or finding him a job in order to strengthen his hand until he no longer needs help."[231] Maimonides was talking about Jews helping other Jews. The society in which he lived carefully preserved social distinctions of all kinds. Differing attitudes toward the lending of money was but one of the religious and social barriers that separated Muslims from Jews. Maimonides regarded charity not as a matter of goodwill, but as a matter of law. To help others was a legally binding responsibility, not simply an appeal to vague moral values. That Maimonides thought of charity in terms of one individual helping another was not surprising. As a doctor his focus was upon helping the suffering individuals who crowded into his office every evening.

Maimonides's taxonomy has become recognized in many charitable circles — recognized but not always understood. The challenge today is not only to help and to heal individuals; it is also to acknowledge the presence of groups of people, of community organizations that are easy to ignore or dismiss as irrelevant. Recent political rhetoric is replete with calls to protect the middle class. It often seems that the poor have become invisible. Society has come to look upon the poor as a pitiable mass of individuals who lack organizational skills. But as John Kretzmann and John McKnight have shown, it is important to look for strengths as well as weaknesses in urban communities, even in poverty stricken urban communities. There are thousands of community groups, even in poverty areas, that are highly organized yet all too often ignored by even the most benevolent of outsiders.[232] Associations as diverse as church choirs or public housing tenant associations reveal the presence of networks that provide vital support for their members. These networks, however, can he easily destroyed by well meaning but misguided planners who often uproot them in the name of urban renewal or who offer "scholarly" solutions to problems that can best be solved by indigenous leaders.

The poor need to be seen as part of a vital community, and not merely as "needy individuals." The individual may be weak. The community offers strength. To enter into a partnership with a community is to do more than offer volunteer projects. It is to seek the cause of poverty, the cause of powerlessness. To build such partnerships is the role of the people who would be positively interstitial.

By suggesting that the donor enter into partnership with the needy, Maimonides was not talking about a super-ordinate and sub-ordinate relationship. As important as it may be to teach a needy person the rules of hygiene for example, or how to apply for a job, it is essential to acknowledge the reciprocal relationships that are so essential to any meaningful community partnership. The poor and powerless are not without their strengths. They have much to teach. And those who seek to help them have much to learn. The unpopularity of the word "charity" may be an indication that this truth is beginning to be generally acknowledged. In this respect, the Hebrew word *tzedakah*, justice, as Maimonides recognized, is a much more appropriate word than charity.

In her appraisal of the pariah, Hannah Arendt exposed the one essential element that would distinguish her model of the pariah from that similar, though vastly different, description of the positively interstitial role. Arendt was keenly aware of what was missing. Her description of the liberal, upwardly mobile Jews of two hundred years ago finds its counterpart in the lives of many modern liberal Jews. Arendt's liberal Jews who attended the fashionable salons, it will be remembered, were "endowed with the attributes that are indeed the privileges of pariahs ... humanity, kindness, freedom from prejudice, sensitivity to injustice. The trouble was that these qualities had nothing to do with the prophets, and that, worse still these Jews usually belonged neither to Jewish society nor to fashionable circles of non-Jewish society."[233]

Clearly Arendt's sympathies lie with those Jews she considers to be pariahs. They are altruistic, genuine, and concerned with the welfare of others. As opposed to them the *parvenu* is selfish, materialistic and prone to seek dangerous alliances with power elites instead of with the masses. As impressive as these distinctions are, they raise important questions about the meaning of "genuine" as it pertains to Jewish life. The thinking Jew may value "genuineness" as much as the phenomenologist that Hannah Arendt certainly was. Her identifiable pariahs, Spinoza, Heine, Borne, as well as Rahel Varnhagen are all admirable human beings, but the term genuine hardly springs to mind in terms of their association with the Jewish community.

The labels that have been applied to Jews from the time of their earliest history provide an evolving record of their interstitial role. In the Bible they are identified as a "peculiar people," a "stiff-necked people." For Hannah Arendt they were a "particular people," and for the Marxists and Abram Leon they were a "people-class." For all of them, this question remains relevant: Can this people survive without the external pressures that have all too often been responsible for its cohesiveness? "Whenever Jews cease to be a class," writes Leon, "they lose their ethical and religious characteristics; they become assimilated."[234]

To turn a people trapped in history's jaws of the negative interstitial role in the direction of positive interstitiality requires confronting precisely those qualities that Hannah Arendt found lacking in so many of the nineteenth-century pariahs. In essence the two factors are related to one another. The rediscovered relevance of the prophets involves not only listening to the voices of Isaiah and Jeremiah, but also exploring new ways to be moral advocates in a vastly expanded and complex universe. An invitation to confront the prophets in modern terms is an invitation to become reacquainted with Judah ha-Nasi and Rashi and Maimonides and to bring their human concerns into modern focus. That these Jewish leaders, were they alive, would hardly recognize the modern applications of their thinking is irrelevant. Jewish religious tradition honors the process of reinterpretation and modernization.

An oft-cited Midrash tells of the martyred Rabbi Akiba who asked God to show him how future generations would view his teachings. Immediately, the heavens opened up and Akiba looked in on a Talmudic Academy. One student said, "This is what Akiba meant." And another argued, "No, this is what Akiba meant." Looking in on this academy of the future, Akiba's became tearful. "O God," he said, I don't recognize a word of it." "Nevertheless," God responded, "these are your teachings." If Maimonides could rationalize the story of Eve and the poisonous serpent, stripping it of its mythology and finding new moral meaning, then surely

American Jews can follow his example by investing the ancient texts with a relevance that meets the need of modern times.

Hannah Arendt complained that there was no connection between the idealized pariah type Jews with either "Jewish society" or "fashionable circles of non-Jewish society." It is precisely this dual connectedness between Jews and "society at large" that is so critically needed in order to confront irrational fundamentalism on one side and spiritual sterility on the other. The Jewish community is called to identify itself as an entity with a purpose beyond the goal of mere survival. The positive interstitial role invites this community to oppose exploitation, fight for righteousness, and help create a universe in which life may flourish and not perish.

Of course, willing individuals have responded to this challenge in the past. The task is to turn the "individual" into the "community." There is a need, in other words, not merely for "good will," but for the conscious creation of Jewish communal organizations that truly can speak the "word," and, more importantly, translate its modern message into action.

Hannah Arendt's search for "fashionable circles in non-Jewish society" also demands to be taken seriously. There are numerous religious and secular organizations in that non-Jewish society eagerly looking for allies as they seek to build a just and sustainable world. They, too, are distressed by the growing inequality and powerlessness that threaten the entire fabric of our democratic society. They too struggle against those forms of egoism that result in vapid self-righteousness. And they struggle, too, against those whose "holy grail" is the dollar and the power it can purchase. We need to join them in the sometimes lonely struggle against the tide of a fundamentalism that esteems "religious values" above a religious search for human value. To stand above the fray may offer its subtle attractions, but the authentic Jew, to borrow Sartre's phrase, and to pursue Arendt's admonition, can remain neither indifferent nor deaf to the one cry that will not be stilled — justice!

Acknowledgments

To the men and women who for so many years have served on the board and the staff of Chicago's Jewish Council on Urban Affairs, I offer my profound thanks. They helped turn the interstitial idea into a practical reality. Combining the prophetic ideas of Judaism with Maimonides's simple insistence that the best way to offer help is to enable people to help themselves, the Jewish Council has been able to confront antisemitism in tangible ways even as it has striven toward the creation of a just and compassionate society. Lewis Kreinberg played a critical role in the creation of this pioneering Jewish organization. His insights, sometimes eccentric, always profound, constantly challenged me to probe deeper into the implications of the interstitial analysis.

The ideas for my understanding of the *People in Between* were germinated first at the Hebrew Union College in Cincinnati with the help of a most remarkable teacher, Ellis Rivkin. They matured during a graduate studies program at Yale University where I had an opportunity to study with H. Richard Niebuhr, Brand Blanshard, Omar K. Moore, F. S. C. Northrop and James Gustafson. In a thousand different ways, their ideas have infused my thinking as I developed the interstitial idea.

I am more than grateful to Michael Brown, Steven Feuerstein, and Jane Ramsey who patiently read my text and offered suggestions that have proven to be invaluable. Their comments and sometimes critical suggestions helped to clarify my own thinking in many areas that I otherwise may have overlooked. As the long-serving director of the Jewish Council on Urban Affairs, Jane Ramsey graciously shared with me the insights she had acquired as a result of her years of fruitful community service. Professor Sandra Bartke was generous in her comments about my manuscript. I am particularly indebted to her for her help in interpreting the Jewish implications of Sartre's *Phenomenology*.

I would be remiss were I not to thank my friend Carol Anne Been for her generous help in shepherding my manuscript through the copyright process. I am also indebted to Penny Hirsch as well as her daughter Jenny, who patiently read my manuscript and offered helpful suggestions related to both grammar and content.

The production of this book could not have been completed without the talent, experience and energy of Mark Hess, Alec Hess and Full Voice Media.

Rabbi Bruce Elder has been my successor as the rabbi of Congregation Hakafa in Glencoe, Illinois. He has been my student my teacher and my friend. I am grateful to him for sharing with me his thoughts about the Jewish commitment to social action, but more for the living example he sets as a courageous rabbi and leader.

The members of Congregation Hakafa have been a constant source of stimulation and encouragement. They taught me so much during the countless study sessions we shared together. In addition, they tolerated my sermons for so many years and never complained that they were tired of hearing about interstitiality. At least — to me — they never complained.

To my wife, K. Ruth Marx I am grateful beyond words. She has not only endured countless hours of conversation regarding the "people in between," but she has read and reread the manuscript, offering fresh and valuable insights with every reading. Her patience and wisdom gave me the encouragement and the strength to continue even during moments when I felt the task would never be completed.

Finally, to my son, Richard J. Marx and my daughter-in-law Eve, I owe a debt of gratitude that can never be repaid. Together they read the text and prepared it for publication. Were it not for Rick this study would never be published. It would rest together with hundreds of musty sermons in one of my neglected file cabinets. It was Rick who prodded me to complete my work and to allow him to proceed with its publication. For this I am truly grateful. More, I am truly blessed.

Notes

1 See, Hannah Arendt, *The Jewish Writings*, xxxiii and footnote #2 to her article, "Antisemitism," 111–112.

2 The Philosophy of Hegel, The Philosophy of History, Modern Library Edition, 50.

3 Babylonian Talmud, Gitin, 56a; Midrash, Lamentations Rabbah, 4:3.

4 Suetonius, Lives of the Caesars, Domitian, 12.

5 F. S. C. Northrop, *The Meeting of East and West*, 160.

6 Writing from a Marxist prospective, Abram Leon argues that it was the mercantile role of Jews in the Roman Empire rather than religious rivalry that stimulated early antisemitism. "The cause for ancient anti-Semitism is the same as for medieval anti-Semitism: the antagonism toward the merchant in every society based principally on the production of use values. Abram Leon, *The Jewish Question*, 71. While it is certainly true that Jewish mercantile roles, interstitial as they surely were, had become an important factor in the expansion of antisemitism, these considerations always need to be viewed in the light of the religious conflicts of the time. These conflicts both preceded and in turn stimulated the economic characteristics which have haunted Jewish history.

7 Romans 2.29; Acts 11.1–9.

8 Lillian D. Wald, *The House on Henry Street*, 302.

9 Mark Penn and Kinney Zalesne feel that warm feelings toward Jews are indications of a microtrend that bodes well for Jews. "The emerging group of non-Jews who seriously favor things Jewish — we call them Pro-Semites — are a perfect example of a microtrend. They are the niche edge of the popularity trend revealed by the Gallup Poll; the small but intense group of non-Jews who not only have warm feelings about Jews, but who want to make Jew's ways their own." The authors go on to suggest that "the growing regard for Jews and Jewish priorities, and particularly the emergence of Pro-Semites, may mean that there is a 'marketing' angle to Judaism that many Jewish leaders are not taking advantage of." "Taking 'Yes' for an Answer." *World Jewish Digest*, vol. 5 No. 5 (February 2008).

10 The number of books and articles dealing with Judaism and social issues is truly impressive. Albert Vorspan and Eugene Lipman published their pioneering work *Justice and Judaism* in 1956. Joseph Soloveitchik brought an Orthodox perspective to the problem with his groundbreaking book, *The Lonely Man of Faith*, which was published in 1965. The list would include Bradley Shavit Artson's, *Love Peace and Pursue Peace*; Richard G.

Hirsch, *The Way of the Upright*; Michael Lerner, *Jewish Renewal*; David Saperstein, *Preventing the Nuclear Holocaust*; and Richard H. Schwartz, *Judaism and Global Survival*. This list is but a sampling. Special mention, however, must be made of Jill Jacobs's book, *There Shall Be No Needy*. Rabbi Jacobs combines Halachic (legal) as well as Aggadic (legend) materials to confront contemporary problems such as poverty, housing, housing and income inequality. In her discussion of our penal system she suggests that the Jewish community spends to much of its time dealing with capital punishment, and not enough on the merits of prisons themselves.

[11] Eugene B. Borowitz, "A Jewish Theology of Social Action," *CCAR Journal*, Spring 2008, 8.

[12] K. Kohler, *Studies, Addresses and Personal Papers*, 228.

[13] Edward Bernard Glick, "Everything is not a Jewish Issue," *Newsweek*, February 25, 2007.

[14] *New York Times*, July 15, 2007.

[15] Yehiel Poupko, for instance, writing in the *Christian Century* challenges non-Jewish critics of Israel. "These are not mere criticisms; they constitute a demonization of Israel of a sort that has had a long career. Some of my ancestors, such as Isaiah, Hosea, and Amos, criticized some of my other ancestors with this very language. These words of the prophets of Israel were then taken up by the New Testament writers." *Christian Century*, July 24, 2007.

[16] Abraham Joshua Heschel, *The Prophets*, 11. "Justice is in need of man," Heschel wrote, and with this sentiment Spinoza would undoubtedly agree. See Heschel, God in Search of Man, 291.

[17] Borowitz, "A Jewish Theology of Social Action," *CCAR Journal*, Spring, 2008, 10-11.

[18] Louis H. Feldman, *Jew and Gentile in the Ancient World*, 45--46. See Peter Schafer, Judeophobia. Schafer "I would opt for a harnessing of both approaches — substantialist and functionalist — in research on ancient anti-Semitism....one always needs both components to 'create' anti-Semitism: the anti-Semite and the Jew or Judaism, concrete Jewish peculiarities and the intention of the anti-Semite to distort and to pervert these peculiarities." 7–8. In his study of Hellenistic Judaism, Victor Tcherikover attributes early antisemitism to three factors; the economic position of the Jews, their religious and public self-segregation, and political antagonism between Jews and their neighbors. See Hellenistic Civilization and the Jews, 369–371.

[19] Schafer, *Judeophobia*, 133.

[20] Isaac Deutscher, *The Non-Jewish Jew*, Introduction by Tamara Deutscher, 21.

[21] Ibid., 51.

[22] Josephus, *The Antiquities of the Jews*, 18.81–84.

[23] Cassius Dio, *Roman History*, Book LXIX.14.

[24] Whether the references to a relationship between Judah and Marcus Aurelius are authentic remains open to question. Emperors of the Severan dynasty visited Palestine several times during Judah's lifetime, and the Jewish leader may well have developed a personal relationship with one of them. What is undoubtedly authentic is that there was an ongoing political and commercial relationship between Judah and Roman government officials. See Jerusalem Talmud, Shevat 6.1. See also Simon Dubnow, *History of the Jews*, vol. 2, 111.

[25] Bereshit Rabbah 20.6. Babylonian Talmud, Berakoth, 43a. See also Dubnow, vol. 2, 111 and Encyclopaedia Judaica, art. Judah ha-Nasi.

[26] H. Graetz, *History of the Jews*, vol. II, 451. Also, Dubnow, *History of the Jews*, vol. 2, 110.

[27] Genesis Rabbah, LXXVIII, 15. Summoned to meet with Roman officials, Judah responds reluctantly. His preference is to travel alone and certainly not escorted by Roman soldiers. See also, Dubnow, History of the Jews, vol. 2, 112.

[28] Solomon Zeitlin, *Religious and Secular Leadership*, 19-20.

[29] Albert Hourani, *A History of the Arab Peoples*, 35. See also 47, 111, 118.

[30] For a discussion of the relationship between Abd ar-Rahman III and the Bohemian slave trade, see James Westfall Thompson, *Feudal Germany*, vol. 1, 395–96. Thompson frequently refers to "Jew Slave traders" without acknowledging other more positive aspects of Jewish social and intellectual life.

[31] Eliyahu Ashtor, *The Jews of Moslem Spain*, vol. 1, 249–51. See also, Yitzhak Baer, A History of the Jews in Christian Spain, 28ff.

[32] H. H. Ben-Sasson, *A History of the Jewish People*, 452.

[33] Graetz, *History of the Jews*, vol. III, 254-260. While acknowledging the corruption of King Badis, Graetz is reluctant to assign any culpability to his vizier and advisor.

[34] Ben-Sasson, *A History of the Jewish People*, 401, 454.

[35] Baer, *A History of the Jews in Christian Spain*, 32–34. See also Ashtor, *The Jews of Moslem Spain*. vol. II, 65ff.

[36] Graetz, *History of the Jews*, vol. III, 275–279. See also Ben-Sasson, op. cit. 454, 458.

[37] Judah Halevi, *Book of Kuzari*, translated from the Arabic by Hartwig Hirschfeld, 260.

[38] Norman Golb, "Jacob Tam's Service on Behalf of the King of France at Reims," 7–8. See also Golb, *The Jews in Medieval Normandy*, 15.

[39] Georges Duby and Robert Mandrou, *A History of French Civilization*, 61–62; 68. Also see Marc Bloch, *Feudal Society*, 69, 90–91.

[40] See Georges Duby, *The Knight, the Lady and the Priest*, 3–53.

[41] Maurice Liber, Rashi, 39. Liber reinforces the view that Rashi was in every sense a representative of the general intellectual ferment that was stirring France by the middle of the eleventh century (89).

[42] Ibid., 202.

[43] Rashi's commentary on Exodus 22.24. See also Duby and Mandrou, *A History of French Civiliation*, 115. See also Liber, Rashi, 21. For a comprehensive picture of Jewish life in Normandy during this period, see Golb, *The Jews in Medieval Normandy*.

[44] Liber, Rashi, 56.

[45] The quotation of Obadiah the Proselyte is to be found in Norman Golb, "The Autograph Memoirs of Obadiah the Proselyte of Oppido Lucano," iv. The quotation from Simon Dubnow is to be found in his History of the Jews, vol. 2, 671. It is unlikely that Dubnow knew of Obadiah the Proselyte, whose memoir Norman Golb found and translated, but Dubnow was certainly familiar with many contemporary accounts which conveyed a similar vengeful theme. See also Golb, *The Jews in Medieval Normandy*, 121. Also, Jacques Le Goff, *History and Memory*, 13. "The Crusaders believed that in Jerusalem they were punishing the true tormentors of Christ."

[46] Rashi commentary on *Bereishit* 1.1.

[47] Joel L. Kraemer, *Maimonides*, 26–27.

[48] Solomon Zeitlin remained skeptical about reports that Maimonides had converted to Islam. Concluding his discussion of the matter, he notes "Others, however, deny that Maimonides accepted the religion of Islam. They point out that at no time could he have been a Moslem; for never did his opponents, even in the heat of the controversies against him, accuse him of being an apostate." As far as Zeitlin is willing to go is to concede that during the month of Ramadan (ninth month of the Mohammadan year) he even joined in the Tarawith prayers. *Maimonides: A Biography*, 5, 13. Joel Kraemer, on the other hand, takes it for granted that in order to

preserve his life, Maimonides did indeed convert to Islam. "Maimonides," he writes, "included himself among the enforced converts who had to seek God's forgiveness. Joseph ben Judah Ibn 'Aqnin, who knew him in Fez, described the period of forced conversion, how he lived as a Muslim with guilt feelings as he secretly observed the commandments and studied Torah with Maimonides." See Kraemer, *Maimonides*, 116–124.

[49] See Sarah Stroumsa, *Maimonides in His World*, 38–52.

[50] Kraemer, *Maimonides*, 191; 216–220.

[51] Zeitlin, *Maimonides*, 52. Zeitlin's analysis of Maimonides's approach to the problem of resurrection, as well as his controversy with Samuel ben Ali, provide insight into the strange combination of strength and vulnerability that characterized the Jewish philosopher's entire life.

[52] Ibid., 54. Maimonides's responses and letters reveal the magnitude of the problems confronted by Jews who felt compelled to abandon their religion in the face of Muslim pressure. While it was still regarded as a sin to leave Judaism, even temporarily, Maimonides sought compromises between the letter of Jewish law and the exigencies of Jewish life in the Muslim world. There is a difference between conversion under duress and one stemming from conviction. "We must make a distinction," he wrote, "between a transgression by mere word and one by deed." See, Graetz, History, vol. III, 451ff.

[53] Maimonides, *Guide for the Perplexed, Part II*, Chapter XXX.

[54] Ibid., Part 2, Chapter 3.

[55] Ibid., Part 3, Chapter 51.

[56] David Hartman, *Maimonides Torah and Philosophic Quest*, 214.

[57] Solomon Zeitlin, *Maimonides*, 177. The insistence by Yeshayahu Leibowitz that Maimonides was not occupied with matters of social justice is interesting, but only in terms of its contribution to an understanding Maimonides's religious and philosophical writings. The assertion is especially surprising since it comes from someone as socially concerned as was Yeshayahu Leibowitz. He argues: "For Maimonides knowledge of the truth in its perfection' is not the improvement of human society. It has a specific religious significance — one could even say it has none but a religious significance." Yeshayahu Leibowitz, *The Faith of Maimonides*, 14. Such arguments as those made by Leibowitz do not in any way mitigate the interstitial significance of Maimonides's life as well as his works.

[58] Simon Dubnow maintains that the name *Mitnagdim* can be translated "Protestants." Whether translated "Protestants" or "Opponents," the name *Mitnagdim* carries little positive connotation. Although both adversaries in

their bitter struggles hurled charges of sedition, it was most often the Hasidim who suffered from accusations about their patriotism. The Hasidic Rabbi Shneur Zalman spent fifty three days in jail, and, following the death of Elijah Gaon, the Mitnagdim in Vilna reported twenty-three Jews to the local authorities. These Hasidim were subsequently arrested and imprisoned on charges of sedition. See Simon Dubnow, *The History of the Jews in Russia and Poland*, I: 235ff.

[59] Niall Ferguson, *The House of Rothschild*, 45.

[60] Fritz Stern, *Gold and Iron*, 9.

[61] Ibid., 6 quotes Borne's acerbic comment about the Rothschilds. For Herzl's feelings, see *The Diaries of Theodor Herzl*, 25, 193.

[62] Ferguson, *House of Rothschild*, 146.

[63] Ibid., 18, 262-265.

[64] Letter from Baron James Rothschild to Gerson Bleichroder, May 25, 1862. Quoted by Fritz Stern, *Gold and Iron*, 73.

[65] Quoted by Saul Friedlander, *The Years of Extermination*, 154.

[66] Amos Elon, *Herzl*, 402.

[67] Quoted in Jean-Dennis Bredin, *The Affair*, 264.

[68] See Elon, *Herzl*, 126ff. Also, Jean-Dennis Bredin, *The Affair*, 260. The reference to Marcel Proust and the umbrellas borne by Parisian ladies may be found in an article, "From Munich through Wannsee to Auschwitz: The Road to the Holocaust," by Jan M. Piskorski in *Journal of the Historical Society* vol. VII, no. 2, (June 2007), 161. Piskorski makes the point that the death chants associated with the Dreyfus trial provided a foundation for the Nazi policy of total extermination.

[69] Ibid., 60–61.

[70] *The Diaries of Theodor Herzl*, 7-8. See also Herzl, The Jewish State, 22.

[71] Julius Carlebach, *Karl Marx and the Radical Critique of Judaism*, 31–32.

[72] Ibid. 36.

[73] Ibid., 20.

[74] Ibid. On August 31, 1903: "Although I was originally in favor of a Jewish State no matter where, I later lifted up the flag of Zion and became myself a 'Lover of Zion. Palestine is the sole land where our people can come to rest." "But," Herzl continued, "hundreds of thousands crave immediate help." Diaries, 409. Paradoxically, as late as 1939, Poland's foreign minister Jozef Beck had a conversation with Hitler in which he suggested the possibility of having Poland's Jews moved to one of the African countries. Cf. Piskorski, *Journal of the Historical Society*, 162.

[75] Elon, *Herzl*, 186. In retrospect it is surprising to realize how little known Herzl was in the Jewish world. Although several of his plays were running in Vienna, Herzl was barely known by East European Jews until the time of the first Zionist Congress in 1896. In his autobiography, Chaim Weizmann, who was later to become the first president of Israel, would write: "We had never heard the name Herzl before; or perhaps it had come to our attention only to be lost among those of other journalists and feuilletonists. Fundamentally, *The Jewish State* contained not a single new idea for us; that which so startled the Jewish bourgeoisie, and called down the resentment and derision of the Western Rabbis, had long been the substance of our Zionist tradition. . . . Apparently Herzl did not know of the existence of the Chibath Zion; he did not mention Palestine; he ignored the Hebrew language." *Trial and Error*, vol. I, 43.

[76] Ibid. 271. Herzl can hardly be blamed for his naïve enthusiasm. After his brief audience with the kaiser in Jerusalem in 1898, Herzl made the following entry in his diary: "That brief reception will live on forever in Jewish history, and possibly may entail world consequences." *Diaries*, 291.

[77] Ibid., 126. Herzl was openly hostile to De Hirsch's plans for settling Jews in Argentina. In addition to his practical objections, Herzl could not help but have seen in it competition with his own Zionist dreams. This is Herzl's reconstruction of his meeting with the Baron. "I said: 'Your Argentine Jews have not conducted themselves any too well, I am told. One incident particularly struck me; about the first thing done was to build a house of — uncertain fame.' Hirsch broke in: 'Not true. That house wasn't built by my settlers.'"

It is important to remember that this was the man Herzl was trying to win over to his cause. The conversation proceeded with Herzl saying: "You will prove nothing with your twenty thousand Argentine Jews even if they prosper. Whereas if the experiment fails you furnish a dreadful argument against all Jews." *Diaries*, 17.

[78] Yoel Florsheim, "What is the Land of Israel for the People of Israel, Petahim, 47-48. September 1979, 66. Quotted by Idith Zertal and Akiva Eldar, *Lords of the Land*, 478.

[79] Ibid., 233.

[80] For Louis Brandeis this realization was of great importance. Brandeis who became the first Jewish justice to serve on the U.S. Supreme Court was for many years recognized as the leader of American Zionists. In trying to win the support of skeptical American Jews, he repeatedly assured them that the Zionist dream does not expect that all Jews will choose to live in

the Jewish State. "Zionism," he declared, "is not a movement to remove all of the Jews of the world compulsorily to Palestine." And later he was to echo the same theme. "To avoid misunderstanding, let me say at the onset what Zionism is, and particularly what it is not. First, it is not a movement to transport all the Jews in the world to Palestine. That would be impossible." But like Herzl, Brandeis saw the creation of a Jewish state as an answer to the sickness of antisemitism. "For when the Jew is there in numbers, there will be no anti-Semitism." It was Brandeis who also insisted: "In the Jewish colonies of Palestine there are no Jewish criminals." Louis D. Brandeis, *The Curse of Bigness*, 209-259.

[81] *The Non-Jewish Jew*, 40-41.

[82] Dubnow, *History of the Jews of Russia and Poland*, vol. 1, 142.

[83] Dubnow, *Nationalism and History*, 86-87.

[84] Ibid., 86. For Dubnow, Jews certainly constituted a nation, but not a nation in the usual meaning of the word. For him the nation's cultural and spiritual qualities were the essence of its nationalism and these qualities were defined by the character of the people. It was in this context that Dubnow distinguished between national individualism and national egoism. National individualism, he wrote "involves the striving by every people to retain its originality and to preserve the necessary internal or external cultural political autonomy in order to insure its own free development. It is the fruitful and creative will of a natural group to remain true to itself, to improve and adorn its historical forms, and to defend the freedom of its collective personality." National egotism was the evil side of national movements. It "means the complete negation of all these progressive principles. It represents the ambition of the ruling nationality to dominate over the dependant national groups. . . . It constitutes the negation of freedom and equality in relations between nationalities." 95-96.

[85] Ibid., 242ff. See also Dubnow, *History of the Jews in Russia and Poland*, vol.3, 45ff. Dubnow maintained this unique conception of Jewish nationalism throughout his life. Toward the end of his study of Polish and Russian Jewish life, Dubnow wrote: "The scholarly endeavors of Russian Jewry constitute an attempt to understand the social development of the Diaspora as a peculiarly, internally-autonomous nation, which , at all times, has sought to preserve not only its religious treasures, but also the genuine complexion of its diversified national life." Ibid., vol. 3, 65.

[86] Ahad Ha-Am: *Essays, Letters, Memoirs*, 265.

[87] Ibid., 89.

[88] Quoted by Koppel S. Pinson in the introduction to Dubnow, *Nationalism and History*, 9–10.20.

[89] Ibid.

[90] Dubnow, *History of the Jews*, vol. 2, 475.

[91] Arthur Hertzberg, *The French Enlightenment and the Jews*, 23–24. Werner Sombart, whose controversial study of The Jews and the Rise of Capitalism, refers not only to Colbert's defense of the Jews of Marseilles, but also points to an incident that took place in Bordeaux in 1675. Mercenaries attacked the city and many of the Jewish merchants fled the city. The town council was terrified, and a report presented to its member contained this statement in which the departing Jews are clearly a source of great anxiety. "We are very much afraid that commerce will cease altogether." And a few years later, the Sous-Intendant of Languedoc wrote these words about the merchants of the area: "Without them (the Jews) the trade of Bordeaux and of the whole province would be inevitably ruined." Both Cromwell in England and Colbert in France were friendly toward the Jews. "In my opinion," Sombart writes, "it is of no small significance that these two organizers, both of whom consolidated modern European states, should have been so keenly alive to the fitness of the Jew in aiding the economic (i.e. capitalistic) progress of a country." See Sombart, *The Jews and Modern Capitalism*, 3–4. Sombart's odd mixture of attraction and repulsion to the Jewish people remains unsettling. "Money was in consonance with the Jewish nature," he writes at one point. "They became lords of money, and, through it, lords of the world." 344.

[92] R. H. Tawney, *Religion and the Rise of Capitalism*, 37.

[93] Dubnow, *History of the Jews*, vol. 3, 136.

[94] Despite its welcome guarantees of protection for the Jews of Austria, the charter offered by Frederick reveals the special relationship between the Jewish community and the duke himself. One of its provisions reads: "Likewise, one shall in no place proceed in judgment against a Jew except in front of his synagogues, saving ourselves who have the power to summon them to our presence." The interest rate, as huge as it now seems, was regarded as both a safeguard against exploitation and a way of encouraging new economic activity. "Likewise, we decree that the Jews shall receive only eight dinars a week interest on the talent." (This amounted to 173.33 percent annual interest) Jacob R. Marcus, *The Jews in the Medieval Word: A Sourcebook 315–1791*, 28-33. Dubnow, *History of the Jews*, vol. 3, 154-55.

[95] Ibid., vol. 2, 668.

[96] Dubnow, *History of the Jews*, vol. 3, 134–149. Also Marvin Lowenthal, Jews of Germany, 78-79.

[97] Ibid., vol. 3, 23-26.

[98] Ibid., vol. 3, 134–135; 137; vol. IV, 226–230. Selma Stern pictures Suess Jud as a complicated man, caught up in court intrigue, conscious of the need to help his fellow Jews, and basically decent in his instincts. See The Court Jew, 34–35; 44ff; 72ff; 257-266. Marvin Lowenthal summarizes his life in one sentence: "He made the social error of conducting himself as an equal among his fellow courtiers. Lowenthal, *The Jews of Germany*, 186, See also, Julius Carlebach, *Karl Marx and the Radical Critique of Judaism*, 19.

[99] Dubnow, *History of the Jews of Russia and Poland*, vol. 1, 44–45.

[100] Ibid., vol. 1, 47–48.

[101] Ibid., vol. 1, 106ff.

[102] Ibid., vol. 2, 22–29.

[103] Ibid., 352–353.

[104] Ibid., 361–362.

[105] Of the Warsaw pogrom in 1881, Dubnow writes: "For events soon made it clear that the anti-Jewish movement served as an unfailing device in the hands of the black reactionaries (i.e. the czarists) to divert the popular wrath from the source of all evil — the rule of despotism — and direct it towards the most unfortunate victims of that despotism." *Jews of Russia and Poland*, vol. 2, 280. See also vol. 3, 68.

[106] Ibid., vol. 3, 164–66. On July 10, 1940, sixteen hundred Jews who lived in the town of Jedwabne were murdered by their neighbors. In searching for the roots of the anti-Jewish feelings which made the massacre possible, Jan Gross writes: "We must remember that in the background of anti-Jewish violence there always lurked a suspicion of ritual murder, a conviction that Jews use for the preparation of Passober matzoh the fresh blood of innocent Christian children. It was a deeply ingrained belief among many Polish Catholics, and not simply among residents of the boondocks. After all, rumors that Jews were engaging in these practices drew incensed crowds into the streets of Polish cities at a moment's notice even after the Second World War. This was the mechanism that triggered the most infamous postwar pogroms in Cracow in 1945 and in Kielce in 1946. Jan T. Gross, *Neighbors*, 80.

[107] Jan T. Gross, *Fear*, 40-41; 178. "Why don't you give me your possessions, — we recall a good friendly neighbor suggesting to Chaja Finkelsztajn — otherwise those who are about to harm you are going to get it all" (251).

[108] Stephen Eric Bronner, *A Rumor about the Jews*, 4. In this work Bronner traces the origins and history of *The Protocols*. His thesis is that *The Protocols*, in addition to accommodating all forms of antisemitism, was also directed against the "progressive political legacy of the Enlightenment and modernity in general." From an interstitial perspective, however, it is important to keep in mind that the original and specific function of *The Protocols* was to divert mass antagonism away from the czar and the reactionary group known as the Black Hundreds and to focus the attention of the masses instead on the treachery of the Jews. "Nicholas and Alexandra ordered a sermon quoting the pamphlet in all the 368 churches of Moscow, and they supported its publication in right-wing newspapers." Ibid., 92.

[109] Citing Sophie Dubnov-Ehrlich's biography, *The Life and World of S.M. Dubnov*, Friedlander describes Dubnow's last days: "Dubnow, who lay ill, had been overlooked during the first massacre. The second time he was caught in the dragnet. The sick and feeble ghetto inhabitants were brought to the execution area in buses; as Dubnow could not board the bus fast enough, one of the Latvian guards shot him in the back of the head. The next day he was buried in a mass grave in the ghetto. According to a rumor — fast turning into legend — on his way to the bus, Dubnow repeated: 'People, do not forget; speak of this, people; record it all.'" Friedlander, *The Years of Extermination*, 262.

[110] Jean-Paul Sartre, *Anti-Semite and Jew*, 69.

[111] Saul Friedlander, *The Years of Extermination*, 117–121.

[112] Quoted by Michael Burns, *Dreyfus: A Family Affair*, 452.

[113] For an examination of the controversy surrounding the Condorset affair, see Jonathan Judaken, *Jean-Paul Sartre and the Jewish Question*. 49–52. "While both Being and Nothingness and The Flies were approved by the Nazi censors, Sartre was at the same time writing for the underground journal, *Les Lettres Francaises*. . . . Sartre's work during the war years thus enacts an ambivalence that I trace within and between the texts and their contexts." 52.

[114] Judaken, *Jean-Paul Sartre and the Jewish Question*, 54–55.

[115] Ibid.

[116] Judaken provides a welcome review of Sartre's wartime reflections on Jewish authenticity, as well as of his correspondence with Simone de Beauvoir, *Jean-Paul Sartre and the Jewish Question*, 54–59.

[117] Ibid., 79–80.

[118] Sartre, *Anti-Semite and Jew*, 71.

[119] Sartre, *Anti-Semite and Jew*, 10. A striking contrast to Sartre's psychological approach is the work of one of Sartre's French contemporaries, Jules Isaac. In his book, *The Teaching of Contempt*, Isaac attributes antisemitism not to the French psyche, but to the zealous actions of early church leaders. "How could the Christians succeed? Only by destroying the prestige of their adversary, by a campaign to discredit him. In this manner was established a kind of so-called Christian teaching which is more accurately called the teaching of contempt, and which I have shown to be the most formidable and pernicious weapon ever used against Judaism or the Jews." Isaac concludes his study of antisemitism on a hopeful note: "God be thanked, a purifying stream exists in Christianity and grows stronger every day." Isaac, 33–34, 146–147.

[120] Ibid.

[121] Ibid., 25.

[122] Ibid., 24–25

[123] Ibid., 33, 53–54.

[124] Ibid., 56–57.

[125] Christopher Clark, Iron Kingdom, 651. Fortunately, Grzesinski was able to flee Germany in 1933. He eventually settled in New York, where he ended his days as an auto repairman. See also Sartre, Anti-Semite and Jew, 40.

[126] Sartre, *Anti-Semite and Jew*, 106ff.

[127] Ibid., 90, 136-7.

[128] Barry Rubin, *Assimilation and its Discontents*, 230–231.

[129] George Herbert, *Mead, Mind, Self and Society*, 154–155. "The attitude of the generalized other," Mead maintains, "is the attitude of the whole community. Thus, for example, in the case of such a group as a ball team, the team is the generalized other in so far as it enters — as an organized process or social activity — into the experience of any one of the individual members of it . . . It is in the form of the generalized other that the social process influences the behavior of the individuals involved in it, and carrying it on, i.e., that the community exercises control over the conduct of its individual members."

[130] Ibid., 141.

[131] Ibid., 11–12, 46.

[132] Ibid. 11–12, 106.

[133] Tom Reiss, "Laugh Riots," *New Yorker*, November 19, 2007.

[134] See Elisabeth Young-Bruehl, Hannah Arendt, *For Love of the World*, 11-12, and Jerome Kohn's preface to Arendt, *The Jewish Writings* — Hannah Arendt, x–xiv.

[135] Geoffrey Wheatcroft, reviewing Tony Judt's book *Reappraisals* in the New York Times Book Review, April 20, 2008. In this book, Judt expressed general enthusiasm for Arendt's work, though he also added that *The Origins of Totalitarianism* was "not a perfect book."

[136] Hannah Arendt, *The Origins of Totalitarianism*, 56.

[137] Ibid.

[138] Ibid., 70–71.

[139] Benjamin Disraeli, *Coningsby*, 227, 233, 261.

[140] Arendt, *The Origins of Totalitarianism*, 68–79.

[141] Ibid., 19, 54.

[142] Ibid., 19.

[143] Ibid., 24.

[144] Ibid., 14ff; 19ff. See also, Arendt's *Rahel Varnhagen*, 180. Once society came to regard the Jewish problem as a disease rather than a crime the fate of the Jews was sealed. Thus, whether they were hated because of their useless wealth or their extreme poverty, the same destiny awaited them. In October of 1939, Hitler visited the Jewish section in Kielce, Poland, and Otto Dietrich who accompanied him summed up the reactions to the visit with these words: "If we had once believed we knew the Jews, we were quickly taught otherwise here. . . . The appearance of these human beings is unimaginable. . . . Physical repulsion hindered us from carrying out our research. . . . The Jews in Poland are in no way poor, but they live in such inconceivable dirt, in huts in which no vagrant in Germany would spend the night." In a report to Hitler that same year, propaganda minister Goebbels described the Jews as "waste product" and as a "clinical issue more than a social one." And after a visit to the Jewish sections of Lodz, Goebbels wrote: "We travel through the Lodz ghetto. . . . It cannot be described. These are no longer human beings, these are animals. Therefore, it is no humanitarian task, but a surgical one. One must cut here, in a radical way. Otherwise Europe will perish of the Jewish disease." Saul Friedlander, *The Years of Extermination*, 17, 19, 21. The theme of Jewish degeneration was one that was repeated ad nauseam by the German propagandists. The impossible living conditions which the Nazis had created for the Jews crowded into the Warsaw ghetto made them an easy target for this form of antisemitism. Thus, for example, Hubert Neun writing in March 1941 could affirm: "There surely cannot be a place on the

continent that offers such a graphic cross-section of the chaos and degeneracy of the Semitic mass. At a glance one can take in the enormous, repellent variety of all the Jewish types of the East; a gathering of the asocial, it floods out of dirty houses and greasy shops, up and down the streets, and behind the windows the series of bearded, spectacled rabbinic faces continues — a dreadful panorama." Friedlander, *The Years of Extermination*, 161.

[145] Arendt, *The Origins of Totalitarianism*, 19.

[146] Quotation from Henry Kissinger's videotaped oral history interview with Louise Bobrow, January 11, 2001, quoted in Jeremi Suri, *Henry Kissinger and the American Century*, 55.

[147] Arendt, *Origins*, 136.

[148] See for example, Hannah Arendt, *The Human Condition* in which the vita activa is examined. Arendt here is more interested in Greek thought than in Jewish theology. As a matter of fact her only comment about Judaism comes toward the end of the book were she criticizes the Ten Commandments for failing to condemn murder more vigorously.

[149] Clark, *Iron Kingdom*, 424–5. Clark notes that such pronouncements tempting Jews with the right to hold office if they converted were not at all unusual during the earlier years of the nineteenth century. The carrot and the stick is an apt metaphor for the relationship between Prussia and its Jews. In 1808, for example, property-owning Jews were allowed to vote, and David Friedlander, a disciple of Mendelssohn, was elected to a seat on the Berlin council. Yet the prevailing feeling was that Jews ought to convert before being granted full rights. Even as liberal a thinker as Wilhelm von Humboldt argued that the emancipation of the Jews was to be desired because it would lead to the voluntary self-dissolution of Judaism. "Since they are driven by an innate human need for a higher faith," the Jews "will turn of their own free will to the Christian religion," 336. All of this would take time — that was the view of another Prussian official. Repression, he concluded, has made the Jews "treacherous" and "the sudden concession of liberty would not suffice to reconstitute all at once the natural human nobility within them," 338. For a discussion of the rewards offered to Jews who converted, see Julius Carlebach, *Karl Marx and the Radical Critique of Judaism*, 32–35.

[150] Arendt, *The Jewish Writings*, 48–49.

[151] See Abram Leon, *The Jewish Question*.

[152] Ibid., 62ff.

[153] See Jonathan Judaken, *Jean-Paul Sartre and the Jewish Question*, 11–13.

[154] Ibid., 85ff. In her biography of Marc Bloch, Carole Fink points out that in 1886, Drumont signaled the birth of modern French antisemitism with the publication of his two-volume hate-filled work titled *La France Juive*. An unprecedented 100,000 copies were sold within a year. Carole Fink, *Marc Bloch: A Life in History*, 17. What these accounts seem to neglect is the persistent strain of antisemitism within the Catholic Church which created the climate for both the antagonism toward Hertz and Reinach as well as Dreyfus. For a large section of the clergy, Jean-Denis Bredin asserts, "the Jews remained the people of 'deicide.' The Talmud was but an 'anticatechism' from which the Jews 'derived like serpents, all their vices. Periodically, the old myth of ritual crime was revived." Bredin, *The Affair*, 24. It would be a mistake to assume that the Catholic Church was totally unconcerned about the antisemitic attitudes of many of its priests. In 1897, the distinguished Catholic economist and historian Anatole Leroy-Beaulieu convened a conference on antisemitism at the Institut Catholique of Paris. Before an audience that was generally, but not totally, friendly, Leroy-Beaulieu underscored the persistent religious roots of anti-Jewish feelings. The Jews, he suggested, were being unfairly blamed for the emergence of "idees moderns" and for the de-Chrisianization of modern society. Anatole Leroy-Beaulieu, *L'antisemitisme*, 9. In this context it should also be added that Dreyfus's own attorney, and a staunch defender of his cause, was Edgar Demange, a conservative and a Catholic.

[155] There is another Jewish connection to the Panama Scandal that Arendt does not mention, probably because it is not relevant to her study of European totalitarianism. In the United States the banking house headed by Jesse Seligman handled the stock issue for the French Panama Canal Company. Seligman, a prominent member of New York's elite German Jewish community, received an extra fee of $350,000 simply "for the privilege of using the Seligman name as patrons of the undertaking." It should be added that other American firms also participated in the doomed stock offering, namely Drexel, Morgan and Company and Winslow Lanier and Company. The Seligman name was given top billing to the delight of Jesse Seligman, whose rivalry with J. P. Morgan was intense. The Senate investigation of the Panama venture was a severe blow to the integrity of the Seligman banking house. Birmingham, *Our Crowd*, 252-261.

[156] *The Origins of Totalitarianism*, 60-61.

[157] Cf. C. Wright Mills and Hans Gerth Character and Social Structure, p. 216. Also Max Weber, *Essays in Sociology*. Weber would apply the word pariah to the entire scope of Jewish history during the Diaspora. "When a

tribe loses its foothold in its territory it becomes a guest or a pariah people."
Essays in Sociology, 399. Again, with reference to the Jewish people, he writes: "Since the exile, Judaism has been the religion of a civic 'pariah people'" Ibid., 269. It should be noted that Weber rejected the genetic stereotyping advocated by Werner Sombart in *The Jews and Modern Capitalism*. Yet in a footnote, he spells out in detail what "pariah capital" may indicate. "To the English Puritans, the Jews of their time were representatives of that type of capitalism which was involved in war, Government contracts, State monopolies, speculative promotions, and the construction and financial projects of princes, which they themselves condemned. In fact, the difference may, in general, with the necessary qualifications, be formulate: that Jewish capitalism was speculative pariah-capitalism, while the Puritan was bourgeois organization of labour." *The Protestant Ethic and the Spirit of Capitalism*, 271.

[158] Bernard Lazare, *Antisemitism, Its History and Causes*, 332ff.

[159] See *The Jewish Writings*, lv, 284–285, 338–50.

[160] Quoted in Christopher Clark, *Iron Kingdom*, 263. It is interesting to note Clark's use of the word interstitial in this context: "This interstitial sphere of enlightened trans-confessional conviviality steadily expanded in the later decades of the eighteenth century."

[161] Arendt, *Rahel Varnhagen*, 214–215. And so, to the very end of her life, Rachel remained a Jew and a pariah, 227.

[162] Arendt, *The Origins of Totalitarianism*, 64.

[163] Arendt, *The Jewish Writings*, 275. As for Gershom Scholem, his opposition to the use of the word pariah was unequivocal. Asked to release his correspondence about the Eichmann trial so that it might be published in a volume to be entitled *The Jew as Pariah*, the editor Ron H. Feldman reports: "Permission to reprint this letter was given by Gershom Scholem although he registers his strong objection to the title of this book which he finds most offensive." Arendt, *The Jew as Pariah*, edited by Ron H. Feldman, 240.

[164] *The Origins of Totalitarianism*, 59ff., 66. In a footnote to an article on Herzl and Bernard Lazare, Arendt seems to approve of Lazare's distinction between the "unconscious pariah," i.e., the non-emancipated Jew and the conscious pariah of Western society, *The Jewish Writings*, 341.

[165] Arendt, *The Jewish Writings*, 47.

[166] Young-Bruehl, *Hannah Arendt*, 331.

[167] Arendt, *Eichmann in Jerusalem*, 117–118; 125–126.

[168] Young-Bruehl, *Hannah Arendt*, 348–351, 352–354.

169 Arendt, *Eichmann*, 230.

170 See, for instance, Arendt's long letter to Gershom Scholem. "You know as well as I know how often those who merely report certain unpleasant facts are accused of lack of soul, lack of heart, or lack of what you call *Herzenstakt*. We both know, in other words, how often these emotions are used in order to conceal factual truth," *The Jewish Writings*, 467. As *Eichmann in Jerusalem* reveals, the subject of evil was never far from Arendt's mind. In an essay dedicated to her memory, Tony Judt quotes her as saying that "the problem of evil will be the fundamental question of postwar intellectual life in Europe — as death became the fundamental problem after the last war." Judt goes on to suggest that "if we wish to grasp the true significance of evil — what Hannah Arendt intended by calling it 'banal' — then we must remember that what is truly awful about the destruction of the Jews is not that it mattered so much but that it mattered so little." Tony Judt, "The 'Problem of Evil' in Postwar Europe," *New York Review*, February 14, 2008.

171 J. Glenn Grey in a letter to Arendt dated March 23, 1963. Jasper's comments about the Eichmann book are contained in a letter he wrote to her on December 13, 1963. Quoted in Young-Bruehl, *Hannah Arendt*, 370. See also p. 526 notes 128 and 129.

172 Arendt, *Rahel Varnhagen*, 7, 28.

173 Arendt, *Origins of Totalitarianism*, 49–50, 56.

174 Arendt, *The Jewish Writings*, 50–56.

175 Ibid., 51 The italics are Arendt's.

176 Georg Simmel, *The Sociology of Georg Simmel*, 146.

177 Ibid., 152.

178 Ibid., 154–155.

179 For an early account of Chicago's Contract Sales battle, see James Alan McPherson, "In My Father's House," *Atlantic Monthly*, April 1972. For a more complete analysis, see Beryl Satter, *Family Properties*. Beginning with an account of her father's ownership of property on Chicago's West Side, Professor Satter carefully documents the complicated legal and moral issues involved in the Contract Sales Battle.

180 Satter. *Family Properties*, 71–72.

181 Internet statement: "Who is Bernard Madoff, the man behind the $50 billion fraud?" posted by Christopher Bollyn, December 12, 2008.

182 Laurence Learner, quoted in the *New York Times*, April 12, 2009.

183 The letter written by the American Jewish Committee's executive director, David A. Harris is worth quoting in its entirety:

To The Editor: "In 'Standing Accused: A Pillar of Finance and Charity,' your Dec. 13 Business Day article about Bernard L. Madoff, arrested in a major fraud scheme, there was a striking emphasis on his being Jewish. It was not just once or twice, but at least three times before the article continued inside. Why?

"Yes, he is Jewish. We get it. But was this relevant to his being arrested for cheating investors or so key to his evolution as a businessman that it needed to be hammered home again and again?

"I have read several accounts in the *Times* of the shenanigans of Gov. Rod Blagojevich of Illinois. Yet have no clue of what his religion is, nor frankly, do I care. Why should I? Unless he was acting in the name of his faith, which I assume he was not, what difference does it make? And if a profile is warranted and the governor's faith matters to him, mention it and move on.

"But to refer to the 'Jewish T-Bill,' the clubby Jewish world,' and 'the world of Jewish New York' within four paragraphs near the top of the article on Mr. Madoff was over the top." *New York Times*, December 21, 2008.

[184] Isaac M. Wise, *Reminiscences*, 37–38.

[185] Robert J. Marx, *Changing Patterns of Leadership*. 264.

[186] Ibid., 33.

[187] Naomi W. Cohen, "Commissioner Williams and the Jews, *American Jewish Archives Journal*, vol. 61, no. 2 (2009), 121.

[188] Robert J. Marx, *Changing Patterns of Leadership*, 17.

[189] Quoted by Jonathan D. Sarna, *American Judaism*, 78.

[190] Isaac M. Wise, *Reminiscences*, 235.

[191] Gary Zola reports this exchange between Leeser and Wise in a fund-raising letter on behalf of the American Jewish Archives, December 10, 2007. Wise's frequent attacks on Leeser's academic background seem ironic for it is doubtful whether Wise himself ever earned an academic degree or a formal ordination. Yet he regularly referred to himself as the "Reverend Doctor." See Sarna, *American Judaism*, 92. See also James G. Heller, Isaac M. Wise, 74; Meyer, *Response to Modernity*, 250.

[191] Isaac M. Wise, *Reminiscences*, 37–38.

[192] Meyer, *Response to Modernity*, 250.

[193] Stephen Birmingham, *Our Crowd*, 316.

[194] Ibid., 24–27. The name Belmont, of course, is the French equivalent of Schonberg — "beautiful mountain." "He spoke," says Birmingham, "some Italian, a little Spanish, a little French, and all three languages with an atrocious accent, but nobody in New York knew the difference," 32.

[195] On the relationship between Nixon and Kissinger, much has been written. See, for example, Robert Dallek, *Nixon and Kissinger: Partners in Power*, 90; 170–171.

[196] Quoted in the *New York Times*, February 1, 2009.

[197] Jeremi Suri, *Henry Kissinger and the American Century*.

[198] Michael Gerson, quoted in *World Jewish Digest*, November 2007.

[199] *Forward*, July 11, 2008.

[200] *Forward*, September 7, 2007, *Reform Judaism*, Summer, 2008.

[201] Raquel Ukeles, "Locating the Silent Muslim Majority," manuscript distributed by Mosaica Research Center, 13.

[202] See, for instance, Norman Podhoretz's dire warning in "The Case for Bombing Iran." "Schools in England are dropping the Holocaust from their history lessons to avoid offending Muslim pupils." And: "much of the world has greeted Ahmadinejad's promise to wipe Israel off the map with something close to insouciance. In fact it could almost be said of the Europeans that they have been more upset by Ahmadinejad's denial that a Holocaust took place 60 years ago than of his determination to set up one of his own." *Commentary*, June 2007. See also, Gabriel Schoenfeld discussing the increasing number of Jews elected to Congress as Democrats: "The Democratic party itself is becoming demonstrably less hospitable to Jewish interests." "Jews, Muslims and Democrats," *Commentary*, January, 2007. One more of the many instances of *Commentary*'s preoccupation with antisemitism can be seen in Joshua Maravchik's article, "Our Worst President, Writing about President Carter," Maravchik observes: "Something of the old fashioned pre-Vatican II Christian animus toward Jews may be at work in Carter." *Commentary*, February 2007.

[203] Jonathan Sarna, *Amercan Judaism*, 75.

[204] Emmanuel Levinas, *Outside the Subject*, 14.

[205] Benedict de Spinoza, "(Tractatus) Theological-Political Treatise," Chapter 8, in *Complete Works*, edited by Michael Morgan, 471–480.

[206] Ibid., Chapter 17, 547. Jonathan Israel suggests a possible economic connection to Spinoza's break with the synagogue. Several ships owned by Michael Spinoza, Baruch's father, had either been seized by the English navy or captured by pirates. The family business was ruined, and by 1656, Baruch Spinoza had stopped paying his synagogue dues. This hardly explains, as Israel notes, the rancor evident in Spinoza's excommunication. "The precise reasons adduced by the community elders for his excommunication remain unknown. But it is plain from the form of

excommunication used in July of 1656, one of altogether exceptional vehemence, and severity only occasionally deployed in early modern times, that he was proscribed for no ordinary deviance, sacrilege, financial irregularity, or heresy but open, systematic, premeditated, and blatant doctrinal rebellion of a fundamental kind that simply could not be ignored or smoothed over." Israel, *Radical Enlightenment*, 172. See also 165–7, 171–3.

[207] Israel, *Radical Enlightenment*, 185–196. See also Chapter 16. "Signs that Spinoza was being watched were especially evident in and around The Hague, where he lived and worked. What principally worried the secular and ecclesiastical authorities were indications that his ideas were beginning to penetrate society more widely," 286.

[208] Steven Nadler, *Spinoza: A Life*, 306. The account of Spinoza's anger at the De Witt assassination comes from Leibniz's account of a later visit with Spinoza. According to this account, the landlord Van der Spyck bolted the door preventing Spinoza from endangering his own life as well, perhaps, of the Van der Spyck family.

[209] Spinoza, *Theologico-Political Treatise*, 18.2.1 and 19.2.27.

[210] Spinoza, *Complete Works*, 553–4. In dealing with the prophets, Stuart Hampshire rightly points out that Spinoza's anger was not directed against the message of the prophets, but against those who take their claims to any special authority too literally. Hampshire offers this paraphrase: "The work of the prophets is achieved if he persuades men to obey the laws of their society and to lead quiet and useful lives. . . . If we appreciate the old Jewish prophets from this standpoint, we find that they were ignorant men brilliantly gifted to instill faith and obedience in an ignorant society by myth and story. As philosophers, we understand their function, and do not regard their writings as making any claim to literal truth. Confusion comes from the false sophistication of those, who like the great Maimonides, try to read philosophic truths into the text of scripture by ingenuities of interpretation." Hampshire, *Spinoza and Spinozism*, 154. Isaac Deutscher found Spinoza's critique of the prophets to lie at the heart of his rupture with Judaism: "Spinoza himself when he started out as independent thinker and as initiator of modern criticism of the Bible seized at once the cardinal contradiction in Judaism, the contradiction between the monotheistic and universal God and the setting in which that God appears in the Jewish religion — as a God attached to one people only; the contradiction between the universal God and his 'chosen people.' We know what the realization of this contradiction brought upon Spinoza; banishment from

the Jewish community and excommunication. He had to fight against the Jewish clergy which, itself recently a victim of the Inquisition, became infested with the Inquisition. Then he had to face the hostility of the Catholic clergy and Calvinistic priests. His whole life was a struggle to overcome the limitations of the religions and cultures of his time." Deutscher, *The Non-Jewish Jew*, 2.

211 *Theologico-Political Treatise*, 13.1.22, Spinoza goes on to specifically praise Jeremiah for his ethical vision: "But let anyone glory only in this: to understand me and to know that I, Jehovah, do charity, judgment, and justice in the land, for I delight in these things, says Jehovah." (Jer. 22.16). See also *Theologico-Political Treatise*, 13.1.30, We see, accordingly, that Jeremiah, Moses, and John comprehended in a few words the knowledge of God which each is bound to know; and as we have meant to say, they place it in this alone: that God is highly just and highly merciful, or the simple model of true life."

212 Jonathan Israel, *Radical Enlightenment*, 159–160. "Exactly like Machiavelli and Hobbes, but unlike almost every other writer, Spinoza was usually referred to by the hundreds of Early Enlightenment authors who cite him by his surname alone." 161. Israel distinguishes between the Radical Enlightenment which Spinoza represented and the more conservative, or, as Israel prefers to call it, moderate mainstream Enlightenment. To mention a few of the names hardly does justice to the variety of views which the Enlightenment elicited. Noteworthy within the radical wing with Spinoza would be thinkers as diverse as Hobbes, Bayle, Diderot, and perhaps a young Rousseau. Counted among the moderates would be Newton, Boyle, Leibniz, Locke and Hume. Both radicals and moderates of course had to face the attacks of counter-enlightenment forces that regarded the ideas Spinoza and his adherents as threats to the established order, i.e., the church and monarchism. See the introduction to Israel's *Enlightenment Contested*.

213 Stewart, *The Courtier and the Heretic*, 11. Adam Rechenberg from his base in Leipzig undertook the task of alerting his fellow clergy to the dangers of Spinoza and Spinozism. Warning against "deism, Naturalism, fatalism, and Neo-Epicureanism," Rechenberg emphasized the special threat posed by the "penetration of radical thought which 'calls God Nature' and equates 'His intelligence, energy, and capability with Natura Naturans,' that is, the most systematically philosophical form of atheism." Cited by Jonathan Israel, *Radical Enlightenment*, 4. In the same work Israel notes that despite Spinoza's estrangement from Jewish life, his enemies

found it convenient to persist in identifying him as a Jew. philosopher, Bertrand Russell in his *History of Western Philosophy*, 569. Johannes Musaeus (1613-81), for example, a professor at Jena, fiercely asserted that no one had wrought greater havoc upon Church and State than this 'imposter.' His name, he declares, is "Benedictus Spinosa, a Jew by nation' but in truth an 'enemy to all religion." 631ff. Of course, the intensity of anti-Spinoza criticism was a tribute to the tremendous impact the heretic Jew had upon contemporary philosophical thought. A much different and wholly positive assessment of Spinoza was offered by the twentieth century philosopher, Bertrand Russell in his *History of Western Philosophy*, 569.

[214] It was in his "Short Treatise on God, Man, and His Well-Being"that Spinoza used the term "born again." He went on to say that "our first birth took place when we were united with the body, through which the activities and movements of the (vital) spirits have arisen; but this our other or second birth will take place when we become aware in us of entirely different affects of love commensurate with the knowledge of this incorporeal object, and as different from the first as the corporeal is from the incorporeal, spirit from flesh. And this may, therefore, all the more justly and truly be called Regeneration." Short Treatise, Chapter XII, in Spinoza, *Complete Works*, 95.

[215] Spinoza first used the terms *Natura naturans* and *Natura naturata* in his "Short Treatise on God, Man and His Well-Being," which was probably completed around 1662. Spinoza, *Complete Works*, 58. See also Spinoza, *Ethics*, Part I. James Martineau in his Study of Spinoza discusses the distinction between Natura naturans and Natura naturata and points out that "this antithesis is much older than Spinoza's time, and is resorted to by him merely to adjust the relation of his philosophy to that of an earlier age." 224-6. It is in his *Ethics*, Jonathan Israel insists, that Spinoza clarifies "his distinction between Natura Naturans and Natura Naturata, the first designating what exists independently in itself, and conceived through itself, namely 'God, insofar as he is considered to be a free cause,' that is nature understood as the creative power or potential of nature . . . the latter, denoting by contrast, the actuality or determinate state of nature." Israel, *Radical Enlightenment*, 231.

[216]Quoted by Eugene Mihaly in *Spinoza, A Tercentenary Perspective*, 106.

[217] Spinoza, *Ethics*, Part I, Appendix, In Spinoza's *Complete Works*, 238 The compatibility of Spinoza's metaphysics with modern biological theories has frequently been noted. Stuart Hampshire, for instance, makes the following observation: "It is probable that the human body served for Spinoza as the

model for physical systems in general, even though he did not have access to the physiology and the anatomy which would conduct him from protein to the cell to the limb to the whole person. He had an extraordinary understanding of the dynamic processes, the conflicts and the delicate balances which are to be found in all living systems." Hampshire then goes on to note that "Evidently Spinoza had no knowledge of the genetic component in the individual's struggle for self-maintenance. But he did provide a framework within which the discoveries of modern genetics and of molecular biology can be fitted without too much strain and without too many changes of emphasis." *Spinoza and Spinozism*, xxxii–xxxiii.

[218] Jonathan Stewart, *The Courtier and the Heretic*, 179. Jonathan Israel maintains that debates about the virtues and dangers of Spinoza's philosophy occupied the great minds of the early Enlightenment period. "The question of Spinozism is indeed central and indispensable to any proper understanding of Early Enlightenment European thought. Its prominence in European intellectual debates in the late seventeenth and early eighteenth century is generally far greater than anyone would suppose from the existing secondary literature." *Radical Enlightenment*, 12–13.

[219] Spinoza, *Ethics*, Appendix, Prop. XII. Spinoza, *Complete Works*, 240.

[220] Jonathan Israel uses Spinoza's words to describe this view of religion. "It is owing to the radical philosophical positions he has already adopted on man, nature, and society that Spinoza can insist that the 'state can pursue no safer course than to regard piety and religion as consisting solely in the exercise of charity and just dealing and that the right of the sovereign, in both the religious and secular spheres, should be restricted to men's actions, with everyone being allowed to think what he will and say what he thinks.'" *Radical Enlightenment*, 117.

[221] Deutscher, *The Non-Jewish Jew*, 30.

[222] Louis Dupre, *The Enlightenment and the Intellectual Foundations of Modern Culture*, 9.

[223] Ibid., *The Enlightenment and the Intellectual Foundations of Modern Culture*, 116.

[224] Stewart, *The Courtier and the Heretic*, 11. Stewart's entire book is based on this one visit with Spinoza, and the impact it had upon Liebniz's later thinking.

[225] Martineau, *A Study of Spinoza*, 104.

[226] Ernest Gellner, *Plough, Sword and Book*, 134–136. Gellner's critique of the Enlightenment understanding of both Nature and Reason is incisive and important. "The new nature left no room within itself for the new

revelation; the new revelation would not vincicate and underwrite nature. The greatest thinkers of the Enlightenment were those who laid bare this internal crisis." 137.

[227] Spinoza, Ethics, Appendix, Prop. XII, Spinoza *Complete Works*, 240.

[228] Spinoza goes on to assert: "Accordingly, they imagine two powers distinct in number from each other — the power of God, and the power of natural things." *Theologico-Political Treatise*, 6.1.

[229] Joseph Soloveitchik, *The Lonely Man of Faith*, 36. Soloveitchik concludes that both Adams are important to God and are destined to be united in a covenant of faith.

[230] Emmanuel Levinas, *Nine Talmudic Readings*, 84-85. Levinas repeatedly emphasizes the importance of "alterity," concern and responsibility for the "other." Nowhere is Levinas more conscientious in asserting both his debt to Spinoza and his differences with him than in a statement he inserts in the conclusion of his philosophical study, *Totality and Infinity*. "To exist has a meaning in another dimension than that of the perduration of the totality; it can go beyond being. Contrary to the Spinozist tradition, this going beyond death is produced not in the universality of thought but in the pluralist relation, in the goodness of being for the Other, in justice. The surpassing of being starting from being — the relation with exteriority — is not measured by duration. Duration itself becomes visible in the relation with the Other, where being is surpassed." 301–302.

[231] Maimonides, *Hilchot Matnot Ani'im*, 10:7.

[232] John P. Kretzmann and John L. McKnight, *Building Communities from the Inside Out.*

[233] Arendt, *The Origins of Totalitarianism*, 66.

[234] Deutscher, *The Non-Jewish Jew* 81.

Bibliography

Ahad Ha-Am. *Essays, Letters, Memoirs.* East and West Library, Oxford, 1946.

Arendt, Hannah. *Between Past and Future.* Viking Press, New York, 1968.

> *Crises of the Republic.* Harcourt Brace Jovanovich, New York, 1969.
>
> *Eichmann in Jerusalem.* Viking Press, New York, 1963.
>
> *The Human Condition*, University of Chicago Press, Chicago, 1958.
>
> *The Jew as Pariah.* Edited and with an introduction by Ron H. Feldman, Grove Press, New York, 1978.
>
> *The Jewish Writings.* Edited by Jerome Kuhn and Ron H. Feldman, New York, Schocken, 2007.
>
> *The Life of the Mind.* 3 vols. Harcourt Brace Jovanovich, New York, 1971.
>
> *The Origins of Totalitarianism.* New York, Harcourt, Brace & World, 1951, 1958, 1966.
>
> *Rahel Varnhagen.* Harcourt Brace Jovanovich, New York, 1974.

Ashtor, Eliyahu. *The Jews of Moslem Spain.* 3 vols. The Jewish Publication Society, Philadelphia, 1979.

> *Babylonian Talmud.* Soncino Press, London, 1960.

Baer, Yitzhak. *A History of the Jews in Christian Spain.* 2 vols. The Jewish Publication Society, Philadelphia, 1961.

Bartke, Sandra Lee. *Femininity and Domination.* Routledge, New York, 1990.

Ben-Sasson, H. H. ed. *A History of the Jewish People.* Harvard University Press, Cambridge, 1976.

Birmingham, Stephen, *Our Crowd.* Harper & Row, New York, 1967,

Blake, Robert, *Disraeli.* St. Martin's Press, New York, 1967,

Bloch, Marc, *Feudal Society.* University of Chicago Press, 1961.

Borowitz, Eugene, *Liberal Judaism.* Union of American Hebrew Congregations, New York, 1984.

Brandeis, Louis D. *The Curse of Bigness.* Viking, New York, 1934.

Bredin, Jean-Denis. *The Affair.* George Braziller, New York, 1986.

Broad, C.D. *Five Types of Ethical Theory.* Routledge & Kegan Paul, London, 1930.

Bronner, Stephen Eric. *A Rumor About the Jews.* St. Martin's Press, New York, 2000.

> *Reclaiming the Enlightenment.* Columbia University Press, New York, 2004.

Burns, Michael. *Dreyfus: A Family Affair.* Harper Collins, New York, 1991.

Caird, John. *Spinoza.* J.R. Lippincott Company, Philadelphia, 1888.

> *Cambridge Companion to Spinoza.* Edited by Don Garrett, Cambridge University Press, Cambridge, 1996.

Carlebach, Julius. *Karl Marx and the Radical Critique of Judaism.* Routledge and Kegan Paul, London, 1978.

Chapman, Guy. *The Dreyfus Trials.* Stein and Day, New York, 1991.

Chumash with Targum Onkelos, Haphtaroth and Rashi's Commentary. Silberman Family, Jerusalem, 1984.

278

Clark, Christopher. *Iron Kingdom: The Rise and Downfall of Prussia, 1600-1947.* Cambridge, Mass.: Belknap Press of Harvard University Press.

Corti, Count Egon Caesar. The *Rise of the House of Rothschild.* Cosmopolitan Book Corporation, New York, 1928.

Cowles, Virginia. *The Rothschilds.* Alfred A. Knopf, New York, 1973.

Dallek, Robert. *Nixon and Kissinger: Partners in Power.* Harper Collins, 2007.

Deutscher, Isaac. *The Non-Jewish Jew.* Hill and Wang, New York, 1968.

Dio, Cassius. *Roman History.* Loeb Classical Library, Harvard University Press, Cambridge, 1925.

Disraeli, Benjamin. *Coningsby.* Wildside Press, Doylestown, Pennsylvania, (First published, 1844).
  Alroy or the Prince of the Captivity. M. Walter Dunne, London, 1904.

Dubnow, Simon. *History of the Jews.* 6 vols. South Brunswick, New York, 1967-69.
  History of the Jews of Russia and Poland. 3 vols. Jewish Publication Society, Philadelphia, 1916.
  Nationalism and History. Atheneum, New York, 1970.

Duby, Georges. *The Knight The Lady and the Priest.* University of Chicago Press, 1981 Duby, Georges and Mandlou, Robert, A *History of French Civilization,* Random House, New York, 1964.

Dupre, Louis. *The Enlightenment and the Intellectual Foundations of Modern Culture.* Yale University Press, New Haven, 2004.

Elon, Amos. *Herzl.* Holt, Rinehart and Winston, New York, Chicago, San Francisco, 1975.

Encyclopaedia Judaica. Encyclopaedia Judaica, Jerusalem.

Feldman, Louis H. *Jew and Gentile in the Ancient World.* Princeton University Press, Princeton, 1993.

Ferguson, Niall. *The House of Rothschild, 1798-1848.* Viking, New York, 1998.
  The House of Rothschild, 1849-1998. Penguin Books, New York, 1998.
  The Ascent of Money. Penguin Press, New York, 2008.

Fink, Carole. *Marc Bloch, A Life in History.* Cambridge University Press, Cambridge, 1989.

Saul Friedlander. *The Years of Extermination.* Harper Collins, New York, 2007.

Gellner, Ernest. *Nations and Nationalism,* second edition. Cornell University Press, Ithaca, N.Y., 2006.
  Plough, Sword and Book. University of Chicago Press, Chicago, 1988.

Golb, Norman. "The Autograph Memoirs of Obadiah the Proselyte of Oppido Lucano" Oppido Lucano (Basilicata), 2004.
  "Jacob Tam's Service on Behalf of the King of France at Reims," European Association for Jewish Studies, Moscow, 2006.
  The Jews in Medieval Normandy. Cambridge University Press, Cambridge, 1998.

Graetz, H. *History of* the *Jews.* 6 vols. Jewish Publication Society, Philadelphia, 1891.

Gross, Jan T. *Fear.* Random House, New York, 2007

Neighbor. Penguin Books, New York, 2002.

Halevi, Judah. *Book of Kuzari*, translated by Hartwig Hirschfeld. Pardes, New York, 1946.

Hampshire, Stuart. *Spinoza and Spinozism.* Oxford University Press, Oxford, 2005.

Hartman, David. *Maimonides, Torah and Philosophic Quest*, The Jewish Publication Society, Philadelphia, 1976.

Hegel, Georg Wilhelm Friedrich. *The Philosophy of Hegel*, The Modern Library, New York, 1953.

Heller, James G. *Isaac M. Wise*, Union of American Hebrew Congregations, New York, 1965.

Hertzberg, Arthur. *The French Enlightenment and the Jews.* Columbia University Press, New York and London, 1968.

Herzl, Theodore. *The Diaries of Theodor Herzl.* Edited and translated by Marvin Lowenthal. Dial Press, New York, 1956.
The Jewish State, Scopus Publishing Co. New York, 1943.

Heschel, Abraham Joshua. *God in Search of Man.* Farrar, Straus & Cudahy, New York, 1955.
The Insecurity of Freedom. Schocken Books, 1972.
The Prophets. Harper Torchbooks, New York, 1962.

Hitler, A. *Mein Kampf.* Houghton Mifflin, New York, 1969.

Hourani, Albert. *A History of the Arab Peoples.* Belknap Press, Cambridge, Mass. 1991.

Howe, Irving. *World of Our Fathers.* Harcourt Brace Jovanovich, New York, 1976.

Huppert, George. *After the Black Death.* Indiana University Press, Bloomington, 1986.
The Style of Paris. Indiana University Press, Bloomington, 1999.

Isaac, Jules, *The Teaching of Contempt.* Holt, Rinehart and Winston, New York, 1964.

Israel, Jonathan I. *Enlightenment Contested: Philosophy, Modernity and the Emancipation.* Oxford University Press, Oxford, 2006.
Radical Enlightenment: Philosophy and the Making of Modernity 1650–1750. Oxford University Press, Oxford, 2001.

Jacobs, Jill. *There Shall Be No Needy.* Jewish Lights, Woodstock, Vermont, 2009.

Josephus. *The Works of Josephus*, Translated by William Whiston, Hendrickson Publishers, Peabody, Mass., 1987.

Judaken, Jonathan, *Jean-Paul Sartre and Jewish Question.* University of Nebraska Press, Lincoln, Nebraska, 2006.

Katz, Jacob, *Tradition and Crisis, Jewish Society at the End of the Middle Ages.* Schocken Books, New York, 1961.

Kirsch, Adam, *Benjamin Disraeli.* Schocken Books, New York, 2008.

Kogan, Barry, ed. *Spinoza, A Tercentenary Perspective.* Hebrew Union College-Jewish Institute of Religion, 1978.

Kohler, K. *Studies, Addresses and Personal Papers.* Jewish Publication Society Press, Philadelphia, 1931.

Kraemer, Joel L. *Maimonides.* Doubleday, New York, 2008.

Kretzmann, John P. and McKnight, John L. *Building Communities from the Inside Out*. Institute for Policy Research, Evanston, Il. 1993.

Lazare, Bernard. *Antisemitism, Its History and Causes*. International Library Publishing Company, New York, 1903.

Le Goff, Jacques. *History and Memory*. Columbia University Press, New York, 1992.

Leibowitz, Yeshayahu. *The Faith of Maimonides*. MOD Books, Tel Aviv, 1989.

Leon, Abram. *The Jewish Question, A Marxist Interpretation*. Pathfinder Press, Inc., New York, 1972.

Leroy-Beaulieu, Anatole. *L'antisemitisme*. Ancienne Maison Michel Levy Freres, Paris, 1897.

Levinas, Emmanuel. *Ethics and Infinity*. Duquesne University Press, Pittsburgh, 1994.

   The Levinas Reader. Blackwell, Oxford, 1989.

   Nine Talmudic Readings. Indiana University Press, Bloomington, 1994.

   Outside The Subject. Stanford University Press, Stanford, 1993.

   Time and the Other. Duquesne University Press, Pittsburgh, 1987.

   Totality and Infinity. Duquesne University Press, Pittsburgh, 1969.

Liber, Maurice. *Rashi*. Jewish Publication Society, Philadelphia, 1906.

Lowenthal, Marvin, *The Jews of Germany*. Longmans, Green and Co. New York, 1936.

Maier-Katkin, Daniel. *Stranger from Abroad: Hannah Arendt, Martin Heidegger, Friendship and Forgiveness*. W.W. Norton, New York, 2010.

Marcus, Jacob R. *The Jew in the Medieval World: A Sourcebook, 315–1791*. Jewish Publication Society, New York, 1938.

Martineau, James. *A Study of Spinoza*. Macmillan & Co., London, 1882.

Marx, Robert J., *Changing Patterns of Leadership in the American Reform Rabbinate, 1890–1957*. PhD thesis, Yale University.

Mead, George Herbert. *Mind, Self and Society*. University of Chicago, 1934.

Meyer, Michael A. *Response to Modernity*. Wayne State University Press, Detroit, 1988.

Midrash Rabbah. Yavneh, Tel Aviv, 1958.

Montaigne, Michel De. *The Complete Works*. Everyman, New York, 2003.

Morton , Frederic. *The Rothschilds*. Atheneum, New York, 1962.

Nadler, Steven. *Spinoza, A Life*. Cambridge University Press, 1999.

   Spinoza's Ethics, An Introduction, Cambridge University Press, Cambridge 2006.

Northrop, F. S. C. *Ideological Differences and World Order*. New Haven, Yale University Press, 1949.

   The Logic of the Sciences and the Humanities. The Macmillan Company, New York, 1947.

   The Meeting of East and West. The Macmillan Company, New York, 1946.

Pearson, Hesketh. *Dizzy*. Harper and Brothers, New York, 1951.

Piskorski, Jan M. "From Munich through Wansee to Auschwitz: The Road to the Holocaust," *Journal of the Historical Society*, vol. 7, no. 2 (June 2007).

Poliakov, Leon. *The History of Anti-Semitism*. 4 vols. The Vanguard Press, New York, 1965.

Randall, John Herman. *The Making of the Modern Mind*. Houghton Mifflin, Boston, 1936.

Rubin, Barry. *Asssimilation and Its Discontents*. Times Books, New York, 1995.

Russell, Bertrand. *A History of Philosophy*, Simon and Schuster, New York, 1945.

Sarna, Jonathan D. *American Judaism*. Yale University Press, New Haven, 2004.

Satter, Beryl. *Family Properties*. Metropolitan Books, New York, 2009.

Sartre, Jean-Paul. *Anti-Semite and Jew*. Schocken Books, New York, 1948.
　　Being and Nothingness, Philosophical Library, New York, 1956.

Schafer, Peter, *Judeophobia*. Harvard University Press, Cambridge, 1997.

Schwartz, Richard H. *Judaism and Global Survival*. Lantern Books, New York, 2002.

Schorske, Carl E. *Fin-de-Siècle Vienna*, Alfred A. Knopf, New York, 1980.

Seltzer, Robert. *Jewish People, Jewish Thought*. Macmillan, New York, 1980.

Simmel, Georg, *The Sociology of Georg Simmel*, translated by Kurt H. Wolff. The Free Press, Glencoe, 1950.

Simonsen, Jon Gunnar Molstre, art. "Perfect Targets — Antisemitism and Eastern Jews in Leipzig, 1919–1923," in *Leo Baeck Institute Yearbook*, Berghan Books, Oxford 2006.

Soloveitchik, Joseph, *The Lonely Man of Faith*. Jason Aronson, Northvale, New Jersey, 1997.
　　Man of Faith in the Modern World. 2 vols. K'tav Publishing House, Hoboken, New Jersey, 1989.

Sombart, Werner. *The Jews and Modern Capitalism*. The Free Press, Glencoe, 1951.

Spinoza, Benedict de. *Complete Works*, translated by Samuel Shirley, edited by Michael R. Morgan. Hackett Publishing, Indianapolis, 2002.
　　Ethics, in *The Collected Writings of Spinoza*. Translated by Edwin Curly. Princeton University Press, Princeton, N.J, 1985.
　　Theologico-Political Treatise. Translated and with an essay by Martin D. Yaffe. University of North Texas, 2004.
　　Tractatus Theologico Politicus. Trubner & Co., London, 1862.

Stern, Fritz. *Gold and Iron*. Alfred A. Knopf, New York, 1977.

Stern, Selma. *The Court Jew*. Jewish Publication Society of America, Philadelphia, 1950.

Stewart, Jonathan. *The Courtier and the Heretic*. W.W. Norton, New York, 2006.

Stroumsa, Sarah. *Maimonides in His World*. Princeton University Press, Princeton and Oxford, 2009.

Suri, Jeremi. *Henry Kissinger and the American Century*. Harvard University Press, Cambridge, 2007.

Tawney, R.H. *Religion and the Rise of Capitalism*. Harcourt, Brace and Company, New York, 1926.

Tcherikover, Victor. *Hellenistic Civilization and the Jews*. Jewish Publication Society, Philadelphia, 1959.

Thompson, James Westfall. *Feudal Germany*. 2 vols. University of Chicago Press, Chicago, 1928.

Vorspan, Albert and Lipman, Eugene J. *Justice and Judaism*. Union of American Hebrew Congregations, New York, 1956.

Wald, Lillian D. *The House on Henry Street*. Transaction Publishers, New Brunswick, 1991.

Weber, Max. *From Max Weber, Essays in Sociology*. Oxford University Press, New York, 1946.

The Protestant Ethic and the Spirit of Capitalism. Charles Scribner's Sons, New York, 1952.

The Theory of Social and Economic Organization. The Free Press, Glencoe, Illinois, 1947.

Weizmann, Chaim. *Trial and Error*. 2 vols. Jewish Publication of America, 1949.

Wise, Isaac Mayer. *Reminiscences*. Leo Wise & Co., Cincinnati, 1901.

Young-Bruehl, Elisabeth. *Hannah Arendt For Love of the World*, second edition. Yale University Press, New Haven, 1982.

Yovel, Yirmiyahu. *Spinoza and Other Heretics*. Princeton University Press, Princeton, N.J., 1989.

Zborowski, Mark and Herzog, Elizabeth. *Life is With People*. International University Press, New York, 1952.

Zeitlin, Solomon. *Maimonides A Biography*. Block Publishing Company, New York, 1955.

Religious and Secular Leadership. The Dropsie College for Hebrew and Cognate Learning, Philadelphia, 1943.

Zertal, Idith, and Akiva Eldar. *Lords of the Land*. Nation Books, NY, 2005.

Index

www.ingramcontent.com/pod-product-compliance
Lightning Source LLC
Chambersburg PA
CBHW021828090426
42811CB00032B/2078/J